THE BROKEN BRANCH

Institutions of American Democracy

Kathleen Hall Jamieson and Jaroslav Pelikan, *Directors*

Other books in the series

*Schooling America: How the Public Schools Meet
the Nation's Changing Needs*
Patricia Albjerg Graham

*The Most Democratic Branch:
How the Courts Serve America*
Jeffrey Rosen

THE BROKEN BRANCH

*How Congress Is Failing America
and How to Get It Back on Track*

Thomas E. Mann and Norman J. Ornstein

THE
ANNENBERG FOUNDATION TRUST
AT SUNNYLANDS

THE ANNENBERG
PUBLIC POLICY CENTER
OF THE UNIVERSITY OF PENNSYLVANIA

OXFORD
UNIVERSITY PRESS

2006

OXFORD

UNIVERSITY PRESS

Oxford University Press, Inc., publishes works that further
Oxford University's objective of excellence
in research, scholarship, and education.

Oxford   New York
Auckland   Cape Town   Dar es Salaam   Hong Kong   Karachi
Kuala Lumpur   Madrid   Melbourne   Mexico City   Nairobi
New Delhi   Shanghai   Taipei   Toronto

With offices in
Argentina   Austria   Brazil   Chile   Czech Republic   France   Greece
Guatemala   Hungary   Italy   Japan   Poland   Portugal   Singapore
South Korea   Switzerland   Thailand   Turkey   Ukraine   Vietnam

Published by Oxford University Press, Inc.
198 Madison Avenue, New York, NY 10016
www.oup.com

Library of Congress Cataloging-in-Publication Data
Mann, Thomas E.
The broken branch : how Congress is failing America and
how to get it back on track /
by Thomas E. Mann and Norman J. Ornstein.
p. cm.
"The Annenberg Foundation Trust at Sunnylands."
"The Annenberg Public Policy Center."
ISBN-13: 978-0-19-517446-5
ISBN-10: 0-19-517446-1
1. United States. Congress. 2. United States. Congress—Reform.
I. Ornstein, Norman J. II. Annenberg Foundation Trust at Sunnylands.
III. Annenberg Public Policy Center. IV. Title.
JK1041.M36 2006
328.73—dc22
2006002568

3 5 7 9 8 6 4 2
Printed in the United States of America
on acid-free paper

To our wonderful families—Sheilah, Ted, and Stephanie;
Judy, Matthew, and Danny (and Harvey and Renee)
—who sometimes joined, other times tolerated, our
fulminations about Congress and American democracy.
And to the memories of two great legislators who
understood: Barber Conable and Pat Moynihan.

Contents

Preface

WE ARE BOTH HARDCORE PARTISANS—institutional partisans. For us, Congress has always been the first branch. We have been fascinated with Congress for four decades, since we began to study it as undergraduates at the Universities of Florida and Minnesota and afterward as graduate students at the University of Michigan. Our bias toward Congress as the linchpin of the American constitutional system grew substantially when we came to Washington together in 1969 as congressional fellows.

We love politics and the legislative process—in spite of their transparently unattractive features. Even the strongest institutional partisans, ourselves included, sometimes wince or gag in the face of individual excess and collective irresponsibility. But those legislative politics and processes are also the essence of democracy, especially in the United States. We each have had close friends who have served in the House and Senate; some still do. They have labored to do the right thing, and in many cases they have changed the country and the world for the better.

We have our differences on matters of policy and politics. But over the thirty-six years we have been in Washington and immersed in Congress, we have singly and together worked hand-in-glove with many Republicans and Democrats—and criticized Democrats and Republicans. We have tried hard throughout our careers, which have been hybrids of involvement in think tanks, academia, public commentary, work in Congress, and reform efforts, to put the institution first.

Over the past two decades, we have grown more and more dismayed at the course of Congress. Our unease began with the Democrats in charge of both houses, when a combination of their arrogance after thirty-plus years in the majority and the increasingly shrill frustration of Republicans who chafed under their seemingly permanent minority status was creating strains different and more ominous than any we had seen before. During that time, we vigorously and harshly criticized many of the practices of the majority Democrats, including shortcomings in the ethics process, the failure to improve the quality of deliberation in committees, and the many moves to restrict the role of the minority Republicans throughout the legislative process, especially on the floor. We applauded many of the steps Republicans made to reform the Congress when they took over after the 1994 election, especially in the House and in particular those actions that promised restoration or protection of minority rights.

But it did not take long before those promises went by the boards, and practices that were more unsettling than those of the Democrats became the norm. Of course, the steps taken by the leaders of the new majority and supported by their members did not occur in a vacuum. The escalation of the permanent campaign, the collapse of the center in Congress, the growing ideological polarization of the parties, the transformation of intense partisanship into virtually tribal politics, and the decline in accountability—all occurring in a new media environment that was *Crossfire* all the time, even after the demise of the show *Crossfire*—contributed to a climate on Capitol Hill that we found unsettling and destructive. The highly unusual era of partisan parity, with very narrow partisan majorities in Congress and majority status up for grabs at every election, relegated bipartisanship on Capitol Hill to a nostalgic, bygone time. Few of the steps Republicans took in the majority were invented by them. But they escalated their use in frequency and breadth. In chapter 1, we offer a good example: the employment of votes on the House floor lasting more than the norm of fifteen minutes. Democrats only once stretched a vote to twenty-five or thirty minutes and incurred as a consequence the sustained outrage of Republicans. Now votes of an hour or more occur so frequently they no longer shock or surprise, fully closed rules are common, and outbursts of partisan outrage occur with depressing frequency. We are not alone in our dismay. Each of us has had current and retired members of Congress we respected as model legislators, both Republicans and Democrats, who have told us that they barely recognize the House or Senate anymore.

Other elements were added to the mix when the Republican majority in both houses of Congress found itself with a Republican president—the first time that alignment had occurred since 1954. The majority saw itself more as a group of foot soldiers in the president's army than as members of an independent branch of government. Serious congressional oversight of the executive largely disappeared, and long-standing norms of conduct in the House and Senate were shredded to fulfill the larger goal of implementing the president's program. The attitude of majority party leaders that the president's program trumped everything, including institutional comity and basic fairness, accompanied a general decline in institutional identity. Here was one area in particular where our institutional hackles were raised. A very aggressive assertion of executive power was met with institutional indifference in Congress. The majority abandoned their institutional identity and independence with barely a second's thought. We did not expect nor would we have welcomed a Whig-like claim of legislative supremacy. We recognize that the American system works best when both the executive and legislative branches are strong and protective of their institutional prerogatives and comparative advantages. But Congress largely abdicated that responsibility as party and ideology trumped institution.

All these feelings combined to motivate us to write this book. To many readers, it will sound particularly harsh on the Republicans. It is meant to be. They are the ones in charge, responsible for the operations of the House, Senate, and Capitol complex, guardians of the integrity of the First Branch who are given the responsibility to make the process work fairly and according to the regular order; and they are the ones who, more frequently and ardently than we would have imagined, have ignored or underplayed that role.

But it is important for us to stress that the seeds of many of the problems predated the Republican majority. Arrogance, greed, venality, condescension toward the minority—all were in significant evidence during Democratic rule and were not invented after 1994. It is also important to acknowledge that while many minority Democrats have offered reform proposals to counter these trends, including some very constructive ones, we have no great confidence that they would behave demonstrably better in the majority than their counterparts. They are no doubt sincere—but so were Republican reformers, such as Newt Gingrich, David Dreier, and Jerry Solomon, when they took over the House in 1995. Within a couple of years, their sincere pledges had disappeared, driven in the cases of Gingrich and Solomon by their successors and no doubt influenced by the larger forces that gripped American politics. Faced with narrow margins, harsh partisanship, and the drive to accomplish a policy agenda, Democrats in the majority will be sorely tempted to bend the rules and norms to their will as well. As soon as an important bill comes up, if the vote count indicates an embarrassing setback on a Republican amendment or the chance of an even more embarrassing setback on the vote on the bill itself, will Democratic leaders submit to the embarrassment or find tools, such as closed rules or extended votes, to help them prevail?

If Democrats do succumb to those temptations when they recapture the majority—if they do not follow through on their pledges to run Congress more fairly and openly and to assert Congress's prerogatives—we will be all over their case. Even if it requires a second edition of *The Broken Branch*.

THE BROKEN BRANCH

ONE

Introduction

THE BILL THAT BROUGHT House members to a fateful vote early on November 23, 2003, was not your average piece of legislation. It was the major social policy initiative of President George W. Bush and the top priority of his congressional leaders. Shortly before six o'clock in the morning on that Sunday, following a debate that began Saturday and a vote that began at 3 a.m., a House of Representatives described by the *New York Times* as "fiercely polarized"[1] passed a bill to provide prescription drug benefits under Medicare. The 220 to 215 vote, begun under the normal procedure that routinely limits votes to fifteen minutes, took two hours and fifty-one minutes to complete; the *Times* piece said it took "an extraordinary bout of Republican arm-twisting to muster a majority."

Extraordinary it was. At exactly 3 a.m., Rep. Richard "Doc" Hastings (R-WA), presiding over the House, announced that the time for debate on the Medicare bill had expired. He said from the chair, "Members will have fifteen minutes to record their votes." As *Congress Daily* described it,[2] the roll call opened at 3:01 a.m., with seventeen Republicans immediately voting no. The official time expired at 3:15

a.m. with no Democrats having voted for the bill, twenty-two Republicans against it, and the nays ahead. At 3:30, the vote still open, the official tally was 212 for and 214 against. At 3:40, Republican Dana Rohrbacher, after intense discussions at the back of the chamber with Speaker Dennis Hastert and fellow California Republicans David Dreier and Duncan Hunter, voted yes, moving the tally to 213 for and 214 against. By 3:48, the vote was 215 to 218; for the first time, the opposition to the bill had an absolute majority of the House on its side. The vote went on.

Over the next fifteen minutes, Speaker Hastert spoke directly to a few of the Republicans who had voted no: Marilyn Musgrave of Colorado, Ernest Istook of Oklahoma, and Nick Smith of Michigan. Musgrave waved the Speaker off; a lengthy conversation with Smith ended with Smith refusing to switch to yes. At 4 a.m., Democrat Ken Lucas changed from present to no. One minute later, after speaking with Hastert, Istook switched from no to yes, making the vote 216 for and 218 against. At 4:20 a.m., Speaker Hastert, joined by Health and Human Services (HHS) Secretary Tommy Thompson, returned to Nick Smith, who had announced his retirement from the House and was hoping his son would be able to succeed him. Hastert sat on one side of him, Thompson on the other, for an extended conversation.

At 5:30 a.m., with no movement in the preceding ninety minutes, Hastert and Ways and Means Committee Chairman Bill Thomas surrounded Nick Smith near the Republican entrance to the House chamber, joined by Thompson and others. He again declined to change. In the meantime, House Majority Leader Tom DeLay and other leaders gathered in the cloakroom with a group of GOP "no" voters, many of whom had been telephoned only a few minutes earlier by President Bush. At 5:53, DeLay emerged, smiling, having persuaded Reps. C. L. "Butch" Otter of Idaho and Trent Franks of Arizona to switch their votes, following which several other members also changed their votes (in both directions), leading to the final margin of 220 to 215. The gavel came down quickly.

Speaker Hastert and Majority Leader DeLay were delighted. House Democrats and some Republicans were outraged. "Never have I seen such a grotesque, arbitrary, and gross abuse of power," commented John Dingell (D-MI), dean of the House and a forty-eight-year veteran of the body.[3] Said Democrat Jerrold Nadler of New York, "They grossly abused the rules of the House by holding the vote open. The majority of the House expressed its will, 216 to 218. It means it's a dictatorship. It means you hold the vote open until you have the votes."[4] *Congress Daily* quoted one Republican who voted against the bill, "It was an outrage. It was profoundly ugly and beneath the dignity of Congress." Even a senior Republican aide acknowledged it was "winning ugly."[5]

The ugliness did not end with the vote. In a newspaper column the day after the vote, Rep. Smith accused his own party's leaders of trying to bribe him. "Bribes and special deals were offered to convince members to vote yes," he wrote.[6] Smith elaborated upon the charges in an interview with Michigan radio station WKZO, saying he had been "pressured by the 'leadership'" and they had offered "$100,000-plus in campaign contributions," and threatened "Some of us are going to work to make sure your son doesn't get to Congress" unless he "relented."[7] Smith subsequently softened his charge, but there was more corroboration. The *Washington Post*'s Jeffrey Smith described a lunch held in the back room of a Capitol Hill restaurant two days before the House vote at which twenty conservative Republican congressmen, including Nick Smith, swapped tales of the pressure they faced on the vote. In this account,

> According to two other congressmen who were present, Smith told the gathering that House Republican leaders had promised substantial financial and political support for his son's campaign if Smith voted yes.[8]

Rep. Tom Tancredo (R-CO), who was at the luncheon, also heard Smith report that someone suggested that if he were to vote for the bill, his son would be the "beneficiary . . . up to the tune of about $100,000." Tancredo believed, "If Nick Smith said it happened, it happened."

Strong feelings about the Medicare vote and questions about the tactics used on the House floor lingered. On December 8, the House ended the first session of the 108th Congress by rejecting, on a party-line, 207–182 vote, a resolution by Minority Leader Nancy Pelosi that condemned Republicans' handling of the Medicare vote. As part of an extraordinarily tense exchange on the floor, Pelosi and Minority Whip Steny Hoyer harshly denounced GOP tactics. To the dismay and scorn of Democrats, none of the top Republican party leaders, including Speaker Hastert and Majority Leader DeLay, showed up for the debate. Pelosi said, "The Medicare vote will be remembered as one of the lowest moments in the history of the House." When she mentioned the allegations of bribery involving Nick Smith, other Democrats shouted, "Shame, shame."[9]

The allegations of bribery were taken up by the bipartisan House Ethics Committee in March 2004. At the end of September, the committee unanimously admonished Majority Leader Tom DeLay and Michigan Rep. Candice Miller for violating House rules. Their report said "Majority Leader DeLay offered to endorse Representative Smith's son in exchange for Representative Smith's vote in favor of the Medicare bill . . . it is improper for a Member to offer or link support for the personal interests of another Member as part of a *quid pro quo* to achieve a legislative goal." The Ethics Committee reached the same conclusion about Candice Miller, who made statements to Smith on the floor that Smith "fairly interpreted . . . as a threat of retaliation against him for voting in opposition to the bill."[10]

The House vote on the Medicare prescription drug bill was the longest roll call in modern House history. As Rules Committee Chairman David Dreier said during the December 8 House debate, this was not, technically speaking, against the rules. House Rule XX, clause 2 (a) says that there is a fifteen-minute *minimum* for most votes by electronic device. There is no formal maximum. A vote is not final until the vote numbers have been read by the Speaker and the result declared. Indeed, after the November vote, Dreier had said in a radio interview that he saw nothing wrong with keeping a vote open for days.

But the norm for such votes was established and clear from the time electronic voting began in January 1973: fifteen minutes is the voting time. Votes have routinely been left open for a minute or two solely to accommodate members who were delayed getting to the floor; that practice was abused enough that successive Speakers, Democrat and Republican, warned members that the fifteen-minute limit would be imposed if they did not show more promptness.

In the twenty-two years that Democrats ran the House after the electronic voting system was put in place, there was only one occasion when the vote period substantially exceeded the fifteen minutes, and that was in 1987 when an important budget bill was one vote short of passage and one of the bill's supporters reversed his vote and left to catch a plane, unaware that his switch sank the bill. Speaker Jim Wright's daring action, described in detail in chapter 3, resulted in passage of the bill but infuriated Republicans.[11]

Their reaction seems ironic in light of what would happen several years later: Then–Minority Whip Trent Lott of Mississippi referred to "Jim Wright and his goons." Then–Rep. Dick Cheney of Wyoming, later to become minority whip before becoming vice president, called Wright a "son-of-a-bitch" and denounced the action as "the most arrogant, heavy-handed abuse of power I've ever seen in the ten years I've been here."

In 1995, soon after the Republicans gained the majority, Speaker Newt Gingrich declared his intention to make sure that votes would consistently be held in the fifteen-minute time frame. The "regular practice of the House," he said, would be "a policy of closing electronic votes as soon as possible after the guaranteed period of fifteen minutes." The policy was reiterated by Speaker Hastert when he assumed the post.

The legislative process that preceded this Medicare floor vote in the House was no less offensive to congressional norms of deliberation and due process. The bill was considered and legislation drafted ("marked up") in the House Ways and Means Committee in a purely partisan fashion, with minority Democrats virtually left out of the process. When the bill went to a House–Senate conference committee to resolve differences between the two chambers, House Democratic conferees—like all conferees, formally elected by the House itself—were excluded from most of the deliberations and all of the negotiations, as were half the Senate Democratic conferees, including the Democratic leader.

The headlong rush in Congress to give the president a victory on Medicare prescription drugs had consequences that went beyond a simple violation of congressional norms and standards. The resulting law was criticized by conservative Republicans and liberal Democrats alike as based on faulty assumptions, filled with questionable cost estimates and flawed in many particulars, problems that came back to haunt the administration as the provisions of the new law began to be implemented.

Institutional Decline

It would be one thing if the Medicare vote was, like the 1987 budget vote, a singular exception driven by unique circumstances. But it was more a punctuation of a growing pattern in the House. Faced with a series of tough votes and close margins in recent years, Republicans have ignored their own standards and adopted a routine practice of stretching out the vote when they were losing until they could twist enough arms to prevail. On at least a dozen occasions before and after the Medicare issue, they went well over the fifteen minutes, sometimes over an hour.

The Medicare prescription drug vote—three hours instead of fifteen minutes, hours after a clear majority of the House had formally signaled its will—was thus not a unique exception to standard practice, but the extension of a now-common tactic that ended up descending into one of the most breathtaking breaches of the legislative process in the modern history of the House. The way in which the issue played out, and the vote itself, are far more a pattern of the House in the new century—a pattern that more closely resembles the House of the nineteenth century than that of the twentieth, of the Gilded Age more than the Cold War era. In its highly centralized leadership and fealty to the presidential agenda, the post–2000 House of Representatives looks more like a House of Commons in a parliamentary system than a House of Representatives in a presidential system.

The problems did not start with the Republican majority in 1995. Signs of institutional decline were much in evidence during the latter years of the longtime Democratic control of Congress. Under pressure from their increasingly ideologically unified members, Democratic leaders resorted to ad hoc arrangements that often circumvented the normal committee process, restrictive rules that limited debate and amendments on the House floor, and behemoth omnibus legislative packages that short-circuited the normal process, limited transparency, and rendered the majority less accountable. Sharp partisan differences on policy created an atmosphere in which the legislative ends could justify any procedural means. Tensions between the parties often reached a boiling point.

By the time the Republicans took control of both ends of Pennsylvania Avenue, it seemed almost natural for the House majority leadership to drive nearly every issue, controversial or not, in partisan ways. It did not take long before procedures guaranteeing adequate time for discussion, debate, and votes—known as "regular order"—in committee, on the floor, and in conference, which are essential if Congress is to play its critical deliberative role, were routinely ignored to advance the majority agenda. Wounds rubbed raw, civility was strained to the breaking point; in mid-2004, Republican Rep. and Hastert ally Ray LaHood of Illinois said, "It's as bad as I've seen it in my ten years in Congress."[12]

The Democratic majority had in its final years begun to restrict debate and amendments on the House floor, but the practice accelerated sharply under Republican rule. Fewer bills were brought up under open rules, which allow members to offer amendments to the pending legislation. The Republican leadership resorted more frequently to totally closed rules on the House floor, shutting off all attempts at amendment. In the 103rd Congress, under the Democrats, 9 percent of bills came to the floor under closed rules. In both the 106th and 107th, under Republicans, the number went to 22 percent—and to 28 percent in the 108th, 2003–2004. Donald Wolfensberger, former Rules Committee staff director under Republican Chairman Gerald Solomon, has also noted the increased reliance by the GOP on "self-executing" rules, which alter bills automatically when they come to the floor, sometimes for technical corrections but often to accommodate the interests of majority members and leaders. Self-executing rules went from an average of 19 percent of all bills in the 101st–103rd Congresses to 29 percent in the 104th–107th.[13] All of these practices, it should be noted, were roundly denounced by Republicans when they were in the minority.

Another change came with the behavior of the Speaker. The Speaker of the House is the first government official mentioned in the Constitution. Even though the practical reality is that the Speaker is selected by the majority party from its ranks and is its leader, the Speaker is elected by a vote of the whole House and represents the whole House. Underscoring their desire to have a Speaker above normal party politics, the framers established that the Speaker does not even have to be a member of the House. The Speaker rarely takes to the floor to speak on an issue and even more rarely votes. The Speaker does not lobby on the floor; that is supposed to be left to the party leaders—majority leader, majority whip, etc.—who are not elected by the whole House but chosen by their party members for that purpose.

Democratic Speaker Jim Wright was not shy about advancing an aggressive party agenda to challenge the Reagan administration during its last years in office. Nor was he reticent about engaging in personal diplomacy in Central America, actions his critics saw as infringing on the constitutional responsibility of the executive. Republicans in Congress certainly viewed Wright as a partisan, not an institutional leader, even if he mostly adhered to the norm of limiting his direct involvement on the House floor.

Fifteen years later, the Medicare prescription drug vote showed how far the House has strayed from that norm. Speaker Hastert actively lobbied and pressured members on the floor, over several hours. Moreover, by allowing Health and Human Services Secretary Tommy G. Thompson on the floor to twist arms during the vote, he violated a long-standing tradition of the House, whereby the floor was off limits to lobbying by outsiders. That he physically escorted Thompson onto the floor to perform a double team on Representative Smith and others was an unprecedented breach of House practice and ethics.

Restricted debate, loose interpretation of the rules, and a distortion of the role of Speaker are not the only problems with today's House. Unified party government threatens to sap the institution of any will to exercise its constitutional independence. Over a decade of Republican control, the House went from shrill opposition to a Democratic president, culminating in his impeachment, to reflexive loyalty to a Republican president, including an unwillingness to conduct tough oversight of executive programs or assert congressional prerogatives vis-à-vis the presidency—on matters ranging from the accessibility of critical information to war-making. The partisanship has bled over into areas where institutional norms have been particularly strong and resilient, such as the appropriations panels and the power of the purse.

The Senate managed in the 1990s to avoid much of the deeper division and acrimony that plagued the House, but it too has shown signs of institutional decline. The Senate evolved from a hierarchical institution that was shaped largely by the preferences of its senior conservative Democrats to one that spread the wealth to accommodate the interests—and whims—of every member. The parties in the Senate, just like the House, became more internally unified and ideologically polarized as voters realigned and turnover in the body accelerated. But Senate rules allowing unlimited debate and an open amendment process on the floor limited the degree of centralization and the power and resources given to party leaders.

The Senate became far more a bastion of individualism than the House. Its members more frequently were inclined to place "holds" on bills or nominations to extract concessions. The filibuster, which for decades had been limited to issues of great national significance, became a routine practice as leaders no longer brought the Senate to a halt for unlimited debate but simply raised the bar to two-thirds, and then sixty votes, not fifty, whenever a filibuster threat was raised. By the 1980s, it was used by the minority party as a core element of its legislative strategy on a wide range of bills.

Faced with a higher hurdle, Senate leaders began to make more expansive use of the budget reconciliation process, which operated under special procedures that barred filibusters and allowed a simple majority to act, and began to employ other forms of unorthodox lawmaking.[14] In the past few years of heightened partisanship and shared party stakes between the President and Congress, the Senate has begun to consider more radical steps to move away from its roots and toward the House model. The willingness of Republican Senate leaders to consider seriously a unilateral act to block filibusters on judicial nominations—the so-called nuclear option—was a sign of a breakdown in comity that could easily fracture any remaining bipartisan cooperation in that body.

Of course, a time traveler from the nineteenth century would laugh at the idea that the Congress has careened out of control. Partisan acrimony? How about a senator caned to within an inch of his life on the Senate floor by a House member who disagreed with his abolitionist positions. Highhandedness by a Speaker? Penny-ante compared to the arbitrary exercise of power by Speakers Thomas Brackett Reed and Joseph Cannon in the era from 1890–1910. But the rough-and-tumble of the first hundred years of American democracy, before Congress became institutionalized to meet the needs of an industrial society,[15] should not minimize the difficulties to the American system caused by a broken Congress in the post-industrial age of terrorism, in a society with a GDP of over $12 trillion and a federal budget approaching $3 trillion.

It would also be a mistake to suggest that the problems facing Congress are all the result of the actions or misjudgments of a handful of Republican leaders. As we have noted, many of the larger problems plaguing Congress, including partisan tensions, the demise of regular order, and growing incivility, began years ago, when Democrats were in the majority and Republicans in the minority. Their roots, and the reasons they have gotten demonstrably worse, are firmly implanted in larger political dynamics.

The Rise of Partisan Polarization

Members, and leaders, have choices. But the performance of Congress is shaped powerfully by the broader context in which it operates. Political developments in the South over the past fifty years, chronicled powerfully by Nelson Polsby in his book *How Congress Evolved,* profoundly changed the partisan dynamic in Congress and the ideological composition of the parties. The House of the 1930s through the 1970s had a Democratic majority populated by many Southern conservatives as well as Northern liberals. Conflicts on issues often crossed party lines, driven more by ideology and regional interests. The House lost virtually all of its Southern conservative Democrats, leaving a more homogeneous and left-of-center party. At the same time, the Republican

Party, partly as a consequence of this secular realignment in the South, has become even more distinctively conservative, with an ambitious agenda revolving around tax cuts, an assertive national defense, and religious traditionalism.

This ideological sorting by party has now extended to voters, activists, and elected officials throughout the country, creating two rival teams whose internal unity and ideological polarization are deeply embedded in the body politic. Increasing geographical segregation of voters and successive waves of incumbent-friendly redistricting have contributed to this development by helping to reduce the number of competitive House seats to a few dozen. With the overwhelming majority of House seats safe for one party or the other, new and returning members are naturally most reflective of and responsive to their primary constituencies, the only realistic locus of potential opposition, which usually are dominated by those at the ideological extreme. This phenomenon has tended to move Democrats in the House left and Republicans, right.

Despite the fact that redistricting plays no role in the Senate, the same pattern of ideological polarization of the parties is present there, albeit shaped in part by politicians moving from service in the House to the Senate. Many senators brought with them to the chamber attitudes toward Congress that were shaped by the contentious combat in the House of the late 1980s and early 1990s.

In recent years a number of factors—the two parties at parity and ideologically polarized, a populist attack on Congress that has weakened its institutional self-defenses, a more partisan press and interest group alignment, and an electoral environment making legislative activity subordinate to the interests of the permanent campaign—have conspired to encourage a decline in congressional deliberation and a de facto delegation of authority and influence to the president.

The passage of the Medicare bill is a vivid illustration of an institution that has strayed far from its deliberative roots and a body that does not live up to the aspirations envisioned for it by the framers. This problem is not just stylistic, or something that offends academics and other analysts. Bad process leads to bad policy—and often can lead to bad behavior, including ethical lapses. Those consequences affect all of us. In this book, drawing on our seventy-two collective years of inside Congress-watching, we will explore the history and political dynamics of Congress's current maladies, weigh the costs of a dysfunctional Congress for the substance and process of national policy making, consider whether public opinion is already prompting some in Congress to reconsider its institutional responsibilities, and propose actions that might repair the first branch of government.

The need for change, we believe, is compelling and urgent. In foreign policy, with an agonizing war in Iraq joining serious problems in the Middle East and elsewhere in the world, the need is clear for some broad consensus on America's role in the world, or at least for an understanding that these issues cannot be shoved aside in a kind of War of the Roses between the parties and the branches. In domestic affairs, unsustainable deficits looming in the next decade without a redirection of taxing and spending policies, along with unsolved problems in areas like pensions and health care, require a return to serious deliberation and measured bipartisanship. The country and its enduring constitutional pact should not, and cannot, endure a broken branch for long.

TWO

The First Branch of Government

Theory and Practice

CONGRESS IS THE "FIRST BRANCH OF GOVERNMENT." That characterization, familiar to all civics students, is there because Congress is empowered and framed in the first article of the Constitution. Its placement there is no accident: the framers wanted it clear that Congress was to be first among equals of the three branches. Article One is twice as long as Article Two, on the executive branch, and four times as long as Article Three, on the judiciary. Each branch is given unique powers, with many overlapping, but it is clear, when push comes to shove, that Congress can trump the other two branches by overriding a presidential veto, by changing the size or jurisdiction of the courts, by impeaching and removing from office presidents and justices alike.

Not that Congress should as a matter of course dominate politics and policy making at the expense of the other two branches. The Constitution is most certainly not a charter for legislative supremacy. But it does build an institutional edifice in which Congress is seen as a powerful, independent body, one expected to represent a large and diverse republic, to deliberate on important policy questions, and to check and balance the other branches.[1] In the words of

Nelson Polsby, the framers intended Congress to be a transformative legislature, not simply an arena in which external forces work their will.[2]

The textbooks of our student years spoke of the informal "norms" of members of Congress, including "institutional patriotism," the sense of loyalty to the larger body. When we came to Washington as congressional fellows in 1969, we observed firsthand, among Democrats and Republicans, regardless of who was president, the widespread appreciation of its members for their unique and independent role. We felt a flutter in our hearts each day as we approached the Hill, seeing the Capitol Dome rising up over Jenkins Hill, even more so at night as it was bathed in dramatic white light. It was second nature to us that Congress really was first among equals.

We are political scientists by training, not historians. But our education and experiences since our first year on Capitol Hill infused us with a sense of Congress's history and of its prime role in the Constitution. One important figure for both of us was D. B. Hardeman, a former journalist from Texas who had served as the top aide to the legendary Speaker Sam Rayburn in his heyday and until his death in 1961, and who then worked for Rep. Hale Boggs of Louisiana. In retirement in Washington, living in an apartment at 2500 Q Street that was filled from floor to ceiling with books about Congress and government, D.B. took new congressional fellows under his wing. He spent hours telling us Rayburn stories and how, from his own front seat, he saw American history in the making; and he gave us free rein over his remarkable book collection.

From D.B. we learned that Congress had to be understood in its constitutional and historical context. We learned to resist myopia—that the way things were when we were there was neither unique nor the way things had always been. We saw that Congress's power and role could ebb and flow depending on the strength, or lack thereof, of personality in its leaders, that the best leaders were those like

Rayburn who had a fierce loyalty to his institution superseded only by his fiercer patriotism. And we saw how easy it was for Congress to stray from its clear role in the American constitutional system, pushed by presidents or the narrowness and venality of its own members or leaders. We learned the reality that Congress needed persistent attention to its own institutional and individual shortcomings—constant institutional maintenance.

Most of this book reflects on the years since we first came to Congress and on Congress today. But no understanding of today's Congress, including how and why the House and Senate each got to be the way they are, the role of parties, committees and leaders, and where they have measured up and fallen short, can be complete without laying out the constitutional foundation and understanding and following the course of its history.

Anyone without our experience or unfamiliar with the framers' design would be excused if their impressions of Congress were based on the post-2000 period—when it looked more like an arm of the Second Branch, a supine, reactive body more eager to submit to presidential directives than to assert its own prerogatives. But even many familiar with that history—including several Supreme Court justices who pride themselves on their "strict constructionism"—have ignored the framers' intent and promoted the primacy of the presidency.

While President George W. Bush and Vice President Richard Cheney have an unusually strong executive-centered view of American government, their administration is hardly the first to flex its institutional muscles. The presidency gained enormous power during much of the twentieth century, particularly over national security, and public expectations about what the occupant of the White House could and should accomplish soared. Congress in turn was increasingly judged by whether it facilitated or frustrated the president's agenda.

The framers had a much more capacious conception of the role of Congress in the American constitutional system.

Congress was placed at the center, not the periphery, of a strong federal government and empowered with democratic legitimacy and institutional authority. That design was of course subject to the struggles and uncertainties of new, fledgling institutions finding their way in the real world of politics and policy making. Congress has had its ups and downs in realizing the intentions of the framers. Sadly, today it is down—very much the broken branch of government.

Article I

Delegates to the 1787 Constitutional Convention arrived in Philadelphia with the official task of drafting proposals for consideration by Congress and the states to revise the Articles of Confederation. While there was a broad consensus among the delegates that the national authority under the Articles was "too weak to raise revenues, provide for defense, or adequately regulate commerce among the states,"[3] they had no authorization for abandoning the system of state sovereignty that had so constrained the confederation during the previous decade. The Confederation Congress, the sole organ of national government under the Articles, was delegated significant powers (e.g., to declare war, enter treaties, regulate coinage, and borrow money) but little means of imposing its will. Members, appointed and paid by the states, were limited to serving no more than three out of six years. Each state had one vote and most actions required the assent of nine of the thirteen states. Lacking authority over taxation and tariffs and without sanctions or administrative and judicial agencies to enforce its decisions, Congress could do little more than cajole states and individuals to meet their responsibilities.

Widespread concerns about the state of the Union under the Articles were counterbalanced by vivid memories of the abuse of power by British authorities during the late colonial period. In adopting new constitutions after the Declaration of Independence, most of the states took care to limit the power of their governments—by explicitly guaranteeing individual rights, separating authority among legislative, executive, and judicial branches, and restricting suffrage to the propertied class. However, their distrust of executive authority under the Crown and royal governors led them to make legislatures the dominant power within these limited state governments.

The challenge for the delegates who came to Philadelphia was to reconcile the pervasive suspicion of authority and commitment to states as sovereign actors with the obvious need to strengthen the Union. Those favoring a strong national government seized the initiative at the Convention with the submission of the Virginia Plan. The decisive rejection of an alternative New Jersey Plan, one that would retain most features of state sovereignty, soon made it clear that the delegates would be writing a new constitution for the United States, not amending the Articles of Confederation. The centerpiece for constructing this new constitutional order, one in which a national government would enjoy a direct relationship with the people, not simply delegated power from the states, was the legislative branch.

Over half of the recorded debates at the Convention focused on Congress—its basis of representation, election of members, enumerated powers, relationship to the executive and judicial branches, and internal organization. Some matters were resolved with relative ease. The legislature would be bicameral, members of the House, but not the Senate, would be directly elected by the people, and Congress would be one branch in a system that ensured separation of powers. But several critical design features emerged only after extended debate and the negotiation of a compromise between small and large states and northern and southern states. Most important, the House would be apportioned on the basis of population (counting all whites and three-fifths of the blacks), each state would have equal representation in the Senate, and a president would be elected independently by the states.

The preeminence of Congress in the constitutional scheme rested primarily on it—more precisely the House—being the only part of the national government directly tied to the people through popular elections. In George Mason's words, the House "was to be the grand depository of the democratic principles of the government." Delegates rejected the initial proposals from the Virginians that the House elect members of the second chamber from persons nominated by state legislatures, on grounds that it would make the Senate subservient to the House. Desiring coequal chambers of the national legislature, albeit with distinctive comparative advantages, they decided that senators would be elected by state legislatures—although, importantly, they would vote in the Senate as individuals, not as state delegations. This electoral feature, along with its smaller size and a six-year term, would allow the Senate, as stated by Gouverneur Morris, "to check the precipitation, changeableness, and excesses of the first branch." That expectation is nicely captured in a famous exchange sometime after the convention. When asked by Thomas Jefferson why he had consented to a second chamber in Congress, George Washington asked "Why did you pour that coffee into your saucer?" "To cool it," said Jefferson. "Even so," said Washington, "we pour legislation into the senatorial saucer to cool it."[4]

Beyond the critical electoral base, Congress was given additional tools to ensure its independence. Each house would be the sole judge of the election and qualifications of its members and determine the rules of its proceedings. Congress, by law, would determine the salary of its members, which would be paid not by the states, as under Confederation, but by the Treasury of the United States. Under congressional immunity provisions, especially the Speech and Debate Clause, its members would be protected from harassment and threats by other branches of the government. Congress would have the power to tax and spend, to regulate commerce, to declare war and approve treaties, to confirm presidential appointees to the executive and judicial branches, and to impeach national officers for "treason, bribery, or other high crimes and misdemeanors." And in a sweeping grant of lawmaking authority, Congress was authorized "to make all laws which shall be necessary and proper for carrying into execution the foregoing powers, and all other powers vested by this Constitution in the government of the United States, or in any department or officer thereof."

As pivotal and powerful as Congress was in the new constitutional order, the delegates did not embrace a framework for legislative supremacy. While their distrust of executive authority was strong, so too was their concern—born out of experiences in the states after independence—of populist legislative excesses. Checks and balances were the order of the day. An effective executive was deemed an essential counterpart to, though not an equal of, the legislative branch. The president, chosen for a four-year term by electors appointed by the states, would lack the political muscle provided by popular election. By being elected independent of the Congress and eligible for reelection, however, he would have incentive for checking the legislature. To that incentive was added institutional capacity. The president was given power to veto bills passed by Congress, subject to an override by two-thirds vote of both House and Senate. He was invested with the authority to negotiate treaties and make judicial and executive appointments with the "advice and consent of the Senate." Additional constitutional language conferred on the president authority as chief executive (to "take care that the laws be faithfully executed"), commander-in-chief of the armed services, and the lead diplomat with the rest of the world.

The framers were especially keen to create a capable executive in the arena of foreign policy, where "decision, activity, secrecy, and dispatch"[5] were deemed essential qualities that naturally reposed in the executive, not the legislature. While Congress was given a more generous grant of specific constitutional authorities in foreign and military affairs, the executive was expected to play a central role, especially in the diplomatic arena. The result was, in the famous phrase of Edward Corwin, "an invitation to struggle for the privilege of directing American foreign policy."[6]

The framers also recognized the importance of an independent judicial branch.[7] "There is no liberty, if the power of judging be not separated from the legislative and executive powers."[8] Lifetime tenure and a prohibition on reductions in compensation were included in Article III to secure that independence. Yet Congress also received considerable authority with respect to the judicial branch. Appointments to the federal bench by the president require the advice and consent of the Senate. Through its power of the purse, Congress appropriates funds and sets salaries for the judiciary. Congress was also given the power to create judgeships, determine the structure and jurisdiction of federal courts, and enact laws that affect the cases brought to the courts and the procedures under which they operate. And as with officers of the executive branch, Congress was lodged with the authority to impeach and remove members of the federal judiciary.

The prominence of Congress in the Convention deliberations, constitutional text, and state ratifying debates speaks powerfully to the framers' belief that the legislature would be the keystone of the American republic, deriving its legitimacy from the people but also able to act responsibly in their long-term interest. As Michael J. Malbin has persuasively argued, the framers tried to design Congress in a way that would attract people of ability to work for the common good.[9] Virtue was insufficient; "ambition must be made the cornerstone of self-government." *Federalist No. 51* captures the essence of their reasoning:

> Ambition must be made to counteract ambition. The interest of the man must be connected with the constitutional rights of the place. It may be a reflection on human nature, that such devices should be necessary to control the abuses of government. But what is government itself, but the greatest of all reflections on human nature? If men were angels, no government

would be necessary. If angels were to govern men, neither external nor internal controls on government would be necessary. In framing a government which is to be administered by men over men, the great difficulty lies in this: you must first enable the government to control the governed; and in the next place oblige it to control itself.

The key was building governmental institutions that channeled the ambitions of elected officials to serve broad public interests. Malbin demonstrates how this calculation, evident in the Convention proceedings and ratification debates, led to the design of an extended commercial republic with a multiplicity of factions—requiring majorities to be built from coalitions of minorities through a process of accommodation and compromise. An essential feature of this large republic is representative, not direct democracy. Representatives would come together in a deliberative assembly not simply to reflect public preferences but, in James Madison's words, to "refine and enlarge the public views." And senators would provide an additional check on the potential excesses of democracy by taking a cooler, longer-range view perspective.

The solution arrived at in Philadelphia for coping with the inadequacies of the Articles of Confederation while at the same time securing liberty was far from consensual. The opposition that emerged in the state-ratifying debates, the Anti-Federalists, argued that a strong national government would abridge rather than secure personal liberties and ride roughshod over the states.[10] They argued forcefully for an institutional design based not on channeling the ambitions of elected officials to serve larger public purposes but instead on vigilant watch and zealous control over the actions of their representatives. The objective was to get as close to direct or plebiscitary democracy as possible and to guard against a natural aristocracy dominating a distant national government. In the case of Congress, this meant small legislative districts, in which representatives were likely to mirror the electorate; frequent (every year) elections; provisions for citizens to instruct their representatives on specific issues and to recall them during their term of office; and mandatory rotation.

The Anti-Federalists lost the initial battle—a constitution embodying Federalist principles and institutions was ratified—but their arguments and the public sentiment they expressed have exerted a powerful force on American politics throughout our history. As Gordon Wood instructs us in his masterful book *The Radicalism of the American Revolution*,[11] the democratic forces unleashed by the American revolution overwhelmed the republican cautions of many of the framers in the years following the ratification of the Constitution. Many of the revolutionary leaders were bewildered and disillusioned by what they saw as the failure of their experiment in republicanism. "By the early nineteenth century, many of the founding fathers had come to share something of Alexander Hamilton's poignant conclusion that 'this American world was not made for me.' They found it difficult to accept the democratic fact that their fate now rested on the opinions and votes of small-souled and largely unreflective ordinary people."

Wood notes that even Jefferson, who much more than Madison placed his trust in ordinary people, lamented features of this democratic revolution. "He was incapable of understanding the deep popular strength of the evangelical forces, of the real moral majorities, that were seizing control of much of American culture in these years." The everyday concerns of ordinary citizens—making money, getting ahead, nurturing their families and their souls—became the driving force in American politics.

In short, the success of the framers in designing a republican form of government that linked the ambitions of public officials to the interests of the institutions in which they served—and, in the full constitutional scheme, to the broader public interest—was no guarantee that their intentions would be realized in practice. Would the division of authority among and within political institutions prove sufficient to curb the excesses of democracy and to control

the potential abuses of government? Would Congress succeed in fulfilling its responsibilities as a powerful, deliberative assembly without shortchanging the legitimate
interests of the citizenry or trampling the prerogatives of
the executive and judicial branches? As we shall see, major
developments unanticipated by the framers undermined
elements of the logic behind their constitutional design. The
ambitions of politicians were often linked through political
parties rather than counterpoised to reinforce checks and
balances. Congress had more competition from the other
branches than expected, especially as the presidency acquired a more popular base. Its bicameralism evolved differently than intended. Nonetheless, the first branch of
government retained sufficient constitutional and institutional resources to play a central role in American governance. Whether and when it would do so often turned on
broader forces in the political and social environment.

From Design to Practice

Political parties are nowhere mentioned in the Constitution. The dangers of factions and strategies for dealing with
their potentially harmful effects were much discussed during the Convention and ratifying debates; not so, however,
the emergence of teams of politicians linked across states,
branches, and legislative chambers to win elections and control government. The rise of the Andrew Jackson–Martin Van
Buren party system, fueled by a dramatic expansion of the
electorate, led to a nationalization of politics that upset
many of the calculations and expectations of delegates to
Philadelphia.[12]

The House lost its exclusive position as the only national
political institution directly linked to the citizenry through
popular elections. As states shifted responsibility for choosing presidential electors from legislatures to voters, presidents developed their own ties to a national electorate and
the legitimacy that came with it. The continued existence

of the Electoral College prevented the link from being formally direct but the presidency unmistakably entered the arena of mass politics. The direct election of senators, formalized by constitutional amendment in 1913, was preceded by decades of developments in which senators built their own political bases apart from the state legislatures that appointed them. The Lincoln–Douglas debates of 1858, part of an Illinois state legislative campaign that became a shadow senatorial contest, set the stage for the widespread adoption by states of the popular canvas for Senate. Even House elections departed from the expectations of the framers. Local, state-centered elections gave way to more national events as Congress moved to require single-member districts and to set a uniform date for presidential and congressional elections and political parties worked to coordinate their electoral efforts across offices and states.

These developments in the electoral arena made the presidency a more powerful rival to the Congress in national policy making and blurred the differences between the two chambers in Congress. They also threatened to undercut the ambition-based institutional competition and loyalty that was a central feature of the constitutional checks and balances. It soon became clear that the external political environment of Congress—the strength of political parties, their coalitional bases and ideological distinctiveness, and the level of electoral competitiveness—would shape how members of both the House and Senate sought to achieve their personal goals of reelection, power within the institution, and preferred policies. These decisions, in turn, helped determine how Congress would organize itself to achieve its objectives and how aggressively or passively the legislature would engage the other branches.

Internal Capacity

The Constitution is relatively silent on the rules and procedures Congress is to follow in going about its work. The House is to choose its Speaker; the vice president shall preside over the Senate (replaced, in his absence, by a president pro tempore); a journal of each chamber's proceedings, including the yeas and nays, is to be kept and made publicly available; and super-majority votes are required for selected purposes, including overriding vetoes, ratifying treaties, removing officials from office following impeachment, and expelling its own members. Most importantly, each chamber is given explicit authority to "determine the Rules of its Proceedings." The latter gives Congress extraordinary scope to determine its own mode of organization.

The organizational building blocks in each chamber are individual members, committees, and parties.[13] Proceedings in the earliest congresses reflected the fact that members entered their respective houses as equals and were suspicious of any concentrations of power that might dilute their influence. Deliberation in both the House and Senate occurred mostly on the floor, with temporary ad hoc committees appointed to draft legislative language only after the topic had been first vetted by the full membership. The chamber then debated the proposed legislation and took whatever action it deemed appropriate. Select committees typically handled only one piece of legislation, so they had no opportunity to develop expertise or influence. Elections for Speaker were contested partly on partisan lines in the early congresses, but the office did not develop the institutional and political resources for setting the House agenda until the Civil War era. The Senate was even slower to develop a party leadership structure to direct the flow of legislation. In short, the organization of Congress early in its history was notably flat, with a premium placed on the equality of members, not on a rational division of labor or an orderly process for managing its agenda.

As Congress struggled to deal with a burgeoning workload, challenges to its authority from the executive branch, and the personal interests of its members, this initial division of labor among individual members, committees, and parties gave way to more elaborate organizational arrangements.[14] The first significant development, the rise of a standing committee system, created a capacity for informed deliberation based on a division of labor within each chamber. The next involved a centralization of power through the party leadership to bring more order and predictability to the legislative process. A reaction against excessive centralization ultimately led to a third phase in the institutional development of Congress, one in which power devolved to committee chairs and cross-party coalitions of members.

The Rise of Standing Committees. In the House the transition from the temporary to standing committee occurred gradually. Several standing committees were created in the 1790s, partly to provide a source of independent information in the face of an assertive Treasury secretary, Alexander Hamilton. Others were added during the Jefferson administration and in the wake of the War of 1812. By 1822, the House had an elaborate set of standing committees with explicit jurisdictions, the right to have bills in their subject area referred to them, and an ability to propose legislation on their own initiative. Moreover, the House adopted a germaneness rule that barred amendments on the floor unrelated to the legislation under consideration.

A similar set of standing committees was created in the Senate during this period, the first in 1807 and then, a decade later, another twelve, including Finance, Judiciary, and Foreign Relations. But the Senate was more protective of the prerogatives of its individual members than the House in creating its standing committee system. Senate committees enjoyed neither a germaneness rule nor assurance that bills dealing with matters under their jurisdiction would be referred to them before going to the full Senate. As a consequence, they had less ability to shape legislation under their purview and the Senate as an institution was less able than the House to develop an orderly and predictable division of labor.

The differences between the two chambers in placing standing committees at the center of the legislative process are noteworthy but the commonalities even more so. By the early 1820s, both the House and Senate were developing an institutional capacity to process legislation and oversee the executive based on the specialized knowledge of its members. Congress strengthened its policy making position by decentralizing authority to standing committees, whose expertise and institutional memory helped cope with an expanding workload and provided the information essential to evaluating requests from the executive.

Party Leadership. The second critical organizational development of Congress was the formalization and expansion of the party leadership. This historical period, the late nineteenth century, has many fascinating parallels with our contemporary politics. Political parties structured public life in all of its dimensions—as a decisive cue to voters, as campaign organizations, and as competing teams of politicians in government. The two major parties developed distinctive electoral coalitions and policy agendas. After a long period of divided party government, the Republicans won control of both ends of Pennsylvania Avenue and were anxious to enact their legislative program. With narrow majorities in both chambers, they felt obliged to work together within Congress to promote their electoral prospects.

In the House the organizational fallout was a remarkable centralization of power. While the Speaker had long enjoyed the power to appoint committee members, his ability to advance a legislative agenda was greatly constrained. Even the House's first powerful Speaker, Henry Clay of Kentucky, who served in the 1810s and 1820s, was often frustrated by the ability of individual members and the minority party to engage in essentially unlimited debate. In 1811 the House adopted the previous question rule, which allowed a majority to shut off further debate on an issue. But it proved difficult to invoke. Managing the flow of business was especially challenging during the turbulent decades leading up to the Civil War, when both parties, the Democrats and the Whigs, found themselves divided on the issue of slavery.

During this period, incidents of physical violence between congressional colleagues spiked in both chambers as the nation drifted toward armed conflict over slavery. Since the founding of Congress, hostile encounters—some violent—had erupted intermittently within and away from the Capitol. Duels between members of Congress were held multiple times, sometimes turning fatal, while physical altercations on the floors of the House and Senate featured punching, choking, and the brandishing of fire tongs and pistols.[15]

For sheer incivility and brutality, however, the events of May 1856—fueled by antagonism over slavery—have gone unmatched.[16] In a floor speech, Sen. Charles Sumner, a staunch Republican abolitionist from Massachusetts, railed against the South (and South Carolina, in particular) and issued vituperative personal attacks against some fellow senators, saving his worst for Sen. Andrew P. Butler, a South Carolina Democrat. Three days later, Rep. Preston Brooks, Butler's relative and a fellow Democrat from South Carolina, walked onto the Senate floor and started viciously beating Sumner over the head with a cane. Caught off his guard, Sumner stumbled about for a minute before he collapsed on the floor, bleeding from the head. Though Brooks was re-elected that November, four years passed before Sumner returned to Congress, the Civil War less than two years away.

Frustration over the inability of the House to act in a timely and decisive manner built up in the years following Reconstruction. Dilatory motions, made solely to delay business, and disappearing quorums, where members refused to vote even though present, thereby denying the House the quorum it needed to conduct business, gave the minority powerful tools to thwart majority action. Thomas Brackett Reed of Maine, initially as a back-bencher, then as minority leader and eventually Republican Speaker, put an end to that.

Reed, one of the most influential Speakers of the House, never fully accepted his role as a career politician.[17] Initially, he expressed little interest even in entering the political arena, running for his first elected office, as a state legislator, only after an acquaintance put Reed's name forward as a candidate. A reluctant Reed finally joined the race after concluding that the post could prove useful in practicing law. Though he remained in politics and spent more than twenty years in Congress, Reed never bought a house in Washington. "Czar Reed" considered Portland, Maine, his home and preferred reading widely from his library—the state's largest private collection—to schmoozing with his colleagues in Washington.

Though an untraditional politician, Reed proved a commanding figure in the House. He was a formidable physical presence, standing six feet two inches and weighing a hefty 275 pounds. His colleagues had to watch out for "a tongue that at one stroke sliced the whiskers off his opponents' faces," an advantage Reed expertly employed.[18] Referring to two verbose members of Congress, Reed once remarked, "They never open up their mouths without subtracting from the sum of human knowledge." Besides sharp sarcasm, Reed was known for his scrupulous honesty, mental agility, and unmatched skill at condensing an argument to its essence. Perhaps most important for the work he chose to undertake in the House, Reed paid close attention to detail and had an amazing capacity for self-control. He consciously, painstakingly, worked to master the Byzantine House rules, a feat for which he would gain his colleagues' respect. To ensure that his knowledge translated into influence, Reed relied on his calm demeanor to weather the storm that engulfed the House after he moved to empower its majority.

His first important initiative was to use the Rules Committee to manage the legislative agenda. The committee acquired the authority to report special orders that, if approved by a majority of House members, brought bills to the floor out of their regular order, limited the time available for debate, and governed the extent to which members might offer amendments. Since the Speaker chaired the Rules Committee and appointed its members, this became a powerful weapon in his leadership arsenal. But not powerful enough. Dilatory motions and disappearing quorums continued to handcuff the majority leadership. So shortly after Reed became Speaker in December 1889, he moved boldly to eliminate both. Facing the absence of a quorum on a bill important to the majority, he ordered the clerk to count as present those members who had refused to vote. After defeating an attempt to appeal his ruling—by getting a majority of the quorum to vote to table it—he then ruled out of order another appeal, declaring he would henceforth refuse to recognize any member rising to make a dilatory motion. A week later the Rules Committee reported and the House adopted changes in the rules that incorporated Reed's rulings on the counting of a quorum and dilatory motions.

While the minority Democrats vigorously resisted these rules changes, they acquired more of an appreciation of them when they returned to the majority. Eventually both parties— in the majority and minority—came to accept the Reed Rules as necessary if the chaos and indecision of earlier years were to be avoided. "By the close of the 1890s, the House was a remarkably centralized institution featuring a powerful Speakership, who controlled committee assignments, regulated obstruction on the floor, and, through the Rules Committee, exerted considerable influence over the chamber's agenda."[19]

The Senate underwent a similar development toward centralized party leadership in the late nineteenth century, but Senate party leaders never gained the tools necessary to effectively control the agenda like their House counterparts. The constitutional anomaly of the vice president serving as president of the Senate, rather than being chosen by senators from one of their own, retarded the development of Senate party leadership. The position of president pro tempore proved an entirely inadequate alternative. Members of Senate committees were mostly chosen by ballot, not appointed by an elected leader, until that power was transferred in the mid-1840s to the party caucuses and each caucus's committee on committees. With its smaller size, longer terms, greater experience in public life, and a more stable membership, the Senate—much more than the House—rewarded its members by allocating committee assignments by seniority and giving senators a freer rein to advance their own agendas.

Indeed, the "Golden Age" of the Senate—the three decades preceding the Civil War—was distinguished not by strong and assertive party leadership but instead by the prominence and eloquence of some of its individual members. Daniel Webster, Henry Clay (who returned to the Senate after serving as Speaker), and John C. Calhoun contributed mightily to the Senate's status as the chief forum for the discussion of national policy, including the all-important issue of the future of slavery.

The dominance of the Republican party in national politics during the Civil War and Reconstruction periods set the stage for the development of modern party government in the Senate near century's end. Lacking any locus of agenda-setting authority, the Senate struggled to set priorities and cope with its expanding workload. A Republican Steering Committee was appointed in the mid-1880s to help schedule legislative business. By the late 1890s, Senators Nelson Aldrich, William Allison, and fellow members of an informal group of like-minded, senior Republican senators used their leadership positions on the party caucus, Steering Committee, and major committees to take effective control of the agenda. A similar power structure was developed by the Democrats under the leadership of Senator Arthur Gorman, but the party's minority status and internal policy differences prevented him from attaining the notoriety and influence of his Republican counterparts in the Senate, much less in the House.

By the end of the nineteenth century, parties came to constitute a central building block in the organization of the Senate. Through their leaders, parties appointed committees, set the agenda for the consideration of bills by the full chamber, resolved in the caucus internal differences on divisive issues, and enforced a remarkable degree of discipline on the Senate floor. Yet even during this period of party government, individual senators continued to enjoy freedom of action based in large part on the right to unlimited debate. Partly as a consequence of its small size, light workload, and the courtesy and informality of its proceedings in the early congresses, the Senate did not adopt restrictions on debate that were embraced over time by the House. For example, the Senate dropped a previous question rule when it revised its rules in 1806. Nonetheless, dilatory tactics were not a serious problem in the early history of the Senate, as members usually exhibited a good deal of self-restraint and determined majorities were generally able to work their will—albeit after delay and a testing of their commitment. The tradition of unlimited debate fostered the oratorical splendor that garnered the upper chamber a reputation for brilliance and leadership in the pre–Civil War era.

That Senate was seldom to be seen in the decades following the Civil War. The slavery question was settled. Membership grew with the addition of new states. The legislative workload increased dramatically. The rise of strong state party organizations produced a new breed of senator, with public statesmen replaced by professional politicians intent on building a career in the Senate. Filibusters grew in frequency and success, rising to epidemic proportions in the 1880s and 1890s. Individual senators and the minority party were increasingly able to frustrate the will of the majority, in spite of the efforts of party leaders to curb obstruction. Party government had its limits in the upper chamber.

Decentralization.   The third phase in the organizational development of Congress is best viewed as a revolt against the second. Speaker Reed, who left the House in 1899 after amazing success consolidating and exercising authority through his office, was replaced (after an ineffectual transition figure) by Joseph Cannon of Illinois. At the time of his election as Speaker in 1903, Cannon was the oldest representative and had served twenty-eight years in the House.

Since his arrival in Washington, though, Cannon had been known primarily for his eccentric speechmaking.[20] One biographer describes Cannon's first speech on the Hill in this way: "His gestures were spectacular. As he warmed to his subject, his arms flailed the air like windmill blades, his left fist repeatedly whacked the palm of his right hand, and the long tails of his unbuttoned coat fluttered out behind him."[21] Rep. Champ Clark of Missouri claimed to see Cannon spin around completely on his heel once during a debate; Clark called him "The Dancing Dervish of Illinois." Raised in a log cabin on the eastern Illinois frontier, "Uncle Joe" Cannon saw himself as a common man, "one of the great army of mediocrity which constitutes the majority."[22] Yet no later than his first speech, he proved himself far from mediocre in enthusiasm, exclaiming at one point, "I have oats in my pocket and hayseed in my hair, and the Western people generally are affected the same way."[23] The press reported this line widely and came to view the thin, blond Cannon as a character, a member of Congress who gave flamboyant speeches occasionally laced with foul language, all while chomping on a cigar.

Of course there was more to Cannon than this caricature would imply. A hard-line Republican, he supported Reed's reforms wholeheartedly and was the quintessential party loyalist. Cannon vigorously sought to preserve the status quo, which he believed made the United States the world's greatest country. When a supporter suggested to President Theodore Roosevelt, a relentless reformer, that he "lay down on Uncle Joe," Roosevelt responded, "It will be a good deal like laying down on a hedgehog."[24] Cannon certainly could be prickly, having no patience for suffragists, conservationists, free traders, or reformers of any stripe. Yet members of the House from both parties universally respected the gregarious Cannon and enjoyed his company.

As Speaker, Cannon grasped the new tools of party leadership with alacrity and, like Reed, set out to rule the House through the Rules Committee, key committee appointments, and his power as presiding officer. Unfortunately for Cannon, however, conditions had changed, leading many members of the House who liked him personally, both Republicans and Democrats, to view him as an autocratic leader whose arbitrary use of the Speaker's powers thwarted the will of the House majority and their individual interests. Teddy Roosevelt was in the White House and pushing a progressive agenda very different from that of the conservative Cannon. Republican progressives were becoming more numerous, in the House and in the country, creating severe ideological divisions within the party. After more than a century of rapid membership turnover and very brief average tenure, members were beginning to view their service in the House as a career. Fewer voluntary retirements and electoral defeats created a growing constituency of members in both parties concerned about their individual prerogatives and resentful of the Speaker's interference in their pursuit of personal goals. Finally, the minority Democrats increasingly chafed at their marginalization under Cannon's aggressive leadership and sought to make him an electorally useful symbol of an undemocratic and unresponsive legislature.

After several abortive attempts to limit his power, a coalition of Democrats and progressive Republicans succeeded in 1910 in stripping the Speaker of his authority to appoint committee members and chairmen and removed him from the Rules Committee. The revolt against "Cannonism" was institutionalized in 1911, when the Democrats took control of the House and adopted revised rules that incorporated these and other changes limiting the Speaker's power. While Democrats experimented briefly with a less centralized form of strong party leadership, by the 1920s they acceded to a much more decentralized body, with committees dominated by seniority and its agenda shaped by an independent-minded Rules Committee.

Facing many of the same changes in its external political environment, the Senate also backed off its experiment in party government and moved in a decentralizing direction. Internal ideological differences in both parties made it impossible to sustain the interlocking party and committee leadership of the 1890s. Cross-party coalitions, in committee and on the floor, frustrated the efforts of party leaders to enact their agenda. Starting in 1911 both parties in the Senate established formal party leadership positions, including majority/minority leader and whip, but the occupants of these offices felt more constrained than empowered. The Senate majority leader had limited control of the committees and few resources to deal with minority obstruction. He became more a manager of an increasingly complex organization than a leader aggressively shaping policy.

Two additional developments during this period left their mark on the internal structure and capacity of the Senate. The first was the adoption in 1913 of a constitutional amendment providing for the direct election of senators; the second, in 1917, was the passage of Rule XXII, the Senate's first cloture rule providing a means of ending debate.

As discussed earlier, the ratification of the Seventeenth Amendment, which shifted the election of senators from state legislatures to the public, was the culmination of decades of developments in which senators increasingly built their own base of popular support. In the early 1900s, these included the spread of the direct primary, whose ballots, especially in one-party states, sometimes included senatorial candidates, and the "Oregon System," which allowed voters to express at the polls their unofficial choice for senator. By 1910, almost half of the senators slated to be selected by their state legislatures had already been designated by popular vote. Nonetheless, the formal shift of authority from legislatures to voters encouraged even more individualism in the Senate and resistance to control by the leadership.

The adoption of the cloture rule came after a series of extended and highly publicized filibusters. The most notorious succeeded in talking to death President Woodrow Wilson's armed neutrality bill in the closing days of the 64th Congress, only months before the country's entrance into

World War I. Wilson responded angrily: "The Senate of the United States is the only legislative body in the world which cannot act when its majority is ready for action. A little group of willful men, representing no opinion but their own, have rendered the great government of the United States helpless and contemptible." Wilson called the Senate into special session and demanded that it amend its rules. The Senate quickly acquiesced, passing a rule permitting two-thirds of senators present and voting to restrict further debate on a pending matter. In doing so, it rejected an alternative to authorize cloture by majority vote. And the following year it defeated a proposal to allow use of the previous question motion to limit debate during the war. Obstruction on the floor could be ended but only with a supermajority vote. Senate leaders soon realized that the filibuster remained alive and well. It would become an even more prominent feature of the chamber in the decades that followed, reflecting and reinforcing the power of individual senators and the leverage accorded minorities.

Relations with the Other Branches

In addition to providing the critical representational linkage with the public and an independent law-making capacity, Congress was designed to keep a vigilant watch over the other branches of the national government.

Congress vs. the Executive. As we discussed previously, the Constitution was designed to foster a healthy rivalry between the legislative and executive branches, but one in which the president was subordinate to Congress. Yet the earliest years of the new government saw the executive the focal point of the republic and the center of leadership.[25] This reflected the uniquely important role George Washington played at the birth of the nation as well as the extraordinary political skills of Thomas Jefferson. Treasury Secretary Alexander Hamilton was the dominant figure in the Washington administration, acting in many respects as a prime minister in a parliamentary system. As his policies became controversial, Congress resisted his initiatives, in part by creating standing committees to provide independent sources of information and expertise. The emergence of a Jeffersonian opposition to the dominant Federalist influence in both branches set the stage for the presidentially led party government after the election of 1800. Jefferson proved adept at using his role as leader of the newly victorious Republicans to hold sway over majorities in Congress. He did this without challenging the constitutional standing of Congress or exercising his veto power. Instead, he worked in tandem with congressional leaders to set and enact a legislative agenda, garnering him the deserved reputation of a strong and effective president.

Jefferson's successors in the presidency—James Madison, James Monroe, and John Quincy Adams—exhibited neither his ambition in the office nor his effectiveness on Capitol Hill. Furthermore, Madison and Monroe were handicapped by their obligation to the congressional caucus that had nominated them for the presidency; Adams was even more indebted to Congress after he was elected by the House of Representatives in the disputed election of 1824. While Madison enjoyed the nominal support of the Democratic-Republican majorities in Congress, he lost control to a group of "war hawks" who eventually pushed him into the War of 1812. Under the House leadership of Speaker Henry Clay and John C. Calhoun, these radicals within Madison's party seized the initiative and shifted power decisively toward the Congress, a swing of the pendulum not reversed until the presidency of Andrew Jackson in 1829.

The Senate also began to flex its muscles during these two decades of congressional ascendancy, making effective use of its treaty and appointment power. Particularly striking was its dictation of executive appointments. For example, the Senate blocked Madison's choice for secretary of state and forced the President to accept a candidate of its choosing. Presidents were well advised to seek the advice before the consent of the Senate in making appointments.

Jackson's inauguration changed the executive-legislative balance abruptly. Elected to the White House with a program and popular mandate, he unabashedly seized the reins of power to advance his agenda. Jackson was not afraid to take unilateral steps to reverse national policy—such as withdrawing government deposits from the Second Bank of the United States—and then to fight congressional efforts to reverse them. His direct appeal to the electorate, the first by a president, gave him a unique public standing and legitimacy, but he faced vigorous opposition to his policies and high-handed tactics from the new Whig party. The Whigs, whose most notable leader was Henry Clay, represented commercial and industrial interests and were dedicated to the principle of legislative supremacy. Their opposition to Jackson's policies and tactics led to major struggles with the Senate over his legislative proposals and executive appointments.

The Whig doctrine of a weak presidency and dominant legislature gained strong supporters at both ends of Pennsylvania Avenue. The two Whigs elected president, William Henry Harrison and Zachary Taylor, cautioned about concentration of power in the executive and promised not to interfere in the legislative process. Even Abraham Lincoln, who would later defy the constitutional power of Congress in responding to the secession of the South and become the most influential president in American history, espoused the Whig doctrine as a member of the House. He wrote: "Were I President, I should desire the legislation of the country to rest with Congress, uninfluenced by the executive in its origin or purpose, and undisturbed by the veto unless in very special and clear cases."[26] Democratic Presidents John Tyler and James K. Polk accepted the strong presidency as a matter of party philosophy and had no compunction wielding the veto on policy grounds. Polk successfully pursued an ambitious legislative agenda and muscular foreign policy through strong party leadership and an expansive conception of presidential authority.

After Lincoln's death, Congress seized power from his successor, Andrew Johnson, enacting its own program for reconstruction, bypassing his authority as commander-in-chief, and coming within a single vote in a Senate impeachment trial of convicting him and removing him from office. As James Sundquist notes, the rest of the century was characterized by a relatively weak presidency and an ascendant Congress.[27] The Whig party had collapsed but its philosophy carried over to the postwar era as the doctrine of Republican presidents from Ulysses S. Grant to William McKinley. Presidents following Johnson and Grant succeeded to some extent in checking the erosion of their office, most importantly by defending their appointment power, but they had little impact on policy development in Congress. As Congress strengthened its agenda-setting capacity through the party leadership in the 1880s and 1890s, it began to fill the power vacuum in national government. When McKinley became president in 1897, the broad policy consensus among Republicans facilitated an unusual period of harmony between the two branches—one, however, in which Congress remained the dominant partner.

The twentieth century, beginning with Theodore Roosevelt and then continuing with Woodrow Wilson, Franklin Roosevelt, and all of his successors, saw the abandonment of the Whig conception of legislative supremacy and the rise of the modern, powerful presidency. Many factors contributed to this transformation: the ambitions and personalities of the occupants of the White House; the expansion of the responsibilities of the federal government during the Great Depression and the rise of the administrative state; the creation of a standing army; the mobilization effort for World War II and the creation of a national security apparatus within the executive; and changes in communications technology facilitating the use of the "bully pulpit" and the public presidency. The question was no longer whether the president would seek a powerful leadership role; he most certainly would. It was rather how the Congress would respond to its ascendant rival. Ironically, Congress was largely, though not entirely, complicit in the expansion of executive power at Congress's expense. Would the incentives facing its members and the resources available to them be sufficient to allow their first branch of government to fulfill the responsibilities outlined by the framers, to "refine and enlarge the public view" and to check and balance the executive?

Congress and the Judiciary. The framers intended an independent judiciary but also an accountable one, a separate branch of government but one embedded in a set of institutions that provided important checks and balances. With its impressive array of constitutional tools for expressing its displeasure with decisions taken by the court, Congress might be tempted to overplay its hand with the judicial branch. The early history of the republic includes a number of highly charged clashes between the two branches, with Congress mostly the aggressor.[28] Legislators sought to bring independent-minded jurists into submission by impeaching and removing them from office, packing and unpacking the courts, restricting their jurisdiction, cutting judicial budgets, defying court orders, and investigating individual judges. Yet these tactics met with minimal success and are now widely viewed as illegitimate and threatening to judicial independence. As law professor Charles Geyh persuasively argues, apart from the judicial appointment process there has been a gradual decline since the nation's founding in the acceptability of all political means of holding the judiciary accountable for its decisions.

Important precedents were set in the very early congresses. In the Judiciary Act of 1789, Congress exercised its authority to create inferior courts. That structure of district and circuit courts remained essentially intact throughout the nineteenth century. However, one very acrimonious partisan battle, ignited during the interval between Jefferson's election as president and his taking office, saw an ominous packing and unpacking of the federal judiciary.[29] The lame-duck Federalist Congress passed the Judiciary Act of 1801, which created sixteen new federal judgeships, and outgoing President John Adams filled the posts with Federalist judges. Jefferson, outraged that the Federalists would enjoy virtually complete control of the judiciary in spite of their election defeat, worked with his Republican majority in Congress to repeal the act and eliminate the new judgeships. Confronted by a constitutional challenge to the act, on grounds that it circumvented the tenure and salary protections of Article III, the Supreme Court, which less than a month earlier in *Marbury v. Madison* had boldly declared its power of judicial review, timidly upheld the statute.

The Jeffersonians went one step further by launching a campaign to impeach and remove Federalist judges. They succeeded in ousting District Judge John Pickering, aided by the fact that even his supporters asserted he was "insane, totally deranged." Their second target, Supreme Court Justice Samuel Chase, an outspoken Federalist, was impeached by the House for judicial misconduct while sitting on the bench. Although Republicans held twenty-five of thirty-four Senate seats, no more than nineteen senators voted to convict Chase on any of the eight charges, short of the required two-thirds. As Chief Justice William Rehnquist was to observe two centuries later:

> Chase was by no means a model judge, and his acquittal certainly was not an endorsement of his actions. Rather, the Senate's failure to convict him represented a judgment that impeachment should not be used to remove a judge for conduct in the exercise of his judicial duties. The political precedent set by Chase's acquittal has governed the use of impeachment to remove federal judges from that day to this: a judge's *judicial* acts may not serve as a basis for impeachment. Any other rule would destroy judicial independence.[30]

Chase's acquittal took the life out of the Jeffersonians' campaign against the judiciary. And the Senate has never removed a judge by impeachment for making an unpopular decision.

Additional confrontations with the judiciary occurred during Jackson's presidency, the Civil War and its aftermath, the populist period at the end of the nineteenth century, the progressive era at the beginning of the twentieth century, and the early years of the New Deal. Yet these clashes resulted in few punitive actions by Congress through changes in Court structure, size, or jurisdiction. Viewed from this historical perspective, the Court appears to have been very adept at diffusing attacks from Congress and the presidency, perhaps with tactical steps designed to diffuse congressional and presidential animus (a prime example is the famous "switch in time that saved nine," when the shift of one Supreme Court justice from opposition to support of New Deal legislation took the steam out of Roosevelt's move to pack the Court) and by being more responsive to public opinion than its justices and judges would care to admit.[31]

The sole exception to the general pattern of interbranch comity—in deeds if not in words—is in the realm of judicial appointments. The debate at the Constitutional Convention and early encounters between the branches on Supreme Court appointments make clear that the Senate was expected to play a substantive role in the process, not merely serve as a rubber stamp for the president's nominees. The Senate rejected a number of judicial appointees during the first hundred years of the United States, starting in the Washington administration, on obviously political and partisan grounds. These included the nominee's views on unrelated political issues, the president's unpopularity, the timing of a nomination late in a president's term of office, and a failure to consult adequately with key senators. The latter underscores the importance of the "advice" part of the Senate's responsibility for judicial, as well as executive, appointments.

Beginning late in the nineteenth century, the focus of confirmation battles began to shift to decisions nominees appeared likely to make on the bench that would be objectionable to senators and the interests they represented. The first Supreme Court nomination rejected largely on ideological grounds was former Senator Stanley Matthews, submitted to the Senate by President Rutherford B. Hayes in 1881. The trend toward an increasing emphasis on ideology extended into the first three decades of the twentieth century, subsided for an almost forty-year period during which no Supreme Court nominees were rejected by the Senate, and then reemerged in the late 1960s to become a signature feature of the contemporary judicial confirmation process.

This emphasis on ideology, by both the president and the Senate, was much slower to come to the nomination and confirmation of district and circuit court judges. Patronage and partisan politics were the driving forces, and presidents typically deferred to the preferences of home-state senators. But this too was to undergo dramatic change.

Toward the Modern Congress

While Congress has responded to forces and developed in ways not fully anticipated by the framers, much of their logic and most of their design remained intact with the dawning of the modern era. The emergence of political parties and the nationalization of politics complicated their plan to channel the ambitions of politicians into patterns of institutional competition to serve broad public purposes. Popular elections for presidents and senators enhanced their institutional positions, altering somewhat the roles they were expected to play and weakening the protections against the "excesses of democracy." The rise of the administrative and national security state afforded the executive much greater responsibilities, resources, and public expectations for strong presidential leadership than planned.

And yet Congress retained a central position in the American constitutional system, drawing on its critical link to the citizenry through direct elections separate from the executive and its impressive arsenal of constitutional powers. Judgments about how well Congress was meeting its responsibilities—to represent and to legislate, to reflect the democratic wishes of its constituencies, to deliberate in a responsible fashion to serve the nation's purposes, to check and balance the other branches without diminishing their comparative advantages—varied over the course of American history. The organizational building blocks of Congress, that is, its individual members, committees, and parties, were rearranged periodically to respond to external forces and to serve personal and institutional interests. Every such adjustment brought its costs as well as its benefits.

Enhancing the prerogatives and resources of individual members affirms the principle that representatives and senators have equal standing within their respective chambers but weakens the ability to set an agenda and act upon it. It also runs the risk of reinforcing parochialism and removing members from any semblance of electoral competition. A strong committee system permits Congress to use specialization and a division of labor to develop its own substantive expertise, an essential resource in legislating and overseeing the executive. But independent, unrepresentative, and constituency-controlled committees can distort legislative outcomes and frustrate chamber majorities and national interests. Powerful party leaders can help overcome the chaos and fragmentation of a legislature dominated by individuals and committees, but their ability to lead is contingent on broad policy agreement within their caucus and their energies might be deployed more in service of narrow partisan than broad institutional interests. Getting the mix right is no easy task.

That challenge was apparent as the modern Congress began to emerge in mid-twentieth century. The fragmented system that replaced the relatively brief flirtation with party government was effectively controlled by a conservative coalition of Republicans and Southern Democrats, who used their control of the floor on key issues and their seniority-based positions on powerful committees to dominate policy making. In the House, divisions within the Democratic party made it extremely difficult for its leaders to take full advantage of the majoritarian features of their institution. In the Senate, the adoption of the cloture rule did little to constrain the use of filibusters and party leaders increasingly came to manage legislative business through unanimous consent agreements, which further enhanced the power of individual senators. Both chambers sought to rationalize and strengthen their committee systems in the face of a burgeoning executive, eventually leading to the passage of the Legislative Reorganization Act of 1946. In this and many other ways, Congress struggled to maintain its position as the first branch of government.

This was the first branch of government we encountered in the fall of 1969. It was an institution struggling under a new set of political forces to realize the intentions of the framers: to represent a large and diverse public, to deliberate independently and responsibly on complex policy questions, and to keep a watchful eye on the operations of the executive and judicial branches. We did not realize until much later that many of the seeds for change to come, for the nature of Congress today, were present then—the partisan conflict that was set in motion by the clashes between Republican President Nixon and the ruling Democrats on the Hill; the partisan evolution of regions like the South and Northeast; the growing discontent of northern liberal Democrats and moderate Republicans that led to an era of major reform. We were soon in our own front row seats seeing congressional history in the making.

THREE

The Seeds of the Contemporary Problem, 1969–1994

WE ARRIVED IN WASHINGTON from the University of Michigan in the fall of 1969, set to work on Capitol Hill for a year as congressional fellows of the American Political Science Association. We shared a townhouse near DuPont Circle with two other colleagues, one of whom had a dog. On a balmy October evening just after our arrival, one of us took the dog out for a short walk. It did not last long. Before we had gone a block, the dog started to yelp and howl, for no apparent reason. Within thirty seconds, the reason was apparent: a tear gas canister spewing its contents was rolling down the street toward us. Soon, it was followed by more tear gas, and a crowd of people running toward us—followed in turn by police in full riot gear. A demonstration at the South Vietnamese Embassy on the other side of the circle had evidently gone awry. We stumbled back to the house through the tumult and choking gas fumes, closed the windows, put wet towels under the door frames, and waited out the storm. "Welcome to Washington," said one of our roommates.

The Vietnam War Congress

He was right. It was a memorable welcome to a Washington that was filled with conflict and tension, including regular protests against an unending and unpopular war in Vietnam. A Democratic Congress faced an aggressive Republican president, Richard M. Nixon, in his first year after a tough, bitter, close, and divisive presidential election. In a three-way race with Democrat Hubert Humphrey and insurgent former Democrat George Wallace, Nixon had won by a nose with 43.4 percent of the votes. Wallace got forty-six electoral votes, all in the South.

That election reflected a sharp division over civil rights, including such issues as voting rights for blacks in the South, that long had been a part of American politics but that had reemerged with Barry Goldwater's Republican candidacy in 1964. Goldwater got trounced but managed to capture five deep Southern states—Alabama, Georgia, Louisiana, Mississippi, and South Carolina. Four of them had voted in 1948 for "Dixiecrat" candidate Strom Thurmond, as four voted in 1968 for Wallace, but voting for renegade Democrats was quite different than actually voting for a Republican. That 1964 result signaled an undercurrent of partisan change in America, a change that was shaping Congress even as it altered the balance in presidential politics. The South had long been the bedrock base of Democrats in presidential and congressional politics; the bedrock was starting to crumble.

Richard Nixon had run and won, in part, by exploiting these ongoing tensions through a sharp focus on "law and order" at a time when the *Washington Post*'s daily reports of crimes committed in the District of Columbia described the race of the perpetrators. But in the year we spent on the Hill, it was division over the continued conflict in Vietnam that reverberated most strongly on Capitol Hill and in the relationship between president and Congress.

The conflict in Washington was sharp and striking. During our tenure in 1970, Democratic Senator George

McGovern of South Dakota took to the Senate floor and condemned its role in the continuing American presence in Vietnam by saying the Senate chamber "reeks of blood." Soon thereafter, freshman Republican Senator Bob Dole attacked McGovern viciously on the Senate floor, a prelude to Dole's appointment as Republican National Committee chair the next year.

That exchange seemed to underscore the highly partisan nature of conflict in Congress. But our year suggested otherwise. At one point we saw McGovern and Dole walking arm in arm in the Capitol, friends and allies in their mutual interest in alleviating worldwide hunger. The conflict over Vietnam did not pit most or all of the Democrats in Congress against most or all of the Republicans. To the contrary. Supporters of a continuing American role in Vietnam included a very substantial share of the majority Democrats in both houses, particularly the more conservative Southern Democrats who made up a third of the Democratic membership in Congress but held half the committee chairmanships—and all of the chairmanships of the powerful "exclusive" committees. Opponents of a continuing American role in Vietnam included a sizable group of moderate Republicans from the Northeast, Midwest, and Pacific regions. The major legislative vehicle to pull the U.S. out of Vietnam was known as "McGovern-Hatfield" for George McGovern and liberal Republican Senator Mark Hatfield of Oregon; a prime cosponsor was moderate Republican Senator Charles Goodell of New York.

The Parties in Congress

The divisions across party lines on Vietnam were not limited to that one overarching issue. Democrats were in their fifteenth consecutive year of majority status in both the House and Senate when we arrived in 1969—they were to maintain that status for another quarter century in the

House and another dozen consecutive years in the Senate—but it did not take long for the two of us to see that the control over policy outcomes was in many cases more nominal than real. Most of the key issues were won by a "conservative coalition" that represented a majority of Southern Democrats and a majority of Republicans voting against a majority of the non–Southern Democratic legislators. In fact, the key vote measure of ideology used by Congress mavens was Congressional Quarterly's compilation of the votes on which the conservative coalition appeared. After the 1966 midterm elections, which resulted in huge Republican gains, political scientist Charles O. Jones wrote in his classic *The Minority Party in Congress* that it sometimes "appeared that the Republicans were the majority and the Democrats the minority."[1]

On many of the key committees, the relationship between the chairman and the ranking minority member was much closer than the relationship between the chairman and his Democratic colleagues on the panel. On the Ways and Means Committee, for example, Chairman Wilbur Mills and Ranking Republican John Byrnes were so close in their policy views and personal relationship that Mills used to say regularly that if he had to leave the committee room for any reason and handed the gavel to Byrnes, nobody would be able to tell the difference. The same kind of policy congruence held true for House Appropriations Chairman George Mahon and his Republican counterpart Frank Bow, and for many others, including the chair and ranking minority member of the key House Rules Committee.

Republicans nonetheless were clearly in the minority, at least insofar as the operations of Congress were concerned. If the Speaker of the House and the Minority Leader tended to get along or even establish close friendships, it was never fuzzy as to who held the power and ran the body. All the chairmanships were held by Democrats. Committee staffs were firmly under the thumb of the Democratic chairmen; the stricture that the minority party was supposed to get one-third of the committee staff was widely ignored. When such key Republicans as John Byrnes were given a policy role, it was by the choice—and sufferance—of the majority. The role of ranking member was not that of an equal cosharing power but that of a subordinate, similar to the status of a wife in an old-line traditional marriage where the husband wore the pants in the family.

But at least many or most ranking members had serious input into policy decisions or found their views in sync with committee chairs. For a large number of rank-and-file members, Democrat as well as Republican, the contribution to policy was limited. Junior members were expected to be seen and not heard. Subcommittee chairmanships were closely held by committee chairs and their favorites, and they had their jurisdictions and freedom circumscribed by the committee chairs; the subcommittee staffs usually were under central control. Floor debate was limited, and few amendments were allowed to reach roll-call votes. The frustration among those rank-and-file members was growing and would provide the impetus for reform.

Stirrings of Reform

The two of us settled into offices on the House side, finding assignments that fit our backgrounds—Mann with James O'Hara, a Michigan representative; Ornstein with Donald Fraser, of his home state, Minnesota. They were two of the brightest lights in the House and among the most energetic. They had something else in common: both were Democrats who felt relatively powerless, with little seniority and being outside the ruling conservative coalition.

O'Hara and Fraser were policy wonks who found themselves frequently at odds with the policies of President Nixon and the predilections of their own party leaders on their committees and on the House floor. They were active dissidents on their committees, O'Hara on education and labor issues and Fraser especially on foreign policy questions. Both channeled their frustration at being minority voices in the full chamber by working to reform the power structure and dynamic of the House, to give more clout to the majority of the majority party, to open up the deliberations, and to decentralize power and resources to rank-and-file members.

Their vehicle of choice was the Democratic Study Group, the informal group of liberal Democrats that organized after the 1958 election brought a large number of them into the House and that grew in size and stature in the succeeding decade. DSG had an impressive staff, built around the contributions many members made from their office accounts. Its main purpose was to provide rank-and-file members with objective research on bills to fill the vacuum left by the centralization of control in conservative committee chairmanships. But the group also sought ways to promote reform of party and House rules and procedures. Jim O'Hara was a former chairman of DSG; Don Fraser was the sitting chair at the time we assumed our posts.

O'Hara, Fraser, and their liberal rank-and-file colleagues had allies in other places. They saw that their frustration with the power of committee chairs, who were predominantly conservative Southerners, was shared by Speaker John McCormack, who had limited authority over the autocratic chairs. And the liberal Democrats' frustration with the closed nature of the policy process, including the inability to get recorded votes on amendments on the floor, was shared by reformist Republicans, whose agitation for change was initiated in the late 1960s by the loose group "Rumsfeld's Raiders," led by Donald Rumsfeld of Illinois.

What liberal Democrats and dissident Republicans alike encountered was a House with rules, processes, and norms stacked against them. The House was a collection of barons— the committee chairs, who had near full control of committee resources and the flow of legislation to the floor, who were selected in an ironclad fashion by seniority and not with any discretion by party leaders or rank-and-file members, and who were virtually immune from removal.

The power of the committee chairs in the House, by rule and custom, was breathtaking. Committee chairs could hire and fire the staffs, set the jurisdiction of subcommittees and refer—or not refer—legislation to them, choose the subcommittee chairs and often set the subcommittee memberships, select members of conference committees that ironed out differences between House and Senate bills, call committee meetings and hearings, decide whether members of the committee could travel, and control debate on the floor when committee matters came up.

Those powers were supplemented by other procedures and long-standing norms. Nearly all key committee meetings—at which bills were "marked up," put together, and amended piece-by-piece, and where conference panels met—were held in secret, behind closed doors. In the absence of the public and press, and with no recorded votes, chairmen could wheel and deal, and cajole or coerce their members, relatively free of outside pressure or influence. On the floor, too, most votes on amendments were unrecorded, and thus there was no formal record of how individual lawmakers had voted. Chairmen might invite dissidents to "take a walk"—simply miss the votes if they disagreed—to avoid incurring the wrath of the great powers.

The DSG pursued reform on two fronts, the House as a whole and the majority-party caucus, the gathering of all the Democratic members of the body. Changes in the caucus were the more intense focus of these reform leaders, as their frustrations stemmed primarily from the way in which power within the majority had been controlled: limiting reformers' freedom, clout, and resources; keeping the majority of the majority in minority status when it came to shaping policy outcomes; and taking away any real opportunities for accountability against the barons, the committee chairs who dominated the process and could not be removed or sanctioned unless they got tripped up on serious ethics violations or illegalities.

The first real step for reform came in January 1969, before we arrived, with the passage of a party rule that called for a meeting of the caucus once a month if fifty members signed a petition demanding it so that there would be opportunities to discuss issues and procedures and air concerns and disagreements. Before the establishment of that rule, the caucus met only at the discretion of the Speaker and the caucus chair; that is, it met once every two years, at the beginning of a new Congress, to vote on leadership vacancies or challenges, fill committee vacancies, and ratify, en bloc, the committee chairs who had been recommended by the party committee on committees, which consisted of the Democratic members of the Ways and Means Committee and always recommended the most senior figures for the chairs.

The party's senior figures had no interest in other caucus gatherings; why meet as a party if the only reason for doing so was agitation? But open resistance to an assertive call to allow meetings if a sizable group of party members wanted them was hard to justify; besides, Speaker John McCormack and Caucus Chair Dan Rostenkowski wanted to find small ways to appease the DSG liberals, since the tension within the majority party was palpable over Vietnam and social issues. So the reformers got their first modest victory. With the rules change, the caucus actually met to discuss policy issues like Vietnam and was able to serve as a vehicle to push for further reforms.

Soon after we arrived, the next shoe dropped. In March 1970, the caucus met—and liberals proposed creation of a caucus committee to consider rules changes. Some militant reformers wanted to propose sweeping reforms and force the caucus to act on them there and then; Fraser, O'Hara, John Brademas, and other DSG leaders instead shaped a less confrontational, incremental strategy that ultimately prevailed. A committee chosen by the caucus likewise seemed nonthreatening. The eleven-member committee, chaired by Julia Butler Hansen of Washington, was put together by Rostenkowski and had regional and ideological balance. The Hansen Committee met throughout the rest of the year and came out with serious recommendations immediately after the 1970 elections.

The proposals were ratified by the full Democratic Caucus at its January 1971 organizing meeting. They included reforms in two major areas, seniority and subcommittees. With regard to seniority, a new rule allowed a separate, secret-ballot vote of the caucus on any individual nominee for a chair if ten members demanded it. This rule eliminated the possibility of an automatic vote on an entire slate, take-it-or-leave-it, and offered an opportunity for separate accountability. The DSG leaders were poised to single out a small number of especially recalcitrant and autocratic chairs as examples for these up-or-down votes. On subcommittees, new reforms limited subcommittee chairmanships to one per member and allowed each subcommittee chair to select one professional staff member if the committee caucus agreed—with no veto by the chair alone. Thus, chairmen could no longer stockpile the power positions among a few cronies or keep all the committee resources to themselves. Reform did not come easy. But, in this case, the unanimous recommendation of the Hansen Committee helped, as did the relatively modest nature of the changes. And the opening up of more subcommittee power slots to more members meant that self-interest played a part.

Soon after the reforms passed, there were petitions signed to challenge several committee chairs. Only one chair came relatively close to removal. John McMillan of South Carolina, the autocratic, arbitrary, and highhanded chair of the District of Columbia Committee, prevailed 126–96 only after he promised new Speaker Carl Albert that he would mend his ways. He didn't—and would undoubtedly have been ousted from the post two years later, except that he was defeated in the Democratic primary for reelection. Even though not one chair was ousted, the impact of the reform was clear, and the power relationships between chairs and rank-and-file members were changed. The stage was set for more revolutionary change after succeeding elections.

As the second reform took hold, sixteen subcommittee chairmanships were freed for junior members, nearly all liberal and non-Southern.

A second front had been playing out on a parallel track during our year on the Hill, and this was the bipartisan reform effort to change the House as a whole through the first major reform effort since 1946. The DSG reformers targeted the long-standing practice of voting on floor amendments by teller. Instead of a roll-call count, members would walk down one aisle if voting aye, another if voting nay, and designated colleagues, *tellers,* would count them as they passed to come up with the total. Teller amendments saved time—they took only five minutes instead of the usual thirty-five to forty-five minutes required for a full roll-call vote of the 435 members—but the procedure made it almost impossible to tell who had voted for or against what, thus destroying accountability and adding to the leverage of the House's power players.

The unhappiness here was bipartisan. Whether bills were jammed through committees on a partisan or bipartisan basis, there were rarely avenues to challenge the outcome on the House floor. Few amendments of any kind to bills reported by committees were permitted to get roll-call votes on the floor, including those offered by liberal Democrats and those offered by Republicans. Without roll calls, even amendments that were popular or hard to vote against publicly could be quashed quietly, by voice vote or teller votes that did not require members to record their positions one way or another; they could merely stay away from the floor without being noticed and thus avoid the wrath of party and committee leaders.

So here, the bipartisan DSG/Rumsfeld's Raiders coalition took hold, using an inside strategy of appealing to those frustrated lawmakers who were shut out of the ruling power structure and an outside strategy of appealing to the press and the public for more openness and less secrecy in the legislative process. It worked. The public campaign, which resulted in multiple editorials in the *Washington Post,* the

New York Times, and other papers across the country, left members afraid to vote for the indefensible status quo that promoted secrecy. The House passed the Legislative Reorganization Act of 1970, in which was included a set of reform amendments: they changed teller votes on amendments to recorded ones; guaranteed time for debate on amendments; required that meetings and hearings be open; allowed members of a committee to call up a bill that a chair was unilaterally sitting on; and required three days between the time a bill was reported and the time it was brought to the floor for debate.

Another reform was also in the works, one that moved from the old-fashioned roll calls whereby names were called one at a time by the clerk—which took up to forty-five minutes— to an electronic voting system in which members could vote by putting a card in a machine on the House floor. Under the new electronic voting system, the forty-five minutes were reduced by two-thirds, to fifteen. By 1973, virtually all roll calls, including those on amendments, were done within a fifteen-minute time frame, some less controversial ones in five minutes.

The other shoe dropped in January 1973, at the new Congress's organizing caucus, after another bout of reform deliberation by the Hansen Committee. In the election, Democrats had lost seats, but, more important, the relative balance between conservative Southerners and liberal Northerners shifted significantly toward the liberal side. The new set of incremental reforms focused in this case on energizing and empowering the subcommittees. The vehicle was a reform package informally called the Subcommittee Bill of Rights.

At this time, we were back in Washington—Mann on the professional staff of the American Political Science Association, Ornstein teaching politics at Catholic University— and we both kept our hands in Capitol Hill matters through the Congressional Fellowship Program, which Mann now ran with Ornstein's assistance. The Subcommittee Bill of Rights was the brainchild of Peter Barash, a canny staff aide to Rep. Benjamin Rosenthal of New York, who was Don Fraser's best friend in Congress, working with another congressional fellow, David Rohde. Whereas before, in many areas chairs of committees had acted unilaterally and emasculated other majority members, making their subcommittee chairs—if they had them—impotent to act or meet, the new Subcommittee Bill of Rights required that power be spread out to the subcommittees, empowering the subcommittee chairs with automatic access to resources that had been withheld at the whim of the committee chairs. The Subcommittee Bill of Rights did the following:

- It took the power of appointment of subcommittee chairs away from the committee chairs and allowed committee Democrats to bid for them, in order of seniority, with ratification votes taken by the caucus of all committee Democrats.
- It gave the subcommittees fixed jurisdictions and control over their legislation.
- It empowered the subcommittees to meet, hold hearings, receive adequate budgets, and hire subcommittee professional staffs.
- It spread out subcommittee assignments, guaranteeing each member at least one choice assignment.

Reforms to spread power to subcommittee chairs and rank-and-file members were not the only changes made in January 1973. Another set of reforms moved in a seemingly opposite, centralizing direction, giving more power to the Speaker—most of it coming, one way or the other, at the expense of the committee chairs. The Speaker was given a more direct role over committee assignments, more power to refer bills to appropriate committees, and a powerful role on a new Democratic Steering and Policy Committee set up to shape party legislative policy and strategy.

These changes, too, were the work of the liberal DSGers, who saw Speakers like John McCormack and Carl Albert as more sympathetic to them than to the committee chairmen. Speaker Sam Rayburn and the DSG had been close allies in the 1960–61 effort to curtail the conservative power of the House Rules Committee that was a key roadblock to President Kennedy's domestic agenda. If Speaker Carl Albert was not exactly a proponent of these reform proposals, neither was he an opponent or an obstacle. And Majority Leader Tip O'Neill, the Speaker-in-waiting, had been the "point man" on the Rules Committee for the recorded teller vote fight in 1970, was an outspoken dove on the Vietnam War, and indicated his sympathy to spreading around power to more junior members.

The reform movement was not just centered around the internal power arrangements in the House. There was also a broader move afoot to give Congress itself a more expansive and assertive role in core policy making vis-à-vis the executive—all, of course, in the context of increasingly contentious relations between the Democratic Congress and President Nixon. This included the disputes over Vietnam and bombing in Cambodia as well as U.S. support for the autocratic Greek military junta, which offended liberal human rights activists in Congress. On the domestic front, members of Congress were in a power struggle with the president over who would control the federal budget, with a particular congressional unhappiness over the tendency of President Nixon to refuse to spend funds in areas, such as environmental cleanup, that Congress had appropriated and directed be spent for those purposes. Instead, the president impounded the funds, which lawmakers saw as a failure on the part of the president of his constitutional duty to see that the laws were faithfully executed.

In 1973–74, Congress responded with two sweeping pieces of reform legislation, the War Powers Resolution, which required presidents to come to Congress within sixty days after dispatching American forces into combat to get approval, and the Budget and Impoundment Control Act. The former passed in October 1973 and was vetoed by President Nixon. In November of that year, Congress overrode the veto by sweeping margins, 284 to 135 in the House and

75 to 18 in the Senate. The Budget Act passed in 1974, creating a congressional budget process with specific timetables and an annual budget resolution, budget committees in both houses, and a Congressional Budget Office as a counterweight to the Office of Management and Budget, and limiting presidential impoundment.

The reform movement at this point had achieved considerable success, albeit at the margins in internal reforms. But it was not an inexorable juggernaut. In 1974, another more major reform effort to reorganize the House's committee system, led by longtime liberal icon Richard Bolling, faltered when the reform coalition splintered. Reforming the committee system, by reducing the number and size of committees and subcommittees and realigning jurisdictions, cut to the core of every member's career and power, not to mention that of outside groups. Organized labor, upset over the plan's proposed breakup of the Education and Labor Committee, environmental groups, upset over the plan to create an Energy and Environment "supercommittee," and the American Legion, up in arms over the plan to eliminate the House Internal Security Committee, were joined by an odd coalition of liberal and conservative lawmakers who saw their own power bases threatened.

California Representative Phil Burton found a way to sidetrack the Bolling Committee recommendations by funneling them through the Hansen Committee in the Democratic Caucus. The Hansen Committee's members were not at all sympathetic to taking major power from their own committees or those of their allies. The result was a deeply diluted plan that made no significant changes in committee jurisdictions, but which did make some small yet highly significant incremental changes in procedure. Perhaps the most important was one that required each new Congress to return in December after an election, instead of January, which allowed more time for the majority caucus to enact reforms and implement changes.

This change became crucial almost immediately. The 1974 elections, in the wake of Watergate, resulted in a flood of new Democrats; with a net gain of more than forty seats, the majority now had a two-to-one margin over the Republicans. With retirements and other departures, seventy-five freshman Democrats were in Washington in December to help the other 215 members of their party organize the House.

These freshmen were an unusual and motley crew. They ranged from twenty-five-year-old Tom Downey of Long Island to Father Robert J. Cornell, a Catholic priest from Green Bay, Wisconsin, to Larry McDonald of Marietta, Georgia, a member of the John Birch Society Council. As a group, though, they shared several characteristics: they were young, liberal (McDonald notwithstanding), and aggressive; and they came to Congress committed to political and congressional reform—many through specific campaign pledges.

The freshmen set up their own organization with a small staff and an office in a Capitol Hill townhouse. When the December organizing caucus convened, they were ready with their votes to push yet another wave of reforms through the body. One set of changes was aimed at the superpowerful Ways and Means Committee, which had jurisdiction over taxes, trade, Social Security, welfare, and much of health policy. Ways and Means had already been stripped of its power over Democratic committee assignments. Now the caucus voted to expand the committee from its traditional twenty-five members to thirty-seven—with the change in party ratio from 3-to-2 to 2-to-1, Democrats were able to add ten new slots; with two vacancies, that meant twelve plum assignments, and liberal freshmen, in a true break with tradition, got four of them. In addition, the caucus forced Ways and Means to create subcommittees, six in number, further spreading out power. When the longtime chair, Wilbur Mills, was forced by scandal to give up his chairmanship, the transformation of Ways and Means was nearly complete.

That was not all. The caucus also struck at another "supercommittee," Appropriations. It required each of the nominees for chairmanships of the thirteen Appropriations subcommittees—each at least as powerful as most full committee chairs—to be ratified by individual votes in the full Democratic Caucus. (Subsequently, Robert Sykes of Florida was deprived of his Appropriations subcommittee chair because of charges of financial misconduct.) And there was a leadership contest for the chairmanship of the caucus, which was no longer merely ceremonial. Phil Burton was elected by a 162 to 111 vote, putting one of the original reform liberals in the heart of the party leadership hierarchy.

There was more to come. The freshmen organized a caucus of their own and invited all prospective committee chairmen to meet with them. Every one accepted the invitation. Freshmen who had not yet served a day in the House were serving notice to members with an average of two decades of seniority that their continuation as chairmen was no longer automatic. Jamie Whitten of Mississippi, stung by freshman criticism for his antagonism to consumer and environmental protection, voluntarily gave up his Appropriations subcommittee's jurisdiction over those areas in order to save his gavel.

After the freshmen meetings with the committee chairs (F. Edward Hebert of the Armed Services Committee bombed the worst, calling the new members "boys and girls"), the Steering and Policy Committee made its chairmanship recommendations. In a dramatic break with past practice, several senior members were passed over. When the dust settled in the caucus meetings in mid-January, three longtime chairs were deposed—Wright Patman, from Banking, Currency, and Housing; Hebert, from Armed Services; and Bob Poage, from Agriculture. Their replacements were not the second in line in seniority, either, but more activist and liberal members further down the line.

When the committees subsequently met to organize, further change occurred. The Energy and Commerce Committee, bolstered by an infusion of new blood via a dozen new reformist liberal members, staged a "mini-revolt" against Chairman Harley Staggers, ousting him from the powerful chair of the Investigations and Oversight Subcommittee and restructuring the rules to create six virtually independent subcommittee fiefdoms.

Soon after the new 94th Congress convened, an old term was revived by Republicans and some conservative Democrats: "King Caucus" had returned. The ability to call a majority party caucus presented an opportunity to the new, activist members, and they frequently seized it. Early on, spurred by junior liberals, the caucus demanded a relaxed rule on a tax bill to allow votes on two amendments on the oil depletion allowance—a sharp change from the long-standing practice of bringing up tax bills under closed rules with no amendments allowed. In March 1975, a caucus convened after junior liberals triggered it with petitions and voted by a large margin (189 to 49) to adopt a resolution proposed by freshman Bob Carr of Michigan to oppose new military aid to Cambodia and South Vietnam.

One other important set of reforms was passed and implemented in the 95th Congress. After the Bob Sykes ethics imbroglio, the House adopted a new code of ethics, with gift limits, caps on outside income, and financial disclosure, among other things. The ethics code, and the focus on ethics, set the stage for a series of ethics scandals involving individual members in the late 1970s and early 1980s—and for the ethics process to become a weapon in the war between the parties that emerged later on.

Conservative Democrats, such as Joe Waggoner of Louisiana, a Ways and Means member, were not happy about the caucus venturing into the policy arena; some senior liberal Democrats privately shared that unease. And Republicans, no longer sharing the same collaborative success that the conservative coalition had enjoyed, also railed against the caucus actions, charging that the new Democratic policy activism, including its intervention on rules, trampled on minority rights.[2]

For all the frustration of Republicans, the move to democratize the House, including empowering rank-and-file members and opening up amendments on the floor to recorded votes, worked to the advantage of entrepreneurial Republicans, especially those who were less tied to the old House power structure. And the emergence of a liberal class in the House did not mean a new liberal coalition, much less liberal hegemony. Nor did it mean a new spirit of party unity. Democrats continued to have a sizable group of Boll Weevils, more conservative Southern members, including several chairing committees, and finding cohesive majorities on key issues remained difficult. The conservative coalition still had some teeth, however, in committees and on the floor. When Democrat Jimmy Carter came into the White House in 1977, he had a more than two-to-one party majority in both houses of Congress, but was often frustrated trying to accomplish his legislative goals. Carter's Southern roots (he had been governor of Georgia) did not bring him the votes he needed from Boll Weevils on budget matters or in energy— and when he made concessions to satisfy the Boll Weevils, as in the energy area, he often found himself facing intense opposition from the more liberal members.

Mr. Gingrich Goes to Washington

In the 1978 midterm election, Republicans picked up fifteen seats in the House; one was a history professor from Georgia on his third try to win a seat in the body: Newt Gingrich came to Congress with a different attitude toward the status quo than most of his colleagues and a well-formed strategy for creating a Republican majority in the House.

In 1978, even as we continued in our other jobs, the two of us (Mann and Ornstein) established the Congress Project, a new entity at the American Enterprise Institute. Working together as adjunct scholars, we set out a plan to track Congress as an institution. Soon after the 1978 elections, we invited a bipartisan group of eight members of the newly elected freshman class to join us for an ongoing series of off-the-record dinners to discuss their perceptions of the institution through their first term. Among them were Newt Gingrich and Dick Cheney.

From the first dinner on, Gingrich outlined and then elaborated upon his vision. It was based on the belief that as long as Republicans went along to get along, cooperating with Democrats to make the House work and focusing on winning seats in the House one by one, the advantages of incumbency and the tendency of the public to hate the Congress but love their own congressman would allow the Democrats to stay in the saddle indefinitely. Republicans were going to have to nationalize the congressional election process and broaden the public hatred of Congress until enough voters became convinced that the place was thoroughly corrupt and dysfunctional and that sweeping change was necessary. Gingrich disdained the kind of majority/minority partnerships that had worked for so long on committees like Ways and Means and between Speakers and Minority Leaders. He wanted to dramatize regularly that the House was run by Democrats, had been run by Democrats for a quarter century, and that the Democrats had been corrupted by their own power.

Gingrich found a number of allies among his colleagues— and a very sympathetic friend in Cheney, a rising star in the GOP House establishment. Some of them characterized themselves as "the bomb-throwers." Like liberal reformers among the Democrats, they pushed within Republican ranks to decentralize power in committees out to the subcommittees and rank-and-file members, thus opening the process to participation by more junior members. But within the House Republican establishment, Gingrich and his handful of allies were largely shunned and viewed with contempt.

When Ronald Reagan beat Jimmy Carter in 1980, bringing with him thirty-three more Republicans into the House, Gingrich found a more hospitable environment for his tactics. Democrats had lost the Senate for the first time since

1954 and were left with only the House for traction—with a much smaller majority than they were used to. Feeling embattled, they turned to their advantage on procedures for leverage. At the same time, Republicans united strongly behind their new president and grew increasingly frustrated with the Democrats' behavior. When Speaker Tip O'Neill split up the president's first-year budget into six pieces, splitting off key parts to deny Republicans the up-or-down vote they wanted, they were furious. With the help of some of the Boll Weevils, they defeated the rule setting the terms of debate on the bill, thus stopping it from debate and a vote, which handed O'Neill a serious setback.

Gingrich's strategy was to use the new openness on the House floor, including the television coverage now provided by C-SPAN, for political advantage. Soon, dissident Republicans were offering regular floor amendments to bills designed to put Democrats in embarrassing positions whereby their votes could be used as campaign fodder; and Republicans began to take to the deserted House floor after regular business, using a procedure called "special orders," to orchestrate colloquies that bashed the majority.

In 1983, five years into his tenure, Gingrich created a group to fulfill his goals: the Conservative Opportunity Society included such key figures as Vin Weber (R-MN), Bob Walker (R-PA), and Dan Lungren (R-CA), all savvy legislators who shared Gingrich's frustration with minority status and the acquiescence of their leaders to it. Together, they reinforced the tactics that Newt had developed and honed, seeking to make Democrats overreact. And the Democrats acted just as Gingrich hoped and expected they would. They began to apply more and more closed and restrictive rules on bills to head off politically motivated amendments. And they grew increasingly agitated at the rhetoric, often overheated and hyperbolic, that the COS members used during the special orders that allowed for debate time on the floor after the House's official business had ended each day. Since C-SPAN cameras were usually fixed on the particular member who was speaking, it was not apparent to viewers that the chamber was largely empty. When no Democrat rose to counter or rebut the charges, it appeared as if they had no defense and that the charges were therefore true.

Minority Report

By 1984, it was clear that the tension between the two parties had grown to a striking degree. First erupting in midyear over the special orders that came to be known as "Camscam," animosity grew even more rancorous in early and mid-1985 over a disputed congressional election in Indiana that was decided in the House in favor of the Democrats to the intense outrage of Republicans who believed the majority had stolen the election from them. In late 1985, Ornstein wrote a piece on this dynamic in the *Atlantic Monthly* that captured the atmosphere at the time. Here are some excerpts:

> On Wednesday, May 1 [1985], the casual TV channel-switcher who came across C-SPAN was treated to the closest thing to [the prime time television soap opera] *Dallas* that public affairs television has yet had. As the House of Representatives prepared to install Democrat Frank McCloskey in the disputed seat for the Eighth Congressional District in Indiana, Republican tempers boiled over, and rank vitriol rose from the House floor, where exaggerated courtesies usually prevail. "You know how to win votes the old-fashioned way, Mr. Speaker," Bob McEwen, of Ohio, said. "You steal them." Georgia's Newt Gingrich accused the Democrats of having a "leadership of thugs." Other Republicans referred to their Democratic counterparts as "corrupt" and "rotten." The House Republican leader, Bob Michel, said, "Might does not make right." This case, he charged, "is but one example of a consistent abuse and misuse of power by the majority." A colleague said this was, "plain and simple, a rape." After the debate Republicans stormed out of the chamber en bloc. A few of the younger and more passionate members vowed to take drastic

action, such as chaining themselves to the House podium or linking arms outside the chamber entrance to prevent anyone from entering.

Passions quickly faded and cooler heads—aware of what anarchy in the House would do to the Reagan program—prevailed. . . . But under the surface the emotions and tensions lingered. . . .

Just after the July 4 recess, as freshman Joe Barton was walking down the center aisle of the House to cast a vote, he found himself in the middle of an angry crossfire of epithets between Democrat Marty Russo, of Illinois, and Republican John McCain, of Arizona. Seven-letter profanities escalated to twelve-letter ones and then to pushes and shoves before the two were separated.

Russo and McCain were wrangling over bitter complaints from Republicans that they had been deliberately "short-counted" by the majority Democrats in the chair when they had asked for roll-call votes, an outrageous abuse of power which the Democrats just as vehemently denied. Right before the July 4 break Dan Lungren, a Republican conservative, took to the floor to charge that Democratic Majority Leader Jim Wright had threatened to punch him and his colleague Bob Walker in the mouth when they complained about short-counting. Democrats previously had urged Bob Michel to curb his members' obstructionist tactics and rhetoric on the House floor.

Little incidents like these ke[pt] popping up. None was serious or approximate[d] the real physical conflict that was common in Congress in the nineteenth century. But each verbal threat or physical confrontation underscore[d] the deep and bitter partisan tension that permeate[d] the House. . . .

Th[e] frustrating development[s] for Republicans [were] not undone by the election of Ronald Reagan in 1980. Democrats in the House were dismayed by a presidential campaign that focused on the House and especially Tip O'Neill, and an election in which they lost the White House, the Senate, and thirty-three seats in the House, leaving them as close as they had been in twenty-six years to losing their majority. The Democrats did not react by offering an olive branch or a share of power to their Republican counterparts. Instead, they tried to shore up their forces to withstand the Reagan-led assault. Among other attempts to exploit the House rules to their full advantage, the Democrats moved to exaggerate their number on key committees like Ways and Means and Budget, in order to give themselves a working majority and offset any defections by "boll weevil" Democrats. In the process, they did the Republicans out of coveted seats, and provoked immediate and long-lasting outrage.

To a party wandering in the desert of the minority for thirty years with no oasis in sight, and burdened further by the indignities of lessened power and cavalier treatment by the majority and even by their own Republican President, 1985 proved the last straw. When on January 3 Democrats refused to swear in Indiana Republican Rick McIntyre along with the other certified freshman election winners, putting the seat on hold for a recount, and then, four months later, declared Democrat Frank McCloskey the winner of the seat by four votes and moved to seat him, the Republicans exploded. To some degree, talking to Democrats and Republicans on this subject is like reliving *Rashomon*. Each side has its own distinct point of view and interpretation of events—and the overlap is meager when it comes to the Indiana case. But there are some areas of agreement. One is that the situation has intensified in the past few years because of a deliberate strategy of confrontation on the part of a cadre of young Republicans.

Republicans—even those with little affection for Gingrich—[were] outraged over the high-handed behavior of the majority, and Democrats, in turn, outraged over the personal attacks and provocative tactics of the COS Republicans. The Indiana debacle and Republican feelings about parliamentary shenanigans . . . provided some measure of vindication for Gingrich and the rest of the COS team, countering the disdain with which they ha[d] been viewed by many mainstream Republicans. Diverse points of view on policy don't stand in the way of Republican unity when it comes to indignation about majority abuses of power. . . .

Tom Tauke, a mild-mannered Iowa moderate, [was] a cochairman of a new group of issue-oriented centrist and moderate Republicans in the House, called the 92 Group. It serve[d] explicitly as a counterweight to the COS group. Its approach [was] low-key, but its aim, like that of the COS group, [was] a Republican majority (the 92 in the name refers to its goal of winning a majority by 1992). Tauke, too, seethe[d] over the treatment accorded Republicans by the majority. About the Russo-McCain fracas he sa[id], "There were several times when Marty Russo was in the chair when he obviously and blatantly gave us short calls on votes." But Tauke s[aw] the problem in broader terms: "It's an arrogance of power. It basically has to do with long-term dominance. It's their House, and has been for thirty years. They have no fear of being in the minority— and therefore, of limitations being put on their power. The Democrats don't say, "We'd better not do this to the Republicans, because they could retaliate and do the same thing to us when they win the majority." Tauke and the 92 Group d[id]n't like guerilla warfare as a strategy. As moderates, they want[ed] to see their party broaden its base and expand its tent in the House, for they believe[d] that a majority in the House w[ould] come only if the Republican Party c[ould] comfortably embrace the kinds of people who get elected from Democratic districts in the Northeast and Midwest. But the thirty or so members [we]re a distinct minority of the minority.

Dan Lungren, a brawny, hard-charging Long Beach conservative whose district include[d] parts of Orange County, [took] a different point of view. Lungren [was] a collection of opposites. He [was] as conservative and aggressive as any member of the House, and . . . a founding member of the COS team, but he [was] also institution-minded. Lungren instinctively wanted to work within the House but [was] passionately bitter over the Democrats and their tactics. To him the COS tactics of pushing for embarrassing roll call votes on the House floor, using the votes to attack targeted Democratic incumbents, and employing harsh and personal rhetoric to provoke Democratic responses and engage C-SPAN viewers [we]re legitimate hardball tactics. . . .

But the Democratic tactics, including, he believe[d], regular short counts of Republican votes, abuse of proxy voting, the indignity of the McIntyre affair, and unfair committee and subcommittee assignments, [wer]e out of bounds. While much of Newt Gingrich's behavior [was] simply strategic, Lungren visibly exud[ed] real indignation. It [was] clear that Lungren's feelings [we]re in substantial part rooted in minority status; in the House he [was] a second-class citizen, and he [couldn't] stand it. He wouldn't abide Democrats who rubbed that in through petty abuses of parliamentary procedure; neither would he be patronized. "Some Democrats have come up to me privately and said, What can we do for you? I said, It's not up to you or anyone else to do anything for me. I'm a member of Congress. I just want to have the same rules apply to everyone.". . .

It is the nature of the House that members do not spend a great deal of time communicating their gripes in encounter sessions with opposing members. The job of a congressman is frenetic and fragmented; there is little time for reflection and no opportunity to stretch necessarily short attention spans. When members relax—for example, by working out or playing basketball in the House gym—they are by tradition off-limits for partisan conflict or discussion thereof. So House Democrats . . . had [no] intimate exposure to Republicans' psychic pain. The Democrats tend[ed] to break down into four types: the hard partisans ("if the Republicans don't like what's going on, the hell with them"), the fight-fire-with-fire tacticians ("they started it, and we have to respond in kind for self-protection"), the oblivious ("I wasn't aware the Republicans felt that way"), and the institutionalists ("I'm concerned about the Republicans' problems, and I worry about what will happen to the legislative process").

Even the institutionalists ha[d] limited sympathy for the Republicans' plight—at least in part because they fe[lt] they ha[d] their own problems. "Sure I sympathize with the Republicans," Les Aspin, of Wisconsin, sa[id]. "But I'm more worried about whether a Democrat can be elected President in this century." Still, some Democrats [were] sensitized by the raw emotions expressed by Republicans of all stripes during the Indiana debate and thereafter. Majority Leader Jim Wright, after that embarrassing confrontation with Dan Lungren, [was] one. Wright immediately apologized to Lungren for any offense taken when he said he'd like to punch Lungren in the mouth, insisting that he'd said and meant it in a jocular fashion (a wholly believable claim, given that Wright [was] sixty-two and that the thirty-nine-year-old Lungren like[d] to lift weights and practice martial arts). But Lungren's reaction stunned Wright and got him thinking, perhaps for the first time, about the deep frustrations of the permanent minority. Despite his apology [to Lungren], Wright too seethe[d] about the tactics and behavior of the COS congressmen. If they wanted to get under the skin of the Democrats' most visible leaders, they . . . succeeded in his case. "Some Republicans aren't fazed if their own colleagues find them thoroughly objectionable. They are more militant than ever before, they try to attribute unworthy motives in a fashion that is nauseatingly prevalent. Gingrich, Weber, Walker, and the others, they're not content to debate issues on their merits. They're constantly in search of opportunities to allege that they're being cheated, mistreated, abused by crass, power-mad Democrats oblivious of the rights of a minority. They are increasingly engaging in a form of latter-day McCarthyism. They attribute un-Americanism, a lack of patriotism, to us. It is simply offensive to the civility that must be a concomitant of the legislative process." The attacks on the Speaker and the leadership [we]re "like drops of water on a rock," perpetrated by people who are trying deliberately to wear the Democrats down.

. . . There is one subject on which Democrats and Republicans agree[d]: the House [was] becoming a much less pleasant place to be. Democrat Tom Downey sa[id], "It's a more frustrating place for everybody—and I can understand where the Republicans are coming from when you have to add minority status to that."

"The House is just not that attractive a place for middle-aged family people," Tom Tauke sa[id]. "It takes a tremendous amount of time—it's a year-round job, you have to go home to the district on weekends, and it puts a real strain on your family. The salary, given the expenses, is not what most members can receive in the private sector." Members constantly assess their options.

Perhaps the most worrisome problem [was] that the members most prone to dismay and frustration over the current situation—those most likely to ditch the House as a result—tend[ed] to be the best ones, [the] institution-minded and leadership-oriented. . . . Many abandoned promising House careers less out of ambition than out of discontent with life in the minority. "For the real ideologues, and for the mediocrities, the House will still be a fine place to spend time," one observer sa[id]. For the C-SPAN viewers looking for a rock-'em, sock-'em, Dallas-like experience, that might be nice. But it won't make much of a legislative body. [3]

In January 1987, at the beginning of the new Congress and after the *Atlantic* article appeared, Jim Wright did succeed Tip O'Neill as Speaker, with Tom Foley of Washington following him into the Majority Leader position and Tony Coelho of California as Whip. For decades, the House Democrats had helped cement their disparate coalition together by twinning a Northern liberal and a Southern moderate in the top two posts—what many called "the Boston-Austin connection." Boston's O'Neill and Fort Worth's Wright had continued that pattern but with a twist. Wright had been a protégé of Sam Rayburn's although his style was very different. Wright was a natural activist, eager to seize the reins of power that the reforms had given the Speaker and to take a more direct policy role himself.

The new Speaker set out an ambitious agenda, from clean water and highway legislation to tax reform, trade, and welfare. And he moved to turn the Steering and Policy Committee into a real policy panel, which he would dominate through appointments and use to shape the agendas of the standing committees. His interests included foreign policy, especially as an active opponent of U.S. support for the Nicaraguan contras. He ruffled the sensibilities of many of his own committee chairs with his aggressive moves to usurp their agenda powers, and he infuriated the Reagan administration and House Republicans with his aggressiveness and direct challenge to the president's foreign policy.

Wright was able to take advantage of his party's greater cohesiveness and its size—numbers large enough that Democrats could still prevail on their own without Republican votes even if they lost some of their own members. Under Wright, Democrats used their committee caucuses and the rules process to write legislation on their own, limiting or erasing Republican input. As Henry Waxman, a leading member of the revolutionary class of 1974 and a power in the House by the 1980s, put it, "If we have a united Democratic position, Republicans are irrelevant."[4] On major bills, Democrats took to using special rules that restricted debate, disallowed most amendments, and provided blanket waivers against points of order. On the key legislation, especially if there was any Republican alternative brewing,

Wright had a hand in crafting the rules strategy; as one member of the Rules Committee said, "Wright had his fingers in just about everything that came through the Rules Committee. He had his opinions, and he sent word down to the Rules Committee that he wanted things handled this way or that way."[5]

Wright's approach quickly put him at loggerheads with House Republicans. Animosity erupted late in his first year as Speaker, on October 29—a day House Republicans came to call "Black Thursday."[6] The issue was the budget reconciliation bill, an important omnibus package that brought together a series of substantive priorities. Wright brought the bill up under a "self-executing" rule that brought ten separate Democratic amendments—including sweeping welfare reform—into the measure without requiring separate votes on them.

Even many Democrats opposed this approach, and the rule was defeated. When the Republicans suggested tabling the issue, Wright got the Rules Committee to write another rule (minus the welfare package) and bring it back to the floor the same day, which would normally require a two-thirds vote. Wright obviated that requirement by adjourning the House and immediately declaring a new "legislative day," a tactic that was at best unusual and at minimum a breach of the normal decorum. Republicans were infuriated.

But it got worse when the bill came to a final vote. The Democrats were one vote short of passage when the normal fifteen-minute time for the roll call had elapsed—in part because Marty Russo of Illinois, unhappy about something else, had voted no and then left immediately to catch a plane to Chicago, thus unavailable to switch back and give the majority its victory. The time of the vote had expired—but another ten to fifteen minutes elapsed without the gavel coming down as the Democrats searched frantically to find someone to change from nay to yea. Finally, Jim Chapman of Texas was located in the cloakroom and persuaded to switch; now with a one-vote victory, the vote was declared official, and Republicans exploded. Dick Cheney, not noted for a temper or harsh public language, said that Wright was "a heavy-handed son-of-a-bitch and he doesn't know any other way to operate."[7]

There were other instances where Republicans chafed under the Democrats' application of the rules to deny them votes, especially on aid to the Nicaraguan contras. On one vote in 1988, where a parliamentary ploy was used to deny a Republican alternative, even Bob Michel exploded in anger.

The Politics of Scandal

Republican frustration was incurred not only by Jim Wright, but he was the focus of their wrath. And ethics charges became the vehicle used by Gingrich to get at him. After Watergate, ethics issues had become a major preoccupation of the press, prosecutors, and the rest of the Washington community; soon afterward, highly publicized scandals involving Wilbur Mills and Wayne Hays resulted in their downfall.

Both houses of Congress, under pressure, crafted codes of ethics in 1976–77 and restructured their ethics committees, but the changes did not dampen outside pressure to hit Congress or others in government on ethics issues. From 1970 to 1979, thirty-six representatives and senators were found guilty of violating laws or ethics, compared with only thirteen in the previous quarter century.[8] It wasn't just Congress—executive officials also became targets of ethics charges, and Congress was not averse to using its investigative powers, especially when faced with a Republican president, to hit officials in the executive branch.

In 1980, Gingrich found the ethics weapon he was looking for when the Abscam scandal hit Congress; in Abscam, prosecutors set up a sting operation that caught a half-dozen members of the House and one senator taking bribes—on video tape. One House member, Michael Myers, was expelled; he and three others served prison terms. On the verge of expulsion, Senator Harrison Williams resigned from the

Senate. In this climate, Newt Gingrich easily made the case that Congress as an institution—after more than a quarter century of unbroken rule by Democrats—had itself become corrupted. It was not difficult to get press attention for ethics charges, nor was it difficult to bring a complaint of ethics violations to the Committee on Standards of Official Conduct. Any member or outside group could do so, using even such evidence as newspaper clippings to bolster their charges.

Soon after Wright became Speaker, Newt Gingrich began a sustained assault on his ethics, relying on investigative reporters' stories questioning Wright's associations with savings and loan officials and other business leaders. When Common Cause joined the attacks on Wright, it forced the ethics committee to open an investigation in mid-1988. By 1989, after Gingrich had ascended to the position of Republican Whip, his attacks on Wright broadened to include charges that Wright had manipulated the rules to benefit financially from bulk sales of his book *Reflections of a Public Man*.

While Wright scoffed at the charges and ridiculed Gingrich, the attacks took a toll. The effect had worsened by January 1989 after Congress and the outgoing and incoming presidents Reagan and Bush combined to endorse a pay raise for Cabinet members and other top executive officials, federal judges, and members of Congress. It was the first significant pay increase in a long time—but the recommended hike, from $89,500 a year to $125,100, triggered a firestorm of populist outrage in the country.

The opposition cut across traditional boundaries; Ornstein appeared on *Crossfire* to defend the pay raise (mainly because few members were willing to support the raise publicly) and took on a tag team of right-wing populist Pat Buchanan and left-wing populist Ralph Nader. Ornstein also accompanied House Democrats that February on their annual policy retreat to the Greenbrier Resort in West Virginia. Leaving Washington from Union Station, the members and speakers had to run a gauntlet of disgruntled public protestors who wielded nasty signs and shouted nastier slogans. The five-hour train ride was remarkably tense; much of the tension was directed by members at Wright for contributing to their politically vulnerable position. Wright in turn was furious with his colleagues for refusing to offer him unquestioned support. Press coverage of the retreat, which invariably mentioned Democrats closeted at the "posh" Greenbrier, fueled the flames of populist resentment of a Congress living high on the hog at public expense.

Under intense public pressure and scrutiny of the press, the House Ethics Committee engaged an outside counsel to investigate the allegations against Wright; his aggressive posture pushed the committee to bring charges of sixty counts of violations of ethics rules and procedures against the Speaker in April 1989. The next month, House Democratic Whip Tony Coelho, facing newspaper accounts suggesting that he had gotten unusually favorable terms on a loan from wealthy party contributors, resigned before an investigation could be triggered. That intensified the pressure on Wright from his own party colleagues in Congress to stop the bleeding. At the end of May 1989, Wright took to the floor of the House and announced that he would step down—as he denounced the "mindless cannibalism" that had overtaken the House.

The focus on scandal did not end with Jim Wright's departure from the House. Congress soon found itself in the grip of the fallout from the collapse of the savings and loan industry, with the Senate's ethics investigation of the so-called Keating Five, senators who had had some dealings with a savings and loan operator named Charles Keating. The House was caught in the middle of a much larger brouhaha over the so-called House bank, when a *Roll Call* story in 1991 referred to a General Accounting Office (GAO)[9] report that the majority of House members had overdrawn their accounts at the bank, some very frequently—what many called "bouncing checks." The scandal was soon dubbed "Rubbergate" in the press, which pursued it relentlessly.

Ornstein wrote at the time in the *Washington Post:*

The House "bank" was not a bank but a cooperative in existence for over 100 years. Its only money consisted of lawmakers' paychecks, which automatically went to the Sergeant-at-Arms Office. There it sat, earning no interest, until members sent the money to their own accounts at commercial banks—often two or three weeks later. But the House bank provided no sophisticated monthly statements or computerized records, making it difficult for members to know exactly when their paychecks were credited and when transfers were debited. Moreover, the House bank had no money machines or automatic overdraft protection—routine services of true banks. Members got cash for daily needs by writing checks against their paychecks to the sergeant-at-arms. Many, perhaps most, ended up inadvertently writing checks not covered by their current balance—generally for small amounts—$20 or $30. But there was no chance of losing the money; the next paycheck, and all future ones, were an automatic safety net. How were the checks covered when there was no money in the individuals' accounts? Not by taxpayers' money but by their colleagues' money—the only funds in this so-called bank.[10]

Even though members of both parties had participated in the overdrafts at the bank, more Democrats did than Republicans—and Republicans moved quickly to exploit the scandal and public outrage, abetted by a press corps hungry to report on and rail against another major scandal. An ethics committee inquiry was attacked by Republicans for not encompassing all the alleged miscreants and not making their names and checking activities public. The major movers here were younger members who had become Gingrich acolytes—in particular, a group of freshmen elected in 1990 known as the "Gang of Seven," led most prominently by Pennsylvania's Rick Santorum and Iowa's Jim Nussle. Nussle forever etched himself in the annals of congressional notoriety by appearing on the House floor to attack the House bank investigation with a paper bag over his head, to proclaim his shame at being a member of a House that would condone or cover up such outrageous misbehavior.

Ultimately, under intense pressure, the ethics panel released the names of the most active overdrafters, but a full 269 sitting members of the House were implicated in greater or lesser measure. The scandal spilled over in a big way into the 1992 elections. The casualties included prominent members of both parties: Gingrich ally and major House Republican strategist Vin Weber of Minnesota decided to retire rather than face a brutal campaign; and key Democrat Steve Solarz of New York, one of the most prominent foreign policy experts in Washington, lost a primary after his district was redrawn to remove his key areas of support, in significant part because of the attacks on him for his bank overdrafts. A full seventy-seven House members who had been implicated in the House bank controversy either retired from office or lost in the elections; the new House contained a remarkable 110 freshmen. Sixty-five House members retired in all, the highest number by far since 1946, reflecting the scandal itself and a broader, ongoing sense of unhappiness with what had happened to the House.

The departure of such a large group of lawmakers did not put an end to the press preoccupation with scandal or to the existence and prosecution of scandals themselves, many of which flowed from the insularity and arrogance of power that came from nearly forty years of unbridled majority. Scandal continued to reach back to corral major figures in Congress, symbols of that insularity and arrogance that punctuated the Gingrich theme.

The House bank was followed in 1993 by the House post office, with allegations that members and staff misused and mismanaged funds. The biggest target here was one of the most prominent and powerful members of the House, Ways and Means Committee Chair Dan Rostenkowski of Illinois. Despite his protestations of innocence, Rostenkowski was indicted by U.S. Attorney for the District of Columbia Jay Stephens in mid-1994—just as the 1994 campaign was moving into full swing. The Gingrich—and press—images of a Congress dominated by a culture of corruption was smack in front of the public's radar screen even as voters were considering their alternatives. And Democrats were nearly oblivious to the growing public outrage.

Change and the Senate

The House was at the center of the tumultuous American political scene from the late 1960s through the early 1990s. But the Senate was not immune from change or insulated from the larger trends. The personal and partisan rancor was not nearly as palpable or as raw as it was in the House—it was common in the Senate for members to slam each other and then work together arm-in-arm, à la McGovern and Dole. But in the Senate of the 1980s, the level of tension and incivility were clearly on the rise. Consider the following observation from veteran Senator Joe Biden in 1982:

> There's much less civility than when I came here ten years ago. There aren't as many nice people as there were before. . . . Ten years ago you didn't have people calling each other sons of bitches and voting to get at each other. . . . As you break down the social amenities one by one, it starts expanding geometrically. Ultimately, you don't have any social control.[11]

What was true in the early 1980s was even more true in the late eighties and early 1990s, not the least reason being the growing ideological polarization in the Senate that paralleled, if with a lag, that in the House. There was no Senate redistricting to create more polarizing and polarized candidates, but there was the same kind of realignment on regional lines in the Senate as in the House. The trend began with the South. In the 85th Congress, 1957–58, the heyday of Majority Leader Lyndon B. Johnson, Southern senators made up 45 percent of the Democratic membership of the Senate. By 1983, the 96th Congress, the Southern wing was down to 27 percent. By 1983, the Southerners represented 23 percent of what was by then a minority party of forty-six senators. As the numbers shrank, Southern Democrats became more like their Northern counterparts.

At the same time, Republicans were seeing shrinkage in the regions that had long fostered more moderate and liberal GOP senators. The New England and Mid-Atlantic regions had made up 37 percent of the Republican membership in the Senate; by 1980, it was down to 19 percent. The confederate South, which had provided zero percent of the Republican makeup of the Senate in 1960, was up to 19 percent of the party in the Senate in 1980. The graphic shift from a Senate in which the center was supreme—with ample representation from both parties—toward one in which the ideological poles began to dominate was striking, and it contributed to a coarsening of the Senate culture.

The Senate began the great era of party change and movement to reform with an already pronounced role for individual members and a natural decentralization that was not evident in the House. Nonetheless, the Senate also found itself forced to respond to demands for change.

A prime area for change in the Senate was the filibuster, the venerable process where a minority of senators could take the floor and keep talking, blocking action on something they did not like even if a majority wanted it. Through the 1950s, filibusters were relatively rare events, often focusing around civil rights issues or other great questions of national significance. Filibusters brought the Senate to a halt, resulting at times in round-the-clock sessions with senators sleeping on cots in the hallways for days on end. When Mike Mansfield replaced Lyndon Johnson as majority leader, he ran the Senate in a different way, empowering individuals more and managing the body more than leading it. Over time, he began to alter the way filibusters were handled, relying on a "two-track system": that is, the Senate would let some of its work go on while relegating the filibustered issue to a separate stream of debate until cloture could be invoked, whereby two-thirds of senators could vote to end debate and get a vote, or fail to get the supermajority and pull the bill from the agenda, effectively killing it.

The two-track approach, designed to expedite action, had the opposite effect. It made filibusters easy to trigger with no larger consequences for the institution or the policy under consideration. As a result the number of filibusters mushroomed in the late 1960s and into the 1970s, constipating action in the Senate. Frustrated presidents often prodded Senate leaders to change the filibuster rule to make it easier to expedite action, with change succeeding in 1975 under Majority Leader Robert Byrd. Cloture, which previously had required two-thirds of the senators present and voting, was changed to a threshold of sixty senators regardless of turnout.

But the rules change did not expedite business in the Senate. Filibusters and holds, often anonymous objections by senators that froze bills and nominations from moving forward, continued to be applied regularly. In the Carter presidency, a two-to-one Democratic margin in the Senate wasn't enough; a filibuster by liberals Jim Abourezk of South Dakota and Howard Metzenbaum of Ohio stymied the Carter energy bill after it had sailed through the House. And conservatives led by Democrat James Allen of Alabama pioneered new tactics of obstruction, including a "post-cloture filibuster." Majority Leader Byrd said in 1978, "It used to be that [the filibuster] was resorted to infrequently and on the grave national issues, most on civil rights, [but] now it's just resorted to promiscuously, I think."[12]

The Senate's internal woes were not limited to filibusters and holds. Frustrated by an overloaded committee system that overextended the members, the Senate began its own committee reform process, under Senator Adlai E. Stevenson III, soon after the House's efforts at committee reform foundered. Ornstein served on the staff, later as staff director, of the awkwardly named Select Committee to Study the Senate Committee System. The Senate was more successful than the House, substantially trimming the number of committees and subcommittees and consolidating assignments of senators—without concentrating power more in the hands of party leaders or a handful of ultra-powerful committee chairs. At the same time, the push for ethics reform as a result of scandal led the Senate to craft a new code of ethics and a revamped ethics committee, and a major process of administrative review led to a large number of reforms in 1976–77.

But the gains of the Stevenson Committee did not last, as the push in the Senate for more resources, more power bases and more freedom for individual senators continued and expanded. Five years later, in 1982, a study group headed by Senators Abraham Ribicoff (D-CT) and James Pearson (R-KS) looked again at Senate practices and procedures. Their 1983 report suggested that limits be placed on filibusters, that the Senate elect a permanent Senate presiding officer, that the Senate consolidate its committees again, and that the budget process be simplified. The Senate did nothing to act on the recommendations. In late 1984, yet another committee to study the committee system was created, this one chaired by Dan Quayle (R-IN). The Quayle panel basically suggested that the Senate actually enforce the limitations on assignments that had been built into the Stevenson Committee report, while also advocating some curbs on nongermane floor amendments and various filibuster tactics. And so there was modest progress, but no fundamental change: the underlying pressure to spread power and resources continued largely unabated.

From the 1970s to the 1990s, the Senate became more open, more fluid, more decentralized, and more democratized—and more polarized. As individual senators benefited from the greater role and power, they also became collectively more frustrated with the institutional consequences of these same trends. Getting anything done became harder, forcing the Senate to spend inordinate amounts of time on a small number of such issues as the budget. Formerly easygoing relations across party lines began to show more signs of strain, in part as the Senate—unlike the House—went from a quarter century of Democrats in the majority to six years of Republican rule during the first six years of the Reagan presidency and then back, in 1986, to control by the Democrats. The oscillations in party control did give all members of the Senate more sensitivity to the rights and role of the minority, but that simply served to make it more difficult to expedite action. And the growing desire by majorities to act, especially during the Carter and Reagan presidencies, led to more partisan tensions—tensions that were not particularly reduced during the six years of divided government under presidents Reagan and Bush from 1987 through 1992. Tension in the Senate expanded sharply after the contentious and unsuccessful nomination by Reagan of Robert Bork to the Supreme Court, a nomination battle that turned personal, enraged many Republicans, and resulted in the new term *Borking* for attacks on individuals nominated to high posts.

During the first Bush presidency a bitter and vicious controversy erupted in the Senate over the nomination of John Tower for Secretary of Defense. Despite Tower's long service in the Senate, his nomination was opposed by many Democrats and a few Republicans, including a number who had served with him on the Armed Services Committee. The allegations against Tower, including excessive drinking and sexual peccadilloes, many based on rumor, were of a different order than the usual charges of incompetence or conflict of interest and ratcheted up the level of rancor yet again. Later in the Bush 41 presidency, the nomination of Clarence Thomas to the Supreme Court, although ultimately successful, focused on allegations of sexual harassment by Anita Hill, a former government employee under Thomas's supervision, and once more partisan animosities ignited. It was becoming a pattern—take a controversial nominee and turn the struggle into an attack on the person and his ethics instead of a debate about qualifications, issue positions, or even philosophy. Each battle ratcheted up the stakes for the next one and left lingering bitterness that went beyond a simple victory or defeat on an issue or a nomination.

The Bork, Tower, and Thomas controversies in some ways reflected the intense focus on scandal during this era. It was not only in Congress, of course. From Watergate on, scandal became a near obsession of journalists, prosecutors, pundits, and politicians. This preoccupation with dirty laundry reshaped American attitudes towards politics and politicians and sharply changed the tone in Washington as well as the behavior of prosecutors. Between 1975 and 1995, the number of prosecutions of federal public officials increased fifteen-fold—that is, by 1,500 percent—during a time when ethics codes were put into place, ethics rules were tightened, and no objective observer of Washington thought that real corruption was actually on the rise.

But the tangible examples of individual corruption, along with a few, such as the House Bank and Post Office, suggesting institutional rot, fueled a populist, anti-Congress, public mood. It also created an atmosphere more conducive to internal congressional reform, an atmosphere that was exploited in 1991 by a core of institution-minded Democrats and Republicans in both houses, led by four stalwarts, Senators David Boren (D-OK) and Pete Domenici (R-NM) and Representatives Lee Hamilton (D-IN) and Bill Gradison (R-OH). Their initial goal was to create a Joint Committee on the Organization of Congress, paralleling those of 1946 and 1970, that could serve as the vehicle for broad-ranging change. The four called upon the two of us to meet with them early in the committee's formative process to brainstorm and to enlist our support in the effort.

As a result, we in turn persuaded several foundations to support our own wide-ranging effort, which we called the Renewing Congress Project, to undertake an independent assessment of Congress and offer recommendations for reform. We set up an advisory committee and conducted a wave of roundtables and conferences with scholars, journalists, and lawmakers. In November 1992, just after the elections that put Democrats in full charge of the machinery of power in Washington for the first time since 1980, under President-elect Bill Clinton, we issued our first report. The Joint Committee on the Organization of Congress was indeed created, and we testified in front of it in both February and April 1993—resulting in a second report in

June of that year. Nine months after that, in March 1994, we issued our third publication, this time a progress report, after the Joint Committee had issued its own recommendations.

The concerns of the four congressional reformers (actually five, since Bill Gradison retired from Congress and was replaced in the "Gang of Four" by Republican David Dreier of California)—and our own—were wide-ranging. As we put it in our first report, "Public dissatisfaction with the first branch of our government threatens to undermine its legitimacy and diminish its authority in national policy making. A healthy skepticism among citizens toward Congress has degenerated into corrosive cynicism. A critical press has resorted to sheer caricature. Members themselves speak of frustrations and diversions that keep them from doing their job."[13]

We eschewed Congress-bashing in our reports, calling instead for Congressional *renewal*—helping Congress do what it has always done best, representing and deliberating. We noted:

> Congress's strength is its representational base—its closeness to the people. Its challenge is to reconcile competing interests through face-to-face deliberation among the people's representatives. "Compromise" and "accommodation" are not dirty words but the very essence of "getting things done" in a representative democracy. Where a consensus exists in the country, or at least the makings of majority sentiment to pursue a course of action, Congress should be structured to articulate, deliberate and act upon that sentiment, enabling the voices of majorities to ring louder than the extremes. Where the public is divided on a crucial problem facing the country, Congress should work to form a consensus rather than hardening those differences and perpetuating policy deadlock.[14]

We decried a series of internal weaknesses in Congress that hobbled these tasks, including a division of labor that hampered coordination and timeliness; institutions for debate that "put a premium on cheap shots and devalue discussions"; a too frenetic schedule; a pattern of catering to individual members at the expense of collective responsibility; a partisanship we described as "intense and destructive," particularly in the House, "born of the near permanent majority status of the House Democrats, the frustration of Republicans . . . and the use of procedure and symbolism to embarrass the opposition in a quest for partisan advantage"; "lax and self-indulgent management of congressional operations and support services"; and "the demise of any principled defense of Congress as the bedrock of American democracy, as an institution in which members have a shared stake, in spite of their different individual and partisan interests."

In the first two reports, we offered extensive recommendations for setting and executing a broad reform agenda for Congress. Our recommendations were detailed and occasionally technical. But we also offered big ideas and new approaches. We called for strengthening the hand of party leaders vis-à-vis committee chairs, giving them a larger role in the referral of bills and floor scheduling. We offered ideas to revitalize debate, including regular, Oxford-style debates in both houses, and to streamline deliberation by reforming the committee system through a further consolidation of assignments, reductions in committees and subcommittees, and reorganization of committee jurisdictions. We offered principles for campaign finance reform and gave suggestions for staffing and administrative reform. We gave a set of ideas for streamlining procedures in the Senate, including restrictions on the overuse of the hold, and a return to the traditional way of dealing with a filibuster—with a twist to allow some delays on issues that were not of overriding importance but still expedited action via a sliding scale of votes from sixty down to fifty-one. We decried the failure of Congress to respond to the criticism that the institution exempted itself from the laws it applied to others, and we offered a responsible way to deal with the problem—the creation of an internal Office of Compliance.

Many of our specific recommendations were embraced by the Joint Committee. Some, such as the Office of Compliance, were incorporated into the key legislation in the area, sponsored by Reps. Christopher Shays (R-CT) and Dick Swett (D-VT). The House did experiment with a series of prime-time Oxford-style debates but did not sustain the effort.

Two areas of change deserve further comment. First was our observation on the role of the majority and the minority, written thirty-eight years into the forty-year consecutive rule of Democrats in the House. In our first report, we noted,

> In recent years the near-permanent majority status of the Democrats and near permanent minority status of the Republicans have led to increasingly hardened and corrosive attitudes on both sides of the aisle: an irresponsibility on the part of many members of the minority, with no stake in governance or institutional maintenance, combined with smugness, a patronizing viewpoint, and arrogance on the part of many in the majority. . . . What may be missing today is any sense on the part of the minority of the demands and responsibilities of government, and any appreciation on the part of the majority of the frustrations and constraints of assuming the role of the opposition. The majority seems to view its power as an entitlement and has set up a structure of patronage that pervades the institution.[15]

We urged an expansion of minority staffing, along with rules changes to make it easier for the minority to offer alternatives. And we noted in our progress report, "closed or modified rules can serve the legitimate purposes of managing debate and protecting the integrity of complex bills; but they should not become, as they have in recent years, the norm for considering all legislation. While there is no good way to write this requirement into the rules of the House, it is imperative that the majority not abuse its authority to set the terms of debate on the floor."[16]

Second, we recommended sweeping changes in the committee system in both houses, but with a particular emphasis on major alteration in committee jurisdictions in the House—focusing on the powerhouse committees of Ways and Means and Energy and Commerce. Some, but by no means a majority, of these specifics made their way into the Joint Committee recommendations. But along the way, we attracted the notice of the powerful House chairmen. The two of us were asked to meet informally with a few of them—a session in which two lonely academics sat on one side of a table, with every major chairman in the House lined up on the other side—including Rostenkowski of Ways and Means, Dingell of Energy and Commerce, and Jack Brooks of Government Operations, who sat directly across from us. They were not happy. The meeting was cordial but tense—in diplomatic terms, we had a frank and full exchange of views. It was not only our call for overhauling the committees that drew their attention but also our critique of the arrogance of the majority.

Speaker of the House Tom Foley was also aware of our critical appraisal and, as a longtime student of the institution, more sensitive than many of his senior colleagues to the danger in the imbalance between majority and minority parties in the House. During the 1993–94 period, the two of us met regularly with Foley for breakfast in a small room off the House restaurant (we ordered traditional fare; he, in the midst of a health kick that resulted in both substantial weight loss and a "buff" physique, brought an elaborate collection of health foods in baggies).

We used the occasions to push our reform agenda, warning the Speaker that failure to act on some of the changes would end up playing into the hands of Gingrich and his allies, would reinforce the public sense of a Congress out of touch, and would lead to the worst of all possible worlds—a House forced by public pressure to act on changes but blamed for inaction instead of congratulated for solving its own problems. In particular, we focused on the need to deal with the issue of Congress insulating itself from the laws it applied to others. While in fact Congress had insulated itself less from the laws than from executive branch supervision of Congress in these areas, for separation of powers reasons, that issue was a thin reed on which to hang any excuse for inaction. The most obvious solution was to create an institution apart from the executive that would oversee Congress in these areas; thus the Office of Compliance.

Foley understood our reasoning and embraced our idea but could not—or would not—act early or proactively in this or other areas of reform. He had been in the middle of the Bolling Committee battles in 1974 and said that some members continued to hold bitter grudges over the efforts to strip their committees of treasured jurisdiction. More generally, the resistance of the other powers in the majority in the House to change—a belief that they needed insulation against minority irresponsibility and a feeling that the anti-Congress mood was transitory and would pass without their loss of power if they merely stood firm—made serious change a steeply uphill proposition.

There was another dynamic at work in Foley's attitude toward committee reform: he had no taste for reopening those wounds or fighting those battles when a larger purpose, enacting a Democratic president's agenda, was at hand. For all these machinations were occurring during a new era.

Be Careful What You Wish For: Clinton and a Democratic Congress

There were many reasons behind Bill Clinton's election in 1992. But surely among them was the focus on scandal at that time. It contributed to the rise of a populist mood and movement in the early 1990s, including the prominent presidential candidacy of H. Ross Perot, who captured 19 percent of the popular vote in the 1992 presidential election. It also contributed to the mood for change that was substantial enough that incumbent president George H. W. Bush was trounced in that election, receiving only 38 percent of the vote as Democrat Bill Clinton—who had to overcome his own set of scandal issues—won the White House and put Democrats in full charge of the machinery of power in Washington for the first time since 1980.

Clinton won by a comfortable margin (370 electoral votes) and had seemingly comfortable majorities to work with in the House and Senate. But it was clear from his Inaugural on that he had serious obstacles ahead. Some were caused by self-inflicted wounds—such as the controversy over gays in the military that dominated the discourse for a good part of his early tenure, causing him to lose momentum and focus. Some were driven by the continuing scandal issues, which were accompanied by regular calls for independent counsel investigations. But the challenge to the new president from the Newt Gingrich–led Republicans was the most significant headache he acquired.

Faced for the first time since Jimmy Carter with an all-Democratic lineup, the attitude of Republicans in Congress was in effect to say to Clinton and the congressional majority—you have all the reins of power, you're on your own; don't count on Republicans for support or votes. Gingrich was able to follow through in part because even those moderate Republicans who had in years past worked with Democrats in the legislative process had become radicalized by the early 1990s, beginning with the Indiana 8th controversy and continuing through the combination of closed rules, abuse by chairmen of proxy-voting authority, and majority arrogance that characterized the period.

After his early stumbles, Clinton focused on the top priority of his first hundred days, an economic plan. Clinton had made the economy his number one issue during the campaign—recall the sign in James Carville's campaign office, "It's the economy, stupid"—and during the primary season had come up with a plan that centered on an economic stimulus package. But after the election, Clinton convened an economic summit in Little Rock; from it and the efforts of his top economic advisers, including Robert Rubin and Leon Panetta, he shifted his early focus more toward deficit reduction.

The new economic plan included tax increases on the wealthy, as well as budget discipline, making for tough votes—and all were going to have to come from Democrats if Gingrich and his Senate counterpart Bob Dole were able to keep the minority party united in opposition. That is how it worked out. Despite having 258 Democrats in the House and 57 in the Senate, enough Democrats from marginal districts uneasy about supporting a tax increase, along with others who did not want to discipline spending, prevented the new president from an early, big victory that would have earned him momentum and political capital to do more.

It took nearly seven months for the Clinton plan to come to a vote in the House; when it did, on August 5, 1993, it was still not clear whether the plan could prevail. As the vote proceeded, Democrats were at least one or two votes short of victory—with not a single Republican supporting it and forty Democrats opposed. Democratic leaders finally managed to convince Pat Williams of Montana and Marjorie Margolies-Mezvinsky of Pennsylvania to switch their votes, and the budget plan made it through by 218–216. As Margolies-Mezvinsky went to cast her vote, a group of Republicans on the floor began to chant, "Goodbye, Marjorie." They were cruel, crass—and correct. Margolies-Mezvinsky, a freshman from a Republican district who had won by an eyelash in 1992, was a top GOP target in 1994, and she lost.

The victory in the House did not provide much boost in the Senate, where the vote was set for the next day. Eight Democrats had announced opposition to the economic plan, and, as in the House, not a single Republican declared support. After another yeoman effort, the president managed to convince Bob Kerrey of Nebraska to support the package, leading to a 50–50 vote, which allowed Vice President Gore to cast the tie-breaking vote in favor.

The presidential victory looked more like a defeat—it took humiliating efforts for a president to bring around individual lawmakers from his own party. Worse, the fact that Marjorie Margolies-Mezvinsky was put into an untenable position to carry the plan over the top was seen by many Democrats in Congress not as a failure on their part to provide adequate support for their own president but as ineptitude on Clinton's part. To be sure, the Clinton administration had stumbled coming out of the box in 1993. But the economic plan was not a radical one—it proved in fact to be an engine of economic growth and prosperity and a vehicle for sharply reducing federal deficits. But the new GOP strategy of trying to deny any votes for crucial presidential priorities, combined with the myopia of Democrats in Congress who cared less about any president's priorities than their own insular needs and viewpoints, created a public perception of a government lacking focus or the ability to act. That sensibility in 1994 spawned the GOP landslide victory.

Not every issue in 1993 broke into two camps—most Democrats for, and all Republicans against. On the North American Free Trade Agreement (NAFTA), Clinton achieved success with significant Republican support overcoming a deeply divided Democratic Party and bitter opposition from organized labor, which only served to increase many Democrats' anger about their president's priorities. The same thing happened in 1994 with welfare reform and the assault weapons ban. The latter passed as part of an omnibus crime bill and became a major campaign theme against Democrats from pro-gun areas, especially in the South and Southwest.

But on several key issues, a united Republican opposition combined with divided Democrats to thwart the president and make the governing party look weak and ineffectual. The crime bill seemed headed to a victory in Congress in 1993 when the rule governing its passage was stunningly rejected on the House floor by a coalition of Republicans and liberal Democrats who objected to some of its tough sections. And, most notably, the Clinton health care plan, the centerpiece of his second year agenda, was stalled early when moderate Democrats led by Jim Cooper of Tennessee refused to support it; at a later stage, when President Clinton was ready to compromise, Republicans in both the House and Senate made clear that they would not come to the table at all. An attempt at compromise in the Senate was filibustered. The plan was doomed, creating a huge embarrassment for the president and his party as well as providing a major campaign tool for Republicans. If congressional Democrats were unhappy with their president, they were also furious at Republicans who refused to deal with them at either end of Pennsylvania Avenue. For more than three decades, the majority Democrats had always been able to find enough Republicans willing to work with them, usually from the subordinate position accorded the minority party. No more.

A witch's brew of difficulties plagued Democrats as the 1994 elections approached. There were sharp partisan tensions as Republicans hit Democrats hard on scandal and corruption issues, often in very personal terms. There was a united opposition, with Republicans refusing to provide any votes or input on issues from the economy to health care. And Democrats, grappling with divisions in their own ranks, frequently were unable to find enough votes to carry budget plans or health policy without Republican support.

The scandal and corruption issue was not confined to Congress. The president's problems were constantly in the news, kept there by aggressive reporting and independent counsel investigations. In addition, the allegations of sexual harassment on the part of Republican Senator Robert Packwood of Oregon garnered headlines just after the 1992 election through the next two years. This, along with the Tailhook scandal of navy fliers and other military personnel who groped women at conventions, underscored the notion of powerful figures in politics and government abusing their privileges.

Despite the obvious public mood, Democrats in Congress continued to resist any preemptive reform action to counter the feelings of an out-of-touch, arrogant congressional elite. Finally, at the eleventh hour in August 1994, the House brought up the Shays–Swett Congressional Accountability Act. It passed, but too late to get Senate approval and too late to look like anything but a lame response to criticism.

In September 1994, Newt Gingrich unveiled the next part of his strategy to take a majority—the "Contract with America," a ten-point reform plan that he and his united

Republican colleagues pledged to enact immediately if they were elected to run the House. From professionalizing House management to enacting accountability legislation, the plan was heavy on a reform agenda that the Democrats who ran the House had rejected or sat on.

Most Americans polled after the elections had no idea what the Contract with America was. No matter. The contrast between the two parties during a time of discontent—and a belief that Democrats, given the opportunity to hold all the reins of power in Washington, had failed—fueled enough voter dissatisfaction to capture a stunning victory for Republicans in both houses of Congress. The first GOP majority since 1955 would take over power in the House, joined by a renewed Republican majority in the Senate. Newt Gingrich would be the first Republican Speaker since Joe Martin. Not a single Republican in the new House had ever been in the majority there, except for a few former Democrats who had switched parties. Only one Democrat, Sidney Yates of Illinois, had ever been in the minority in the House. A new era hit Congress, one promising dramatic change in its operations and dynamics.

FOUR

A Decade of
Republican Control

THE ELECTORAL TSUNAMI that swept across the country in November 1994 left the once seemingly permanent Democratic majority in Congress stunned and dispirited. Forty years of uninterrupted Democratic control of the House—more than double the previous record—had created a widespread sense of entitlement and more than a trace of arrogance. Many Democrats had long believed that being in the majority was their birthright, not their temporary good fortune. Going into the election, they believed they would take a hit, even a substantial one, but with no real chance of losing enough seats to cost them that birthright. Equally stunned was the Democratic occupant of the White House. The magnitude and consistency of the swing to the Republicans left no doubt whatsoever that the electorate had repudiated President Clinton and his party of government. Clinton would soon feel it necessary to insist that, under the Constitution, the president is not irrelevant.

But how were the self-styled Republican revolutionaries in the House—not one of whom, as a Republican, had ever been in the majority in the body—to interpret their victory and to develop a strategy of governance?[1] And with what

discussions with him in the weeks before the election.
the request of Representative Chris Shays, Mann met
October with Gingrich in the Minority Leader's Capitol
ce to discuss preparing for majority responsibility after
1996 election. Gingrich quickly corrected him: "You mean
er the 1994 election." He then proceeded to outline his
ategy for leading the new majority the day after the elec-
n. Ornstein ran into him at an airport a week before the
ction. Gingrich did not flatly predict a GOP sweep, but
made it clear that he was deep in thought about how he
uld handle his new role if it happened.

A former history professor, Gingrich was also a scholarly
ntor to his new brood. He sent them a list of recommended
dings so they would be prepared for the challenges ahead.
ey were to read the Declaration of Independence, the U.S.
nstitution, the *Federalist Papers*, and de Tocqueville's
mocracy in America, all staples of civics education in
erica, and also additional books that revealed Gingrich's
re eclectic interests in futurism, management, and self-
provement. What was missing, however, was *The Anti-*
deralist, the collection of writings by those who opposed
ratification of the Constitution, preferring a more direct,
biscitary form of government. In many respects, Gingrich
d the new Republican majority were the modern-day
ti-Federalists. A pronounced disdain for Washington and
political class, an embrace of term limits, fealty to the
tructions of the citizenry embodied in the Contract, and
eep suspicion of deliberative processes that would at-
uate the direct expression of popular sentiment charac-
ized the Republican Class of 1994. Their strong links to
ngelicals and the business community were reminiscent
the democratic forces that gathered in the new republic
o centuries earlier.

Gingrich moved with alacrity to claim a mandate from
e election. It was not simply a matter of voters reacting
gatively to problems encountered by President Clinton
d the Democratic majority in Congress—from gays in the
litary to controversies surrounding Whitewater and the

consequences for Congress as an institution?
was far from obvious that the Republicans wou
control of Congress for the next decade (except
cratic interlude in the Senate during 2001–200
ington would experience the first extended pe
Republican government since the 1920s. No
that in the following years partisan polarizat
crease in scope and intensity, power woul
centralized, and, with the election of a Repu
dent, Congress would abdicate its position
and independent—branch of government.

Speaker Gingrich and tl
Contract with America

The political architect and spiritual leader of
Republican victory, Newt Gingrich, assumed
modern-day Moses, delivering his tribe from y
tude under the Democrats with ten command
ten on tablets of stone, a "Contract with Amer
people must obey over the first one hundred day
of the 104th Congress.

The press and public reaction to the Repu
over was striking. An unprecedented flood of p
congressional figure—far outstripping that
O'Neill or even Sam Rayburn—made the Speak
famous national figure overnight. Gingrich
graced the covers of every news magazine, w
with similar prominence in such popular culture
as *People, Parade,* and *Us,* got full-blown front-
age in every major newspaper in the U.S. and
was profiled on every conceivable television
Much of the coverage portrayed the new Sp
counterforce to the president—almost an ant
equal to the chief executive in prominence and

Gingrich was not as stunned by the election
were the Democrats, the press, and the pundit

White House travel office to the collapse of health care reform. Instead, Gingrich insisted that the election represented a public embrace of the agenda set out explicitly in the Contract with America (e.g., welfare reform, anticrime measures, tax cuts) and of the related pledge to balance the budget. The Republicans had run on a clearly annunciated platform, they had won a huge victory, and they now would use their new majority status to deliver that agenda to a grateful electorate.

Mandates are not objective realities but subjective interpretations of elections posited by victorious candidates or parties and accepted by the broader political community. Their force depends partly on the clarity and magnitude of the election outcome, partly on the plausibility of the claims about public opinion. Gingrich and his colleagues had ample supporting evidence on the first count. The fifty-two-seat pickup was the largest since 1948. Not a single Republican incumbent lost. A forty-year House majority was vanquished. House Republican candidates publicly embraced the Contract and pledged their support if elected.

On the other hand, the public was much less attuned to the Contract than were the candidates. One poll released on the eve of the election revealed that 71 percent of the respondents had never even heard of the Contract. And a majority of those who had claimed it would have no effect on how they voted.[2] Moreover, the election results for offices not linked to the Contract—senators, governors, state legislatures—were as lopsided for the Republicans as were those for the House. The Contract may have helped to nationalize the midterm election, energize Republican candidates, and sharpen their critique of the Democrats. But far more important was the widespread disgust of voters with gridlock in Washington, partisan bickering, and the elitist arrogance of congressional pay raises and repeated scandals, all on the Democrats' watch. It is more than a stretch to claim that the Republicans vaulted to the majority because of their policy agenda.

Is this a distinction without a difference? What is the harm in reading more into public support for the Contract than is justified? One risk is that the reification of a set of policy commitments shortchanges the need to deal with other influential players in the policy process and preempts normal processes of bargaining and compromise.

Both effects were much in evidence during the 104th Congress. Gingrich kept the House in session until 2:30 a.m. the first day of the session, enacting a series of procedural reforms promised in the Contract. He then directed a forced march through the ten substantive elements of the Contract, including bills with such compelling titles as "The Taking Back Our Streets Act," "The American Dream Restoration Act," and "The Senior Citizens Fairness Act." In only ninety-three days, during which it clocked nearly four times as many hours in session as the average during the same period over the previous ten sessions, the House enacted nine of the ten bills, falling short only on a constitutional amendment to limit the terms of members of Congress, which required a two-thirds vote for passage. Republicans had promised within the first one-hundred days of the 104th Congress to bring to the House Floor each of the ten bills for a "full and open debate" and a "clear and fair vote." They delivered on that promise and more. It was a heady time, one for celebration. And, as recounted by Linda Killian, celebrate they did on the west front of the Capitol in a "spectacular display of pomp, patriotism, and self-congratulation."[3] The unprecedented success for a proactive one-hundred-days agenda set by Congress, not the president, reinforced for Gingrich his role as counter-president and built up heady expectations of much bolder policy success.

What followed was a bit more mundane. The Republican revolutionaries had anticipated that their blitzkrieg would be followed by equally swift action in the Republican Senate—with a cowed president forced to sign bills and implement the conservative opportunity society. They soon ran into the realities of legislative life in the Senate—and into the savvy counterpunching of a strong president. In the second hundred days, and the third and beyond, they saw their agenda largely founder in the Senate and run aground in budget confrontations with the Democratic president. The Senate, even under the hand of the Republicans, simply could not be moved to action with the same ruthless efficiency as the House, even had a majority of its members been committed to the substance of the Contract. A president armed with a veto, backed by a sizable partisan minority in Congress, and endowed with skill in using the bully pulpit could wreak havoc with the agenda of the congressional majority. Their exclusive focus on the Contract had indeed led them to discount other critical parts of the policy process.

Here is what Ornstein wrote in *Roll Call* at the August recess of the first year of the Gingrich Congress:

> The numbers are staggering, especially compared with the historic 97th Congress, in 1981, which was responsible for the "Reagan Revolution." Consider the number of hours in session— 74 for the Reagan one; 531—seven times as many—for the Gingrich one. Fifty-three measures passed in the Reagan-era Congress, 124 this year. Twenty-three roll-call votes in 1981; 302—more than 13 times as many—this year!
>
> . . . As the House moved like a hare on adrenaline, the Senate crept like a tortoise on Nembutal. Well, the analogy isn't quite accurate; the Senate was active—it just went nowhere. . . .
>
> [T]he actual outputs of the 104th Congress through the August recess are the lowest of any of the past eight Congresses. Talk about ironic: The much-maligned 103rd Congress—the one summarily rejected by voters because of its gridlock and drift— had enacted 81 public laws by the August recess of its first year. This heralded 104th Congress that replaced it passed 20. . . .
>
> Quantity is not the only issue, of course—there is quality. The Reagan Revolution 97th passed only 43 bills by the August recess—more than twice what this one has but only half of the output of the 103rd Congress. But the 97th could have passed but one law—the massive reconciliation bill that encompassed Reaganomics and continues to reverberate in the nation—and still be among the most significant Congresses in the 20th century. . . .

Among the 81 bills enacted in the last Congress was the Clinton reconciliation bill, with far-reaching policy implications; family leave; "motor voter" registration; direct student loans; and fast-track trade authority for the president.

The 104th Congress has as its major achievements three small pieces of the "Contract with America": the Congressional Accountability Act, unfunded mandates legislation, and a paperwork reduction law.[4]

The conflict between the House and Senate was predictable. On December 1, 1994, more than a month before the new Gingrich Congress convened, Ornstein wrote in *Roll Call*:

Forget the relationship between Speaker Newt Gingrich (Ga) and President Clinton. The most interesting relationship in Washington for the next two years will be that between Speaker Gingrich and Senate Majority Leader Bob Dole (Kan). . . .

Two years ago, Democratic Rep. Al Swift (Wash) made a pointed and insightful comment on Congress: In the midst of the most bitter partisan acrimony between House Democrats and Republicans in modern times, Swift said, "The Republicans, they're just the opposition. The Senate is the enemy." . . .

I have never seen more hostility in politics than that felt by House Democrats toward their Senate counterparts. When they acted, the Senate dithered. When they made tough choices, the Senate ducked. When they got into trouble, the Senate piled on. Don't expect things to be dramatically different under the Republicans.

Gingrich has a vision, an agenda, and a timetable. His risk-taking, combative, and radical approach worked and has generated a large group of Gingrich progeny in the House—combative, confrontational, sharply ideological conservatives in a hurry. . . .

The Senate is very different. When an ebullient Gingrich was outlining his blitzkrieg approach to governance the day after the election, Dole's reaction was more along the lines of, "Been there. Done that. Slow down." . . .

The fact is that the Senate remains an institution of 100 individualists, all prima donnas, all with their own independent power bases. Filibusters, holds, and threats of filibusters are a way of life in the Senate, but are the least of the problems facing the House Republicans and their agenda. The Senate simply doesn't provide any hope of regular 51-vote majorities for a tough, pure, and hard-line conservative policy approach.

Newt's problem with the Senate is not really Dole. It is the Senate Dole will try to lead. There are 53 Republicans in the body—including among them Specter, Cohen, Jeffords, Snowe, Hatfield, Packwood, Chafee, and Kassebaum. Jeffords is the only one among them who could be called "liberal," but none of the eight listed above is a Gingrich-style Republican. And there are precious few conservative Democrats remaining who can be counted on regularly to join a GOP-led conservative majority. . . .

Newt's strategy is clear, and clever—pass a lengthy string of tough conservative measures on economic, budgetary, and social policy, and send them to the President to face a Hobson's choice. He can accept them and face the outrage of his liberal base. Or he can veto them and become the "do-nothing president." . . .

With what may well be impressive party discipline in the House, that strategy can work—if the Senate cooperates. But the likelihood is that Speaker Gingrich will have to contend with a Senate that will sit on some items, reject others, and dilute others yet, moving according to its own peculiar rhythm. . . .

Bills that pass will probably have enough amendments added to make the purist approach of the new Speaker less workable than he would like, and to make some of the bills that reach the President's desk perfectly palatable to him. . . .

In many ways, the frustrations of modern governance in Washington—the arrogance, independence, parochialism—could be called "The Curse of the Senate." The curse has now been transferred from Speaker Foley and the Democrats to Speaker Gingrich and the Republicans. . . .

We'll see if Newt has any better antidote. [5]

He didn't. Bicameralism and separation of powers rendered the parliamentary-style leadership of Gingrich and followership of House Republicans ineffectual, at least with respect to writing new law. The failure to anticipate the incentives and constraints of the other key players and to accept—if not welcome—the need for strategic positioning and compromise came at a substantial political cost as well. Clinton used his conflicts with the Gingrich-led House Republicans, especially their willingness to shut down government in disputes over the budget, to rehabilitate his political standing and virtually guarantee his reelection.

While Speaker Gingrich encountered severe turbulence in achieving his policy objectives and maintaining the political momentum from the 1994 election, he did succeed in consolidating power within the Republican conference, producing the most centralized majority leadership since the 1910 revolt against Cannon. The promises embedded in the Contract provided both the rationale and the legitimacy for a shift from a committee-based to a party leadership-based process. Gingrich seized the power to name committee chairs, disregarding seniority to choose Bob Livingston of Louisiana, ranked fifth on Appropriations, as its chair, and bypassing Carlos Moorhead of California on two committees, Commerce and Judiciary, to pick Tom Bliley of Virginia and Henry Hyde of Illinois as respective chairs. Gingrich also extracted loyalty pledges from those he appointed. He selected committee members—reserving an unprecedented number of slots on the most prestigious House committees for freshmen—and controlled committee staffing. A new rule limiting chairmanships also spread power positions to even more junior members.

He reduced the discretionary authority of subcommittees and their chairs, set committee agendas and schedules, and monitored committee compliance. He also created a number of leadership task forces to write key legislation normally done by the standing committees. Key bills like Medicare reform were fashioned in the Speaker's office by leadership staff, not in committees such as Ways and Means. Majority Leader Dick Armey of Texas, whose pet legislative idea was a flat tax, floated the idea of bypassing Ways and Means with his bill and going straight to the floor. Taking legislative draftsmanship away from committees and centralizing it in leadership offices would become a common practice on controversial legislation by the Republican majority, one that diminished the quality of deliberation.

Gingrich's dazzling consolidation of power within the House was not without costs. First, in mobilizing the revolutionary zeitgeist of the large Republican class of 1994 to legitimize his assertive leadership and build pressure for strict party unity on the substantive planks of the Contract, he made himself dependent on the acquiescence of the ideologically driven, politically inexperienced freshmen. Many would turn on him when the going got much tougher than passing the Contract through the House. The Speaker, who had been a regular thorn in the side of his party's leader when he was an insurgent, had no clear strategy on how to deal with a passel of junior Gingriches. When freshman Mark Neumann of Wisconsin, appointed to the Appropriations Committee with a promise to maintain party discipline under Chairman Livingston, regularly defied his chair, Livingston removed him from a prestigious subcommittee slot and replaced him with even more conservative Ernest Istook of Oklahoma to show that the issue was loyalty, not ideology. The freshman class vigorously protested—and Gingrich, instead of backing his chairman to underscore the need for loyalty, gave an even bigger subcommittee plum to Neumann and undercut his own leadership capacity.

Gingrich also struggled to reconcile his minority rhetoric of fairness in the House with his desire to run a tight ship. It did not take very long for the rhetoric to be replaced by a different and more restrictive reality. Procedural fairness was not dropped immediately upon the Republican ascendance to the majority. Many key Republicans believed that they could govern in a fashion different—and fairer— than the Democrats, in part because they were more cohesive. Two weeks after the 1994 election, Pat Towell wrote in Congressional Quarterly:

> For more than a decade, Republicans have raged with mounting vehemence that Democrats were hijacking the legislative process, abusing their control of the House to abort GOP initiatives that would have fractured the majority party's fragile coalition.
>
> The central allegation is that Democrats have manipulated floor proceedings with [rules] intended not merely to organize the debate on a bill but to stifle it by precluding key GOP amendments.

In the new regime, prospective Speaker Newt Gingrich, R-Ga., and his lieutenants all insist that the Republicans will abjure those instruments of control, including unduly restrictive [rules].

"We're going to have fair [rules] . . . free and open debate," Gerald B.F. Solomon, R-N.Y., told reporters Nov. 16, after Gingrich tapped him to take the Rules Committee chair. "We're going to let the House work its will."[6]

Solomon emphasized that the norm would be floor rules that are open or include only reasonable restrictions on the number of amendments that have been negotiated between the majority and minority leadership.

Towell also quoted political scientist Bill Connelly, co-author of the definitive book on the House Republicans in the minority, as underscoring the view that the GOP would govern differently. Said Connelly, "No party is in a permanent majority. So the possibility that they will be a minority will restrain them, as the Democrats were not restrained."[7]

As we discuss in the following chapter on institutional decline, adherence to regular order—the rules, precedents, and norms guaranteeing opportunities for genuine debate and deliberation in the House—was trumped by the overriding desire of the new majority to produce legislative results. While Solomon struggled to fulfill his pledge of openness and fairness, he did not by and large succeed. And when David Dreier succeeded him as Rules chair, any pretense of openness and fairness melted away. In our Renewing Congress Project and at other times in the late 1980s and early 1990s, both of us worked closely with Dreier to fashion means of protecting minority party interests and strengthening the House as an institution. Even the lip service to those ideals was dropped—by 1998, he and the other Republican leaders embraced processes that set the stage for the virtual collapse of genuine deliberation in the House and fomented bitter and destructive relations between the two parties.

The Senate Is Not the House

The 1994 elections also catapulted the Republicans into the majority in the Senate. The consequences for the chamber and its leadership, however, were much less striking than for the House. Senate Republicans had experienced the rewards and responsibilities of majority status during the first six years of the Reagan administration, after the 1980 elections ended their quarter century of banishment from power. Regaining control after another six years in the minority was less dramatic, and Senate Republicans made a more sober assessment of the possibilities and limits flowing from the 1994 electoral sweep.

Moreover, the individualistic nature of the Senate helped to contain its leaders' exuberance. Permissive rules governing debate and amendments give individual senators and the minority party ample opportunity to frustrate the policy ambitions of the majority. The Senate schedules its business on the floor largely on the basis of unanimous-consent agreements negotiated between the parties with deference to the interests of individual senators. In the face of substantial controversy, the only alternative is to use cloture to cut off debate—a demanding process requiring sixty votes. As Barbara Sinclair has demonstrated, beginning in the 1970s and then accelerating in the early 1990s, the Senate with increasing frequency experienced extended-debate-related problems, including filibusters and filibuster threats.[8] The latter is typically exercised in the form of a hold, which is a notification by a senator of his or her intention to object to a unanimous-consent agreement. Initially, this trend was fueled by the decline of norms constraining the use of obstructionist tactics by senators, transforming the Senate from an exclusive club or community into an assembly of one hundred individuals. As the parties became more ideologically polarized and nationally competitive, these tactics became critical weapons in the arsenals of party leaders as well as levers for rank-and-file members of both parties. The temptation to place a hold, usually anonymous, on an executive or judicial nomination—sometimes because of problems with the person, sometimes merely as a hostage to pry other concessions from the administration—grew sharply in the 1980s and into the 1990s. By the start of the Clinton administration, half of all major legislation not protected by budget or other "fast-track" rules encountered some type of filibuster-related problem, as did a growing share of presidential nominees.

Senate Majority Leader Bob Dole personified the Senate's historical and institutional distinctiveness and viewed the Gingrich revolution in the House with some skepticism. Although a conservative party loyalist, he was also pragmatic and wary of a Republican legislative strategy built around the Contract with America. A decade earlier, when Dole publicly speculated about the need for additional revenues to deal with exploding budget deficits, Gingrich had dismissed him as "the tax collector for the welfare state." Dole got in his own gibes, often with acerbic humor. One early Dole joke was based on the good news that a bus filled with tax-cut happy, deficit-disdaining supply-siders had gone over a cliff. The bad news was that there were three empty seats.

Dole was much less confident than Gingrich that the Democratic president could be rolled by the newly empowered Republican majority in Congress. And as a certain candidate for the presidency in 1996, he had no interest in helping Clinton demonize the Republican party by making Gingrich and his firebrand freshmen its national symbol. Dole's worst fears were realized, however, in the budget confrontations between the president and the Gingrich-led Republican Congress.

Clinton and the New Republican Majority

The 104th Congress had started out with an assertiveness unparalleled in modern American history, the lead dog in policy agenda-setting and passage. But when the goal of

Speaker Gingrich—to force conservative legislation onto the president's desk and leave him with the Hobson's choice of signing the bills and alienating his base or vetoing them and being labeled a "do-nothing president"—failed, Congress turned partisan and combative. By late 1995, Republicans were spoiling for a showdown with the president, and they engineered one over the budget.

As the fall approached, the House Republicans believed that they could put together a strategy that would force the president into a corner. They were set to pass a giant reconciliation bill that promised a balanced budget in seven years, using somewhat pessimistic economic projections from the Congressional Budget Office and leaving it up to the president to find the cuts once he agreed to the seven-year timetable. That would mean a presidential commitment to deep cuts in Medicare and Medicaid along with serious cutbacks in discretionary domestic spending. The president countered by agreeing to the seven-year commitment but with numbers derived from a more optimistic economic forecast by the Office of Management and Budget, meaning smaller cuts in discretionary spending and no serious whack at Medicare and Medicaid.

The GOP strategy was to send the president the reconciliation bill along with a bundle of all thirteen appropriations bills, the complete package coming as the new fiscal year was under way and when a new budget would have to be set in place to keep government functioning. They could then rely on the endgame squeeze to force the president to capitulate. Eager to force the issue, the House Republicans moved more quickly—sending the president on November 13 a short-term stopgap spending bill and a temporary extension of borrowing ability for the Treasury as the debt limit was exceeded. To their great surprise, he vetoed both.

The Republicans said they would not vote on a veto override until December 1—forcing a government shutdown on November 14. Eight-hundred thousand "non-essential" federal workers were sent home that day, shutting down such government activities as the processing of Social Security applications and closing such attractions as the National Gallery of Art and the Grand Canyon National Park.

Within days, the House Republicans blinked, at least temporarily; they passed another continuing resolution to keep the government operating until December 5. The blink came after a major public relations gaffe on the part of the Speaker. Gingrich had accompanied the president and other dignitaries to Israel to attend the funeral of slain Prime Minister Itzhak Rabin. Afterward, he complained to the press that he had been snubbed by Clinton, forced to exit the plane through the rear door, and that action had spurred him to force the government shutdown.

The fit of pique became a huge story, leading the evening news shows and prompting the New York *Daily News* to run a caricature of the Speaker in a diaper next to a huge headline *CRY BABY*. As a *Washington Post*/ABC poll showed the standing of House Republicans on the budget plummeting to 21 percent, GOP leaders, led by the Senate's Bob Dole, forced the retreat on November 19.

But it did not stop the House Republicans from pushing for more confrontation. Their attitude was typified by freshman senator James Inhofe of Oklahoma: "As time goes on, the President is going to . . . finally come around." [9] House Budget Committee Chairman John Kasich said, "I'd be prepared to carry this thing until hell freezes over."[10] Another set of unpalatable bills sent to the president resulted in more vetoes and no stopgap plan—and another shutdown beginning on December 16. Three days into the second shutdown, the president vetoed a string of appropriations bills that had been sent to him, indicating that he would not back down. This time, 260,000 federal workers were furloughed and once again popular government services were stopped. This time, the shutdown lasted until January 6. When Congress came back to Washington, its members relaying tales of being berated by constituents for their actions, the leaders immediately began negotiations with the president for a seven-year balanced budget plan acceptable to both sides—an agreement achieved on January 26, 1996.

When the budget showdown resulted not in a cowed president but in a humiliated Speaker and humbled Congress, the strategy and climate shifted again. Both the Democratic president and Republican Congress shared a goal—each wanted to win reelection, and each knew that would require some public embrace of those governing. Thus, grudging cooperation was the watchword for most of 1996, and the output of legislation turned more respectable.

The centerpiece of the agenda for both sides was welfare reform. Clinton had called for "ending welfare as we know it" in his 1992 campaign. House Republicans had featured welfare reform as "The Personal Responsibility Act" in their Contract with America. Their collaboration was an uneasy one. After vetoing the first two welfare reform bills passed by Congress, Clinton signed a slightly modified version despite his objections to several of its parts and in the face of substantial criticism from members of his cabinet and Democrats in Congress. Had he pursued welfare reform instead of health reform in the first two years of his administration, when Democrats controlled the Congress, he may well have gotten a bill more to his liking. However, support among Democrats for a number of key elements of Clinton's welfare reform proposal was tepid at best. Divided government may have been essential to the passage of welfare reform. And Clinton, like the Republicans in Congress, used this legislative success to advantage in running for reelection.

In 1996 Clinton also reached agreement with the Republican Congress to increase access to health insurance. Known as the Kennedy-Kassebaum bill (its co-sponsors were Senators Ted Kennedy (D-MA) and Nancy Kassebaum (R-KS)), this legislation limited the extent to which preexisting health conditions could disqualify new employees from receiving immediate and full insurance coverage. It made health insurance more portable for those who changed jobs. While falling well short of Clinton's goal of achieving universal coverage, the legislation addressed a serious problem and dealt with it in a responsible fashion. Both parties and branches were eager to claim credit for its passage in the 1996 campaign.

House Republicans lost seats in the 1996 elections—while their Senate colleagues picked up two—but not enough to relinquish their narrow majority. Shifting tactics after the government shutdowns helped to limit the political damage as did the campaign fund-raising scandal dogging Clinton and Vice President Gore in the weeks before the election, which overshadowed any publicity about the Speaker's ethics problems.

Chastened by their near-death experience but determined to extend their control of Congress, Republicans approached the 1997 budget negotiations in a more pragmatic fashion. Though the ensuing talks were not without tension and temporary setback, both sides avoided the rancorous partisanship of 1995 and 1996 and managed to reach middle ground. Tension was no doubt eased by a timely report from the Congressional Budget Office that predicted an additional $225 billion in revenues over five years. The windfall permitted negotiators to remove two of the deal's most controversial provisions, a cap on Medicaid and a change in the Consumer Price Index, which would have reduced Social Security outlays. The ultimate result was the enactment of companion bills, the Balanced Budget Act of 1997 and the Taxpayer Relief Act of 1997, which together called for a balanced budget by 2002 and provided the largest tax cut since 1981. The former measure reduced expected federal outlays over the next five years by about $260 billion, largely by lowering Medicare reimbursement to hospitals and doctors and by extending the caps on discretionary spending. The latter, which cut taxes by about $95 billion over the five-year period, included child and education tax credits, a reduction in the capital gains tax rates, increased estate tax exemptions, more generous tax-advantaged retirement accounts, and the extension of expiring business tax provisions.

The legislation received wide support in the Congress, and Clinton and Republican leaders hailed the agreement as a bipartisan triumph. To House Budget Committee Chair John Kasich the deal was "[A] dream come true," while the president modestly characterized it as "the achievement of a generation and a triumph for every American." Not everyone was as optimistic, however. Conservative opponents insisted that the deal spent too much, while their liberal counterparts, including House Minority Leader Dick Gephardt, asserted that it did not go far enough and that it disproportionately benefited the wealthy. Meanwhile, nonpartisan policy analysts groused that the agreement did very little to address the solvency of the social insurance programs soon to absorb the baby-boom retirees.

The critics may have been right, but the accomplishment itself, requiring significant compromises on all sides, was a signal one, and the more proximate goal of a balanced budget was met much earlier than anticipated in the agreement, thanks to a cooling of health care inflation and, most importantly, a surge in federal receipts. An economic boom and bullish stock market during the second half of the 1990s dramatically improved public finances, turning budget deficits into surpluses and removing a major source of friction between the parties. Clinton and the Republican Congress could disagree over what to do with the surplus—bank it in order to "save Social Security first" or cut taxes. But the positive-sum nature of the game combined with the public's growing satisfaction with the performance of the economy limited the intensity of their battles over economic policy. Since neither side was in a position to pursue successfully its most ambitious policy proposals, each felt obliged to limit its legislative objectives. In this environment, Clinton increasingly relied on executive orders and administrative actions while Republicans in Congress used the legislative process to engage in message politics: framing choices to improve their prospects in the next election.

The shotgun wedding between the Democratic president and Republican Congress forced policy accommodation by both partners but could not impose anything approaching marital bliss. Partisan tensions remained high during this period of divided party government, fueled by the growing ideological polarization of the parties, particularly between the activists in their core constituencies. Judicial appointments and scandals prompted some of the bitterest engagements between the parties.

Judicial Appointments

President Clinton enjoyed a relatively high degree of success in garnering Senate confirmation of his court appointees during his first two years in office. His two Supreme Court nominees—Ruth Bader Ginsburg and Stephen Breyer—were both unanimously approved by the Senate Judiciary Committee and overwhelmingly confirmed by the full Senate by votes of 96 to 3 and 87 to 9, respectively. The Senate also confirmed 91 percent of his district court nominees and 86 percent of his circuit court nominees.[11] Part of Clinton's success no doubt stemmed from the Democratic majority in the Senate, which gave him an advantage in moving nominees through the Judiciary Committee and in getting timely votes on the Senate floor. But it went well beyond unified party government. Clinton consulted widely on his Supreme Court appointments and gave special consideration to the views of ranking Judiciary Committee Republican Orrin Hatch. He largely avoided partisan battles over his district and circuit court appointments by nominating moderates and giving due deference to the sentiments of individual senators, sometimes to the chagrin of liberal interest groups.

The change in party control of the Senate following the 1994 election did not produce an immediate reversal of this success. Clinton chose not to squander precious political capital on judicial battles and nominated noncontroversial judges. White House Counsel Abner Mikva noted that the administration would not nominate those who "won't get hearings or . . . will end up with a fight."[12] When Clinton was rumored to be ready to nominate two of Senator Barbara Boxer's district court choices, Samuel Paz and Judith McConnell, Hatch said he would refuse to accept either one. Clinton then asked Boxer to recommend alternate California judges and asked Paz and McConnell to withdraw their nominations. By the middle of 1995, the Associated Press noted that judges were enjoying "smooth sailing" in the Republican-controlled Senate and that the hearings were low-key.[13]

The pace of judicial confirmation slowed markedly in 1996. Majority Leader Bob Dole, who had voted for 182 of 185 Clinton court appointments between 1993 and 1995, was now the likely Republican presidential nominee and thus led a chorus of Republicans in sharply criticizing Clinton nominees sent to the Senate. Hatch openly acknowledged that the confirmation process would stall in hopes of a Republican victory in the presidential election and hence the nomination of more conservatives to fill federal vacancies. Only seventeen judges were confirmed in 1996—the lowest number in an election year since 1976; twenty-eight nominees were returned at the end of the session. Clinton's success rate for the entire 105th Congress dropped to 75 percent for district court, 58 percent for circuit court nominees.

Partisan conflict in the judicial confirmation process did not abate once the presidential contest was settled; to the contrary, it intensified after Clinton's reelection and the return of a Republican majority in Congress. Hatch became increasingly outspoken about unacceptable levels of "judicial activism" among the nominees and officially ended the allegedly liberal American Bar Association's advisory role in the judicial confirmation process. Majority Leader Trent Lott was slow to schedule votes for those reported favorably out of committee. This was part of a broader attack on the federal judiciary by such conservative groups as the Judicial Selection Monitoring Foundation and the Federalist Society. House Republicans also engaged in this ideological struggle for control of the federal courts with threats to limit their jurisdiction and to impeach judges who had issued rulings beyond their authority.

By the end of 1997, Clinton had begun criticizing Republicans for a crisis of federal judicial vacancies. In December, eighty-two of 846 federal judgeships were vacant, and twenty-six of those vacancies had existed for more than eighteen months. Chief Justice William Rehnquist felt obliged to speak out on New Year's Day: "Vacancies cannot remain at such high levels indefinitely without eroding the quality of justice that traditionally has been associated with the federal judiciary."[14]

A temporary respite in the judicial wars followed. The public found the sharp attacks on the federal bench unsettling. The White House restructured its staff to make more timely and orderly appointments. And Clinton engaged in ongoing consultations with Hatch. As a consequence, the pace of confirmations quickened in 1998, producing an improvement in the president's success rate in the 105th Congress. He won confirmation of 85 percent of his district court and 73 percent of his circuit court nominees.

That record deteriorated considerably during the last two years of his presidency. The impeachment trial in 1999 and election-year politics in 2000 contributed to the sharp decline in the percentage of Clinton's court nominations that were confirmed by the Senate in the 106th Congress: 69 percent for district court, 43 percent for circuit court appointees. Although Clinton almost always opted for quiet negotiations and bargains with conservative senators over public fights for liberal nominees, his ability to work constructively with the Republican Senate was constrained by the high stakes attached to federal court appointments by each party's core constituencies. While scholars salute his success in filling vacancies with judges known for their moderation and judicial temperament, liberal and conservative activists found in his record much to criticize.

Scandal and Impeachment

If judicial appointments provided a setting for tough partisan battles, scandals surrounding President Clinton precipitated all-out warfare between the branches. Congressional investigations of alleged misbehavior began shortly after Clinton took office, when Democrats were still the majority party in Congress. Controversy surrounding Whitewater, an investment made by the Clintons years earlier, led to the appointment in January 1994 of a special prosecutor, Robert Fiske, Jr. His replacement in August of that year by independent counsel Kenneth Starr, after the underlying statute appointing the special prosecutor was reauthorized, led to an inexorable expansion of the targets of this investigation over several years. These targets included the White House travel office, the death of deputy White House counsel Vince Foster, the use of confidential FBI files, and payments to former Associate Attorney General Webster Hubbell. The expansion culminated in Clinton's affair with White House intern Monica Lewinsky and its links to a civil suit brought against him by Paula Jones.

After the Republicans took control of Congress, the range and intensity of congressional investigations of the "Clinton scandals" increased markedly. Hearings were held on all of the charges eventually included in Starr's portfolio as well as on alleged drug use in the White House, foreign travel of Energy Secretary Hazel O'Leary, and campaign finance abuses. The Republican Congress also requested the appointment of independent counsels to investigate HUD Secretary Henry Cisneros (for allegedly misleading the FBI during background checks), Interior Secretary Bruce Babbitt (for allegedly misleading Congress about a casino proposal), Labor Secretary Alexis Herman (for alleged questionable campaign finance deals), Commerce Secretary Ron Brown (for alleged personal financial improprieties), and AmeriCorps director Eli Segal (for alleged conflicts of interest). But none matches the extraordinary impeachment and trial of the President.[15] Surely 1998 will not go down in the annals of American history as a year ennobling for the president, productive for the Congress, or triumphant for other members of the Washington community. Clinton's reckless behavior with Monica Lewinsky, his dissembling under oath, and the seven-month lapse between his initial public lie and his ultimate acknowledgment demeaned the presidency, eroded critical privileges of the office, betrayed his staff and allies, squandered his opportunity to shape the congressional agenda, and embarrassed the nation. There is no avoiding the conclusion that Clinton himself deserved much of the blame for the whole tawdry business.

But he had a big supporting cast. The Supreme Court contributed with its inexplicable unanimous ruling that the Jones civil suit could go forward while Clinton served as president. Seldom have the Court's words—"It appears to us highly unlikely to occupy any substantial amount of the president's time"—looked so foolish so quickly. The president's personal attorney failed to persuade his client to settle with Jones or to plead no contest and thereby avoid an invasive discovery and deposition. By virtue of its active pursuit of expanded jurisdiction and its aggressive investigative tactics, the Office of Independent Counsel Starr managed to raise more questions in the public's mind about the political roots of the prosecution than it answered about the president's misbehavior.

The *coup de grace* was Starr's referral to the House, which through its open advocacy for impeachment and numbing detail on the president's sexual encounters destroyed any hope that the investigation would garner the credibility intended by the Independent Counsel statute. As for the press—with its breathless forecasts of the president's imminent departure from office, weakly sourced "investigative reports," partisan food fights on cable news channels, and scores of editorials and columns dripping with contempt for the president and the public—suffice it to say that media coverage of this presidential scandal and its appropriate place in national politics and policy making was a wasteland.

Then came the House itself, which ignored every constructive precedent set during the Nixon impeachment process in 1973–74. We were both in Washington during the Nixon period, and one of us, by the accident of circumstance, ended up spending a good deal of time with House Judiciary Committee Chairman Peter Rodino as the committee moved toward resolution of the earlier impeachment. When the House of Representatives dealt with the investigation and impeachment hearings into Richard Nixon, Judiciary Committee Chairman Rodino worked extremely hard to make sure that the result would be broadly bipartisan.

For anyone not around Washington in 1973, it is hard to convey how tense the atmosphere was. We were into uncharted territory. Many people saw the impeachment process as a test for the constitutional system—a test in which it was not foreordained that the system and the Constitution as we knew it would prevail. There was dark talk, and not by the usual conspiracy theorists, of a constitutional coup. It could easily have degenerated into partisan warfare or into a challenge to the role and power of Congress.

But several key people stepped up to the plate and ensured that Congress and the country survived it without a hitch—indeed, with a greater commitment to the rule of law. On the House Judiciary Committee, they included Republicans William Cohen of Maine, Charles Wiggins of California, and Caldwell Butler of Virginia, and Democrats Paul Sarbanes of Maryland, Don Edwards of California, and Barbara Jordan of Texas. Judiciary Chairman Rodino was the glue. He managed to keep some of the more restive and partisan Democrats in line even as he worked patiently with committee Republicans to sift through the evidence and reach consensus, or at least bipartisan conclusions. Ironically, Rodino's success at averting a constitutional crisis in 1974 made it easier a quarter century later for the impeachment process against President Bill Clinton to move in a different direction—a harshly partisan and increasingly petty direction—because members did not feel there was any risk to doing so.

At the outset, it appeared that the second impeachment hearings in the House Judiciary Committee would proceed very much like the first set. Chairman Henry Hyde said directly and openly that it would not be possible to proceed without bipartisanship—a partisan presidential impeachment, one far more like that of Andrew Johnson after the Civil War than of Richard Nixon, would be disastrous for all the parties.

But Hyde's early assurance of bipartisanship evaporated. The hearings and the votes were divided purely on partisan lines, resulting in party-driven votes for impeachment on the House floor. To some degree, the dynamic on the House committee was led by an outside counsel brought in by Hyde from Illinois, who became a rabid Clinton-hater and aggressively lobbied the Republican members of the committee to hit the president hard. But the driving force in the House was Majority Whip Tom DeLay.

As impeachment talk heated up, many Republicans and most Democrats believed that it would be destructive for everybody; it was a punishment nowhere near commensurate with the crime and would not in any event result in removal from office, given the makeup of the Senate. The alternative was a resolution of censure, which would likely have garnered strong bipartisan support while still being a serious rebuke of the president. But Tom DeLay would have no part of a censure and insisted on a full-force drive toward impeachment. He succeeded, while further dividing the parties in the House and causing a significant public backlash against the Republican Congress.

The majority Republicans' decision to release Starr's referral immediately after they received it, without first reviewing its contents or giving the president an opportunity to respond, raised questions about basic fairness. Subsequent data dumps, including videotapes of the president's grand jury testimony, all rationalized by the public's right to know, seemed more like an abdication of congressional responsibility, especially in light of later protestations that "we must fulfill our constitutional duty whatever the views of the public." The hurried decision to open a formal impeachment inquiry, made in the politically charged period just before a national election without any real deliberation on the charges, the evidence, and what constitutes an impeachable offense, certainly reinforced that impression.

Congressional Democrats were hardly the model of dispassionate judgment and stability. After initial disbelief and then disingenuous acceptance of the president's public denial, they reacted angrily to his August 17, 1998, speech acknowledging a sexual relationship with Lewinsky. Many spoke emotionally about their feelings of betrayal and shame and contributed to the escalating pressure on the president to resign. Later, when it became clear that the public's resolute opposition to impeachment or resignation was unlikely to diminish, Democrats charted an entirely different course, one designed primarily to impeach the president's chief accuser.

What was most striking about this entire affair, however, was the House Republicans' response to the historic November election results and to polls documenting the strong public sentiment against forcing Clinton from office. A last-minute advertising blitz orchestrated by Speaker Gingrich failed to make the impeachment debate an electoral liability for the Democrats. It may, in fact, have had the opposite effect. Democrats gained five seats in the House, the first time the president's party avoided House losses in a midterm election since 1934. While very few incumbents in either chamber were defeated and the party balance in the Senate remained the same, Republicans interpreted the results as a major setback. Seldom has so little electoral change been so pregnant with political meaning. Facing his own ethics issue, including a book-deal scandal, and under pressure from his party colleagues concerned about the shrinking Republican majority and a challenge for his office from Appropriations Committee Chair Bob Livingston, Gingrich announced his resignation from the Speakership. (Six weeks later, Speaker-designate Livingston would himself resign from Congress in the face of rumors of extramarital affairs.) Once again, Clinton and Gingrich experienced a sudden reversal of fortunes.

And yet the Republicans pushed forward with impeachment. The House Judiciary Committee reconvened and moved inexorably by party line to report articles of impeachment. Majority Whip Tom DeLay pressed the other House leaders to deny the censure option on the floor, which almost certainly would have been widely embraced and rendered impeachment moot. DeLay also mobilized outside groups of conservative activists to put pressure on the fifty or so House Republicans who were thought to oppose impeachment. Since the constitution requires a two-thirds majority in the Senate to convict the president, there was little chance of his being removed from office. Nonetheless, House Republicans produced the votes needed to approve two of the four articles of impeachment written by the Judiciary Committee, with only five voting against the perjury charge and twelve against the obstruction of justice charge. However much the public thought it was time to bring down the curtain on this national soap opera, the country would be put through an extended run. The spectacle finally ended on February 12, 1999, when the Senate rejected both articles of impeachment by votes of 45 to 50 and 50 to 50.

The failure of the House to pull back from the precipice spoke volumes about the bitter partisan polarization that had come to shape life in the Washington community. Impeachment was just another weapon in the partisan wars, a further escalation of the criminalization of political differences.[16] Activists in the party base would be courted, not ordinary citizens. James Madison would be turned on his head: rather than the mob whose passions had to be cooled by their more deliberate leaders, the public struggled to contain the sectarian obsessions of their representatives in Washington.

Bill Clinton, the ultimate survivor,[17] completed his term with favorable ratings from a grateful nation enjoying an extended period of economic and social prosperity, but also with a palpable sense of lost opportunities and underachievement. He had failed to rebuild the political center, Republicans now controlled the House and Senate, and both the presidency and the Congress were diminished as the central institutions of American democracy.

George Bush Leads a Unified Republican Government: An Escalation of the Partisan Wars

George Bush entered the presidency facing formidable challenges.[18] His election was the most controversial in more than a century; he won by a razor-thin margin in the electoral college after thirty-six contentious days beyond Election Day and then only by a 5 to 4 decision of the Supreme Court. Seething unhappiness about the controversial election outcome was widespread among Democrats. While his party maintained majority status in the House and Senate, giving Republicans control of the White House and both houses of Congress for the first time since Dwight Eisenhower in 1953–54, it was by the barest of margins; the Senate was divided 50 to 50 with Vice President Cheney breaking the tie, and Republicans narrowly controlled the House 221 to 212—the closest margins in both houses of Congress in seventy years. In fact, Bush's election had provided negative coattails in both houses, including the largest loss of Senate seats by a president's party in a presidential election in recent history.[19]

To many observers, the above conditions would have suggested a cautious, incremental, and bipartisan approach to Congress. On the surface, so did Bush's experience in Texas, where he had worked closely with Democrats who controlled at least part of the legislature for his entire time as governor. In May 2001, when Senator James Jeffords of Vermont switched parties, control of the Senate switched to the Democrats, and caution and bipartisanship seemed even more likely. After the shock of September 11, as both parties and their leaders rallied around the president, symbolized by the warm embrace in the House chamber between the president and Senate Majority Leader Tom Daschle (D-SD), bipartisanship via a kind of "government of national unity" appeared inevitable.

But those predicting consistent bipartisanship, or a cautious and incremental approach to policy making, were wrong. Bush emerged as an exceptionally bold president in the legislative arena, governing as if he had won in a landslide. For most of his first term in office, and in the early months of his second, George W. Bush chose a tough-minded, often confrontational, and sharply partisan approach to making policy—tossing aside conventional wisdom of how to approach a closely divided Congress with a weak electoral mandate. His audacious and partisan tactics often worked—both in achieving legislative success in such areas as tax cuts and in blocking the Democrats in the Senate from achieving many of their goals or from gaining significant leverage over policy negotiations.

Inheriting a sharply polarized political environment, the new president chose to make the intense partisanship work to his advantage rather than try to diminish it. This entailed demanding unity from his fellow Republicans on Capitol Hill based on shared political stakes; encouraging House leaders to produce the strongest possible version of his legislative proposals; circumventing Senate Democratic leaders by seeking a handful of Democratic defectors on an issue-by-issue basis; and then dominating the conference committee process to write legislative language that delivered most of what he sought. This strategy worked to near perfection with his highest priority of cutting taxes.

Bush had proposed a large tax cut during the 2000 campaign, a central campaign theme that resonated with his conservative base. After the election, there was widespread speculation that he would cut back on the size and dimensions of the tax cut to respond to the close partisan margins in Congress. But in January of 2001, before taking office, Bush signaled that he would not scale down his tax cut—around $1.6 billion over ten years—and might propose accelerating parts of the tax cut to stimulate the economy. The major features of the plan were a reduction and consolidation of income tax rates, a doubling of the child tax credit, reduction of the marriage penalty, and repeal of the estate tax. Bush made it clear that he would make the tax cut his top priority and push for early action in the Congress.

The legislative strategy was clear: start with the House, go for broke, and use the momentum of a victory there to persuade—or bludgeon—the Senate to go along. The strategy was understandable; the rules of the House, after all, give the majority much more leeway to set the agenda, time action, and limit options, allowing the leadership to set strict rules on debate and to limit or ban amendments by the minority. But with the small margins, the president would need virtually perfect party unity in the body. The Senate, however, was even less favorable terrain; the rules were too loose and Republican unity, given the larger proportion of moderates, was more shaky.

The strategy cut House Democrats entirely out of the process. It meant dealing with individual Democratic senators, but not the Democratic Senate leadership, to avoid excessive dilution of the ultimate product. Republican leaders in the House were eager to take up Bush's tax cut. Despite their bare, six-vote margin, the House Republican leaders aimed to achieve that perfect or near-perfect unity among their members. The Democratic congressional leadership opposed the size, breadth, and duration of the Bush tax cut. But unwilling to appear opposed to all tax cuts, they offered an alternative. The Senate Democratic leader, Tom Daschle, indicated in January that Democrats would support a $300 billion tax cut. By late February they had coalesced around a plan more than double that size. The issue was not tax cut or no tax cut—it was how deep the tax cuts would go.

Thanks to the tough maneuvers of Bill Thomas (R-CA), the chairman of the House Ways and Means Committee, the House moved quickly, sending to the floor a plan that closely mirrored the president's. To expedite action and maximize support, Thomas split Bush's proposal into parts. The Ways and Means Committee first addressed a bill that included the largest portion of the Bush tax cuts, the income tax rate cuts, which amounted to about $950 billion over ten years. On March 1, the committee voted to approve the rate cuts by a 23 to 15 vote, with all Republicans voting in favor and all Democrats against. As the House committee was voting in favor of the tax rate cuts, Bush went public, going directly to voters in states that he had won where there were wavering Democratic senators. Bush traveled to more states in the early part of his presidency than any other president.

On March 8, the tax-cut plan came to the floor of the House, and it was passed 230 to198. Every Republican voted for the bill, and all but ten Democrats opposed it. (By contrast, the Reagan tax cut of 1981, which was much larger adjusting for inflation, garnered significantly more Democratic votes.) Bush attracted very few of the conservative Democrats, who call themselves the "Blue Dogs," some of whom, like Charlie Stenholm of Texas, had voted for Reagan's tax cuts. Thus the major part of the tax-cut plan was passed with scant Democratic support and with virtually no Democratic input.

The House Ways and Means Committee then quickly took up another part of the Bush tax cut, the marriage penalty and child tax-credit provisions. The bill passed out of committee on March 16, once again on a strict partisan vote (23 to16). On March 29, the House voted 282 to 144 in favor of the bill. But the key vote was one to reject a substitute by Democrat Charles Rangel, which would have made the package smaller and more heavily targeted toward lower income earners. Voting against the Rangel amendment were 231 members, including twelve Democrats; 196, all Democrats, voted for it.

That same day, March 29, the Committee on Ways and Means voted for a third part of the Bush tax proposal, the elimination of the estate tax ($192 billion over ten years) by a vote of 24 to 14, with only one Democrat supporting the proposal. On April 4, the House passed the bill 274 to 154 with fifty-eight Democrats voting for the measure and three Republicans voting against it.[20] The bill totally eliminated the estate tax—or as Republicans preferred to call it, the death tax—but phased in its demise more slowly than the president's plan, thereby lowering its cost.

Bush's tax cut was thus passed more or less as he had asked for it, with the House making only marginal changes. The House package was approximately the same dollar amount as the Bush proposal, and it encompassed the major areas the president had proposed. While a few parts of the plan garnered some Democratic support, it was the unanimous Republican backing, combined with the restrictive House procedures, that made for the early and thorough presidential victory.

However, it was clear that the president's bill could not pass the 50 to 50 Senate without at least some change. Only a handful of moderate Democrats—perhaps only Georgia's Zell Miller—might support the House-passed plan, while some moderate Republicans might oppose it. In this atmosphere, Majority Leader Trent Lott (R-MS) and Minority Leader Tom Daschle exerted pressure on their rank and file to hold their lines.

Daschle was less successful. Before long, the ranking Democrat on the Finance Committee, Montana's Max Baucus, began working openly with Chairman Charles Grassley to put together a compromise bill. The timing of Baucus's move upset Democratic leaders as much as the move itself. Daschle and his colleagues had hoped to slow down the bill's progress in order to dull the president's early momentum, but Grassley and Baucus quickly came to a compromise plan, one much closer to the president's than to anything Senate Democratic leaders had contemplated. The plan called for $1.3 billion in tax cuts over ten years; compared to the House version, it was slower and less generous in lowering the rates for the highest income brackets and slower in phasing out the estate tax. On May 15, the bill passed out of the Finance Committee with the votes of all ten Republicans and four of ten Democrats. Majority Leader Trent Lott brought the bill to the Senate floor for debate on May 17, where a number of amendments to the Grassley-Baucus compromise were defeated.

Republican leaders expected that the debate would conclude the week of May 21 and the Senate would pass a bill that would go to conference rapidly to iron out differences with the House. But the week turned out to be more momentous than anyone had expected. On May 21, there were rumors that Senator James Jeffords, a Republican from Vermont, would switch parties, thereby shifting control of the Senate to the Democrats. The following day, Jeffords met with Vice President Cheney and then later with President Bush and made it clear that he would leave the party. Bush asked him to delay the date of the switch until after the tax cut had passed. The Senate voted on the Grassley-Baucus tax package on May 23. All of the Republicans, including Jeffords, and twelve Democrats voted for the package, sending the bill to a House-Senate conference. On May 25, the conference met to work out the details of a compromise; given the reality of a now-Democratic majority in the Senate, the size of the package and the major features of the tax cut were inevitably going to resemble the Senate's version. The only surprise was how quickly the conference worked matters out. Final passage of the tax-cut bill was on May 26. In the House, no Republicans voted against the package and twenty-eight Democrats voted for it. In the Senate, twelve Democrats voted for the tax cut and two Republicans voted against it.

In a substantive sense, the president had a huge victory. The tax cut that was enacted into law was more than 80 percent of the size he proposed and much larger than Democrats had wanted. Both the overall thrust and most of the details resembled the president's original plan. The political victory for Bush was enormous as well: he had achieved his top legislative goal more rapidly than Ronald Reagan had achieved his in 1981, following his landslide election in 1980, with huge coattails in both houses. But whether Congress had done its job—scrubbing the legislative proposals to ensure some reasonable assessment of cost and benefits—was another question altogether.

President Bush's proposal for education reform moved on a parallel track but a far different path to passage. The No Child Left Behind legislation—which emphasized standards, testing, and accountability, with a substantial role for the federal government—had a natural constituency among congressional Democrats but elicited skepticism among many Republicans, who had recently proposed abolishing the Department of Education.

With a tough partisan and ideological approach on tax cuts and a straightforward bipartisan and centrist approach on education, Bush seemed, after his first several months in office, as if he would be able to strike an exquisite balance in his dealings with Congress. That impression was underscored and amplified in the weeks after September 11, when a series of measures, including the authorization to use force in Afghanistan, the airline security bill, and the Patriot Act, got broad bipartisan support.

Democrats felt a surge in warmth toward the president after 9/11, one made evident to the nation when President Bush, after giving a stirring address to the country from the House chamber, went down onto the floor and gave Senate Majority Leader Tom Daschle a warm embrace. Relations between House party leaders also became much less icy when the leaders, who had barely communicated with one another for the entire year, were thrown together in the tense hours after the attacks and had at least some common bond. But if one scratched beneath the surface, it was clear that even in this time of national unity, there were deep-seated differences and animosities between the parties.

The airline security bill brought a sharp division between Democrats and Republicans—and the House and Senate—over whether the airport screeners would be federal employees or privatized; the Patriot Act brought its own divisions both over its tough law enforcement provisions and whether it would be made permanent. Despite the divisions, however, the rally-round-the-flag sentiments of the nation and Congress ensured near unanimous votes on final passage. While highly controversial, the resolution authorizing the president to take military action against Saddam Hussein passed comfortably in both the House and Senate, with near unanimity among Republicans and sharp division among Democrats. On a number of other issues—including agricultural subsidies, energy, transportation, and trade—geographical and sectoral interests represented in Congress cut across party lines, leading to somewhat different legislative strategies and congressional alignments.

Nevertheless, Bush's efforts to reach out to Democrats were limited and short-lived. The president still wanted to rely on the congressional strategy that had worked on the tax cut, one by which the House would be the president's chamber of support, dealing a tough, bedrock conservative hand for him to use as leverage with the Senate—but a Senate operating under a changed dynamic with a Democratic majority that could use its own agenda control to influence events.

Bipartisan cooperation on No Child Left Behind gave way to bitter battles between the parties over its financing. The glow of national unity after September 11 faded within months as the president resumed a more partisan approach to Congress.

The key issue that served to deeply inflame Democrats' hostility toward the president was the proposal to create a new Department of Homeland Security. The original idea for such a department had come in 2000 from a commission on threats to the United States, co-chaired by former Senators Gary Hart (D-CO) and Warren Rudman (R-NH). That recommendation was turned into a bill, introduced by Senator Joseph Lieberman (D-CT). However, the report and this recommendation were largely ignored by the public, the president, and Congress until after September 11.

After September 11, Lieberman renewed the call for enactment of his bill, using his position as chairman of the Senate Governmental Affairs Committee as a platform. The Bush administration strenuously resisted the move to a department, settling for a homeland security adviser, former Pennsylvania Governor Tom Ridge. Many members of Congress in both parties repeatedly challenged the efficacy of an office in the White House with an adviser lacking Cabinet rank or line authority. There was widespread public support for the idea of a department, leaving the White House on the short side of the political argument. While still publicly opposing a department and defending the Ridge office, Bush asked several senior aides to begin a top-secret effort to come up with a plan for a major reorganization that would create a Department of Homeland Security and transfer existing functions from other departments to it.

Bush unveiled the plan on June 6, 2002, the same day that FBI agent Colleen Rowley was scheduled to testify to Congress on the pre-9/11 failures of the agency to heed her warning calls for action after the arrest of Zacharias Moussaoui in Minnesota. The new Bush plan—far more aggressive, ambitious, and wide-ranging than those of Congress—dominated the news and instantly moved to the top of the policy agenda. Designed to have the greatest political impact, the Bush proposal took twenty-two separate bureaus, agencies, and offices, encompassing 170,000 employees and functions as disparate as plant and animal inspection, border patrol, and emergency management and pulled them together into one mega-department. Among opponents and proponents of such a department, there were significant arguments about jurisdiction and logistics as well as security and privacy concerns.

With only a few months before the midterm elections, there was barely time to consider a massive government reorganization. The House decided to bypass the committees of jurisdiction that might have a vested interest in the status quo and instead created an ad hoc Select Committee on Homeland Security, chaired by Majority Leader Richard Armey. His panel, pressed to act quickly and seize the political momentum, ignored many proposed changes recommended by various committees and came up with a bill very close to the White House's original proposal. The House passed its version 295 to 132 on July 26.[21]

In the Senate, the Government Affairs Committee had jurisdiction over the bill. Although chairman Joe Lieberman, the original champion of a department, had fashioned a bill more restrained in its breadth than the president's, he gave Bush much of what he sought structurally but proposed strong worker and union protections, in contrast to the House bill, which granted the president extraordinarily broad flexibility in personnel matters. Besides this difference, there were other signs in the Senate that the issue might take a different path than in the House. In particular, Senator Robert Byrd (WV), president pro tempore of the Senate and chairman of the Appropriations Committee, made it clear that he had grave misgivings about the entire enterprise and favored moving slowly to make such a sweeping change. That was not what the president wanted—his stated goal was to have a bill ready for signature by September 11, 2002— the one-year anniversary of the terrorist attack. But in part because of Byrd's ability to extend debate on the Senate floor, the bill moved slowly in the chamber.

On September 3, as the bill neared the Senate floor, the White House issued a threat that it would veto the Senate version of the bill because it did not provide the president enough personnel flexibility to ensure national security protection.[22] The original Lieberman proposal gave greater protections to workers in the Department of Homeland Security than in other departments. The president's proposal, by contrast, gave the president much greater flexibility in transferring, rewarding, or removing personnel than he had in other departments, even for other national-security related functions, and extended that discretion to all 170,000 employees, whether their functions were national-security related or not.

On the Senate floor, the battle was over which version of the Homeland Security Bill could get the fifty-one votes needed for passage. During the Senate debate, a small group of moderate Republicans and Democrats proposed a middle ground. The White House agreed to modest modifications in its flexibility proposal to satisfy most of the moderate Republicans.[23] Moderate Democrats John Breaux (LA) and Ben Nelson (NE), however, were not satisfied with the president's modification. The partisan battle lines were drawn.

Since Democrat Zell Miller supported the president and chastised his own party for not giving the president what he wanted (Miller said the party would be slitting its throat if it did not vote for the bill), the vote of Republican Lincoln Chafee (RI) became the tipping point. Chafee ultimately sided with the Democrats giving them the one-vote majority needed to get the bill to a conference committee with the House version.

To prevent that occurrence—and deny the Senate Democrats a declaration of victory on this important issue—Republicans invoked a filibuster, and this action managed to block cloture and prevent a vote on the Democratic plan. Democrats retaliated in kind and prevented a vote on the Republican version.[24] Ultimately, no agreement could be reached, and both parties went into the November midterm elections without a deal.

In the meantime, the midterm election campaign was heating up, with the majority in both houses of Congress up for grabs—a GOP margin of only six seats in the House, and the Democrats having no margin for error in the Senate. President Bush made a bold and risky decision to put his own reputation and prestige on the line and campaign vigorously for Republican candidates for Congress and against Democrats. Bush's continued high approval was clearly due to his standing as commander-in-chief in the war against terrorism, a nonpartisan role. If he emerged as a partisan leader, it could easily tarnish his public image and his approval ratings.

Other presidents had campaigned for congressional candidates in midterm elections, but the scope of Bush's effort was unprecedented. He made a record ninety campaign appearances, including campaign stops for twenty-three congressional candidates, sixteen Senate hopefuls, and a number of hotly contested gubernatorial races. Along the way, he attended nearly seventy-five fund-raisers and raised a record $144 million-plus. His campaign trips had him on the road nearly nonstop in the weeks leading up to the November 5 election, including a whirlwind tour of fifteen states in the last five days before the election.

Enough time had passed since September 11 that domestic concerns, many of which favored Democrats, were back on the agenda. But the president still used September 11 as a rallying call. Congress's agenda before the election had been taken up by homeland security, but more visibly by the vote to authorize force in Iraq. There was some division on the Iraq vote, but many Democrats who had tough re-election prospects had voted in favor of the war, and the vote itself was not a major factor in the election.

Bush focused instead on the Homeland Security Department, criticizing Democrats for blocking the measure. It became a standard theme as he traveled the nation to campaign for Republican Senate candidates, bolstered in the message by a barrage of television ads run by individual candidates and the Republican Senatorial Campaign Committee, under chairman Bill Frist (TN), that aggressively attacked individual Democratic incumbents for failing to support homeland security. Some of these ads juxtaposed pictures of the Democratic target (in Georgia, for example, Max Cleland) with those of Osama bin Laden and Saddam Hussein.

The attack themes and ads enraged Democrats but worked in many states, including Georgia. Going against every historical trend, Republicans picked up seats in the House, retook the majority in the Senate, and did well in gubernatorial and state legislative races. While the overall change in seats in the Republican direction was not large, Bush and Republicans had exceeded expectations and gained seats in a midterm election where almost all presidents had lost them. Bush had personalized the election, asking voters to put in a team of Republicans who would help him succeed. To most observers, his efforts—his coattails—made the difference.

After the election, Congress returned for a lame duck session, and the president moved quickly to take advantage of his new political leverage. He insisted that his homeland security bill be passed immediately by the lame duck Congress, and it was, with nearly all the flexibility for dealing with workers that Bush had sought. Bush also got the Senate to confirm a number of judges who had been nominated earlier in the Congress.

When the new Congress convened, the atmosphere was tense and contentious, particularly in the Senate. Senate Democrats had been stunned soon before the election when one of their most popular colleagues, Paul Wellstone of Minnesota, died with his wife and one child in a plane crash in northern Minnesota. In part because of the backlash from a memorial service that seemed to be politicized, their replacement candidate, Walter Mondale, lost the seat to Republican Norm Coleman. Before his death, Wellstone had also been excoriated in ads for softness on homeland security, as had freshman Senator Jean Carnahan of Missouri, another 2002 loser. They, along with Max Cleland, became rallying cries for Senate Democrats, who were enraged and frustrated by what they saw as presidential perfidy, misusing the homeland security issue to challenge the patriotism of their colleagues—and winning with the tactic.

But any sense of resentment on the part of Democrats in Congress did not faze President Bush. He began an ambitious agenda for the 108th Congress by proposing a new tax cut–economic stimulus plan that would cost $726 billion over ten years. The centerpiece was the abolition of the double taxation of corporate dividends, a move favored by many economists, but which was not a populist message nor one that would do anything to stimulate the economy in the short run. Republicans in Congress had not vetted the Bush tax plan. Its announcement by the White House was the first they knew of it.

Ways and Means Chairman Bill Thomas led many of his colleagues in an initial, negative reaction, even though the plan also included a laundry list of cuts favored by nearly all congressional Republicans, including an acceleration of the cut in personal income tax rates and the child tax credit.

Many of the president's advisers, surveying the close margins in both houses of Congress, had recommended a much smaller tax-cut plan, in the range of $350 billion—a suggestion rejected by the president for a bold alternative more than double in size. Given the expanding deficit, the looming war with Iraq, the expected opposition of Democrats, and the stated position of many moderate Republicans that they would not support a large tax cut, this was a very risky approach. But it reflected the approach to governing Bush had assumed regularly in the White House, along with his belief that now, with GOP majorities in both houses and the momentum of a midterm win, he could replicate and expand on his successes in 2001.

The early signs were not very favorable. A range of pundits and politicians had predicted that the new Republican monopoly on the reins of power in Washington would quickly open the floodgates on Bush judicial nominees, moving them through the Republican Senate and onto the courts. Wrong. Using a variety of Senate procedures and customs, and a new, disciplined cohesiveness driven in part by their outrage after the election, Democrats held up several nominees and effectively blocked the president's top judicial priority, Appeals Court nominee Miguel Estrada, with a filibuster on the Senate floor that new Majority Leader Bill Frist tried repeatedly, but without success, to overcome.

House Republicans did manage to prevail on a budget resolution that included the president's tax cut, but barely, and only after Herculean efforts by the new Majority Whip Roy Blunt (MO) and Majority Leader Tom DeLay. In the meantime, moderate Senate Republicans Olympia Snowe (ME) and George Voinovich (OH) signed a pledge to oppose any tax cut greater than $350 billion, joined with Democrats in blocking a larger tax cut in their budget resolution vote, and then held firm against intense White House pressure to increase the number to at least $550 billion. In May and June of 2003, Bush's tax cut passed through Congress. In the end, the president had to settle for less than 50 percent of the amount in his original proposal, and there was significant tinkering with the details, including a reduction, rather than an elimination, of the tax on dividends. In similar fashion to many of his earlier initiatives, Bush used a narrow majority strategy, attracting nearly all Republican votes and few Democratic ones. Although in the end,

Bush had to settle for half a loaf on the size of his tax cut, the president showed his political agility by embracing the plan, declaring victory, and successfully maintaining that perception of victory.

He moved on to his next bold initiative, a Medicare prescription drug bill that he and other Republicans had been loath to embrace while Democrats had championed it, but where the president and other key Republicans saw a need to seize the agenda in much the same way as he had taken over the idea of a Department of Homeland Security.

Bush approached Ted Kennedy and agreed to craft a bill that would include many provisions suggested by Kennedy and his allies. When the bill reached the Senate floor, it got seventy-six votes, including those of Kennedy and many other liberal Democrats—although some were furious that Kennedy had cut a deal with the devil. But Kennedy's expectation that this issue reflected a president chastened by his inability to get the full tax-cut plan the second time around, who would revert to the bipartisan education strategy, was soon derailed. In the House, there was no bipartisan negotiation, no George Miller-equivalent. Instead, the Ways and Means Committee marked up and passed a bill on a partisan basis, and, despite serious conservative opposition to a sharply expanded new entitlement, got the bill through by a single vote on the House floor by extending the vote to one hour and then dragooning a near-weeping Joanne Emerson of Missouri to change her vote from nay to yea.

In the conference committee, the Republicans excluded Senate Majority Leader Tom Daschle and his colleague Jay Rockefeller from the deliberations and reported out a bill much closer to the partisan House version than the bipartisan Senate one. This time around, the bill passed the Senate with only fifty-four votes—and moved to the remarkable scene on the House floor we described in detail in chapter 1.

For the White House and congressional Republicans, the dilemma they faced in Bush's third year was twofold: finding a way to get anything significant through a Senate in which the realistic hurdle was sixty votes, not fifty; and keeping enough Republican unity in the House on controversial issues to maintain the conservative leverage in conference committees.

The president's capacious ambitions—to change the role of government at home and America in the world and to build an enduring Republican majority—led him to eschew broad-based compromises that might produce only incremental policy changes and dilute the perceived differences between the parties. His Republican lieutenants in Congress were charged with finding the means to achieve those ends. They took on that charge eagerly and uncompromisingly.

Bush's approach to Congress was not merely partisan; it was also aggressively executive-centered. While to some extent all presidents aspire to maintain and extend the prerogatives of their office, Bush and Vice President Cheney shared especially strong beliefs about presidential power. During the 2000 campaign, Bush lamented the weakening of the office during his predecessor's tenure and promised to restore the authority, as well as the dignity, of the White House. After September 11, he assumed personal responsibility for responding to the attacks and leading a broader war against terrorism. The president would have little patience for those who sought to constrain him in fulfilling this mission.

Cheney, with considerable experience at both ends of Pennsylvania Avenue, had long espoused the expansive views on presidential power associated with Alexander Hamilton. As the chief architect of the minority report of the congressional committees investigating the Iran-Contra affair, Cheney argued that the president has inherent powers under the Constitution that give him power to act on his own in foreign affairs—as the "sole organ" of the government in negotiation, intelligence sharing, and other forms of communication with the rest of the world—and to protect the lives and interests of American citizens abroad. After a year as vice president, Cheney said: "I have repeatedly seen an erosion of the powers and the ability of the president of the United States to do his job. . . . We are weaker today as an institution because of the unwise compromises that have been made over the last thirty to thirty-five years."[25] Cheney appointed to his vice presidential staff one of his key aides on congressional committees on intelligence and the Iran-Contra affair, David Addington, in order to aggressively defend executive prerogatives on a wide range of issues.

The partisan and executive-centered approach to governance embraced unequivocally by Bush and Cheney shaped the way in which the Republican majority in Congress defined its role and went about its work. The institutional rivalry designed by the framers gave way to a relationship in which Congress assumed a position subordinate to the executive. Party trumped institution. The president set the agenda of Congress and made clear he expected Republican leaders in Congress (his "lieutenants") to deliver.

Speaker Hastert was just fine with this relationship. He proclaimed that his primary responsibility was not to lead and defend the first branch of government but to pass the president's legislative program. Regular order in the House was an institutional luxury that a unified Republican government could not afford. As majority whip and then majority leader, Tom Delay built a formidable political machine—in the House, on K Street, and among conservative activists around the country—to produce the Republican unity essential to that task. Bill Frist, who replaced Trent Lott as Senate Republican Leader in December 2002, was especially solicitous of the president's agenda. He was even willing to break with Senate precedents to use a simple majority vote to eliminate the filibuster on judicial appointments. While individual Republicans in both chambers chafed under the administration's niggardly sharing of information, the congressional leadership deferred to the executive on almost every interbranch dispute. Congressional oversight of the executive diminished significantly under a unified Republican government.

The major chafing points in the Bush presidency were between the Republican president and the Democrats in

Congress. But the way the two parties interacted inside Congress, with Republicans on both sides of the Hill eager and willing to play the role of loyal lieutenants to the president, with House Republicans happy to use and exploit the rules and norms of the body to ramrod through legislation regularly on party-line votes and with virtually no input by Democrats, and with Senate Republicans regularly deferring to the House and the president and downplaying the prerogatives of their Democratic colleagues, caused relationships inside Congress to deteriorate as well. For both of us, watching the House go through the impeachment fandango against President Clinton in 1998 marked the low point in our three-and-a-half decades of Congress-watching. We didn't think they could sink any lower. We were wrong.

FIVE

Institutional Decline

EIGHT YEARS OR MORE IN THE MAKING, the Bankruptcy Abuse Prevention and Consumer Protection Act of 2005 was signed into law by President George W. Bush on April 20, 2005. But in the weeks leading up to its effective date of October 17, the reaction to the impending law was not the usual mix of dread and anticipation. Instead, there was a mad political scramble in the aftermath of Hurricanes Katrina and Rita.

The changes in the law make filing for Chapter 7 bankruptcy harder for individuals, as they are required to undergo a means test and produce such documents as tax returns to prove their economic status. "How does the means test apply in a situation where you've lost your job due to the hurricane and you don't know whether you're going to be employed?" asked Lawrence Anderson, a Louisiana bankruptcy lawyer. "Also, how do you fill out paperwork if you lost records in the flood?"[1]

The two devastating hurricanes left at least 400,000 people without jobs and close to a million refugees without habitable residences. The problem was acute in the period directly after the two natural disasters, but it was clearly going to get worse in the months ahead. A study conducted by a University of Nevada professor before Katrina documented, over a twenty-five-year period, a sharp surge in bankruptcies between twelve and thirty-six months after flood or hurricane disasters, with one-and-a-half times as many filings in the affected states as in neighboring ones.[2] The Katrina situation was expected to be even more acute because so many of the victims lacked flood insurance.

Members of Congress in both parties quickly proposed a waiver of the new law's provisions for hurricane victims. But a blanket waiver would not have been necessary if a prescient amendment offered to the bankruptcy bill during its consideration in the House Judiciary Committee had been accepted. Rep. Sheila Jackson-Lee, a Democrat from Texas, offered the amendment, which would have exempted aid and relief money received after a natural disaster from the income counted in a means test under the new Chapter 7 bankruptcy rules. As with virtually every other amendment offered, this one was summarily rejected in the committee without debate by the committee chair, Mr. Sensenbrenner, after a perfunctory voice vote.

Rep. Jackson-Lee's amendment would not have solved all, or even most, of the problems for the huge number of victims of Katrina and Rita. But they are not the only ones stymied by the new bankruptcy law. What the hurricanes did was to put a sharp spotlight on the nature of the new law, the gaps, inconsistencies, and burdens it would impose on poorer Americans and the challenges it poses to bankruptcy lawyers and judges. While the law made creditors happy, it infuriated consumer groups and the bankruptcy bar.

Every complex law has perceived winners and losers and emerges only after a journey through the meat-grinder that is the legislative process. There is no such thing as a perfect statute. On an issue such as bankruptcy, the journey was especially tortuous. The need for reform of a bankruptcy process that had not changed significantly since 1978 was clear, but the road was blocked in four separate Congresses before a law emerged. In 1998, in the 105th Congress, the House and Senate passed separate versions and could not agree on reconciling them; an attempt to attach a bill as a provision of an omnibus (i.e., overall) spending bill died when congressional Republicans and President Clinton could not agree on language. In the 106th Congress, a conference report reconciling the differences between the houses on bankruptcy emerged and was approved by both chambers, but it was then pocket vetoed (i.e., killed without being signed) by Clinton because a Senate provision drafted by Senator Chuck Schumer of New York—to block convicted protestors, including abortion opponents, from avoiding court judgments by filing for bankruptcy—was removed in the conference between the two houses. A bill once again got to conference in the 107th Congress but was hung up by the abortion-protest language, this time by anti-abortion lawmakers in the House. In the 108th Congress, the Republican majority chose not to bring the bill to the floor because it could not find a way around the Schumer language.

All that changed in the 109th Congress. The bill put together in the Senate, with the active involvement of the credit industry, was fundamentally the same as that drafted eight years earlier. When it came to the Senate floor in March 2005, it was accompanied by a pledge from Senate Republican leaders to shun all amendments. Their strategy was to bypass a lengthy conference committee by passing a bill the House would accept in toto. House Republican leaders in turn had made it clear that they would not accept any changes from the creditors' draft—flexing their muscles while also giving more credibility to the no-amendments strategy.

Two weeks on the Senate floor saw a parade of amendments, many of which had been earlier rejected in the Senate Judiciary Committee, fall by the wayside. One amendment, for example, offered by Russ Feingold (D-WI), would have given older people special homestead exemptions that allowed them to keep their homes after filing for bankruptcy—a particular problem for retirees who lose all their assets after an illness or other problem but have homes owned for many years with mortgages paid off. Orrin Hatch, the bill's manager, said that this issue belonged in the states, and, its merits aside, passage of the bill would be jeopardized by the amendment's acceptance because of the flat warning by House Republicans against any Democratic amendments.

The Feingold Amendment went down 59 to 40. So did an amendment offered by Daniel Akaka (D-HI) to require credit card companies to show on their statements how long it would take their customers to pay off their debt if they only sent the minimum monthly payments. So did an amendment offered by Bill Nelson (D-FL) that would exempt debtors from means testing if their financial problems were caused by identity theft. And so did an amendment offered by Dick Durbin (D-IL) to protect service members and veterans from means testing in bankruptcy and from usurious interest rates. And many others went down also. Each amendment was opposed by every Republican, with three to five Democrats breaking ranks to join the opposition. In each case, the core rationale for rejection was not the worth of the amendment but that the House Republicans would not accept it.

Perhaps the most egregious rejection came on an amendment that would limit the ability of rich bankruptcy filers to use "asset protection trusts" to shelter most of their net worth from creditors. Five states—Utah, Rhode Island, Nevada, Delaware, Alaska—allow anybody, including nonresidents, to set up unlimited-size trusts of this sort. An amendment to limit trusts' size to $125,000 was rejected. Reason? See above.

Not far behind was a Republican-sponsored amendment, this one offered by John Cornyn of Texas, who as Texas attorney general had been frustrated when Enron filed for bankruptcy in New York, a state with looser standards. His amendment, to limit "judge-shopping" and require companies to file in their principal place of doing business, was opposed by the bill sponsors because to accept it would be to lose the votes on final passage of Delaware's two senators. He withdrew the amendment without a vote.

The Senate's actions prompted normally mild-mannered *Washington Post* columnist David Broder to accuse the body of "blatant hypocrisy":

> This "reform," which parades as an effort to stop folks from spending lavishly and then stiffing creditors by filing for bankruptcy protection, is a perfect illustration of how the political money system tilts the law against average Americans. The simple fact that for eight straight years it has gained a place on a crowded congressional calendar is testimony to the impact of the millions of dollars that banks and credit card companies have spent on lobbyists and campaign contributions.... For two weeks the Senate sponsors shot down virtually every attempt to separate the sheep from the goats and carve out protections for the average family trapped by circumstances.[3]

When the bill got to the House, it was rammed through the Judiciary Committee with sharply limited debate and brought to the floor under a closed rule that allowed no amendments. Since the bill that passed was identical to the Senate version, no conference committee was necessary and the bill went right to the president for signature.

An extensive review of the statute after its enactment in the *American Bankruptcy Law Journal,* by noted bankruptcy lawyer and critic of the act Henry J. Sommer, pointed out that the statute's problems include "atrocious drafting." Unlike the 1978 legislation, "no true expert in bankruptcy participated in drafting the consumer provisions sought by the financial services industry... perhaps it is just an indication of the arrogance of the bill's drafters who throughout the legislative process steadfastly resisted even the smallest technical corrections to their handiwork."[4] Sommer added, "It is no secret that the bill's proponents sought to limit the discretion of bankruptcy judges. . . . Ironically, the bill's poor drafting will require judges to exercise their judgment simply in trying to determine what it means."

Working off an industry-created draft that was eight years old—and based on a far-different financial services world—blocking any significant input from those directly engaged in the bankruptcy process, denying any perfecting or corrective amendments, even when it was clear that they eased flaws or gaps in the bill, and actively seeking to prevent any deliberative process, the leaders of the House and Senate obtained a law—but one that was filled with holes and problems, many easily anticipated, and that would bring substantial upheaval and injustice to large numbers of Americans.

The bankruptcy bill is in some ways a special case, but it highlights a pattern—the eschewal of the regular order, the abandonment of deliberation, the core value that the political ends justify the legislative means, the lack of concern about legislative craftsmanship—that results in the production of poor laws and flawed policy.

Of course, it has always been true—and always will be true—that the legislative process is messy and often distasteful; the old saw about law-making and sausage-making is on point. Nonetheless, the contemporary Congress is different, and worse than its predecessors, certainly from its predecessors in our lifetime. The differences are centered on a number of clear-cut trends.

The Decline in Institutional Identity

When he wrote his pathbreaking book on the U.S. Senate in 1960, Donald Matthews examined the norms prevalent in the institution; high among them was "institutional patriotism."[5] Senators were intensely loyal to the Senate as an institution; they identified first as senators rather than as partisans or through their ideology, and they were fiercely protective of their prerogatives vis-à-vis the president or the House of Representatives. The rules and procedures of the Senate were a key to its unique role as the world's greatest deliberative body; and even those who were frustrated by them and by their application, especially when an intense minority thwarted the will of the majority, were respectful of their centrality to the Senate itself.

Norms are not laws. Many individual senators in the 1950s and 1960s, such as Paul Douglas and Wayne Morse, took on the institution, thumbing their noses at what they saw as outdated concepts that upheld an unacceptable status quo. Their successors in the body included such liberals as Jim Abourezk and Howard Metzenbaum and conservatives James Allen and Jesse Helms. But it was obvious to us from the moment we each entered the Senate's environs in 1969 that these kinds of senators were the exception, not the rule. Most senators wore their pride in being in the Senate on their sleeves. Nothing short of a challenge to the primacy and integrity of the body itself could unite them across all conceivable lines.

Moreover, most House members had a heavy dose of institutional patriotism, often accompanied by a contempt, borne in part by jealousy, for the Senate as the so-called upper body. House members and leaders took immense pride in their status as the people's chamber, the first of our constitutional institutions mentioned in Article 1 of the Constitution, and in their legislative craftsmanship and expertise. Senators, in their view, were dilettantes, even if many of their House colleagues yearned to make the move to the other side of the Capitol—only one senator in modern times, Claude Pepper of Florida, had made the *reverse* move, and that not out of choice but driven by his Senate defeat. When an average member of the House was elected to the Senate, the typical line used by his former colleagues was that the move had increased the IQ in both chambers.

During the 1970s and 1980s, we participated regularly in orientations for newly elected members of Congress, put on by our two institutions and the Congressional Research Service of the Library of Congress as well as the Harvard

University Institute of Politics. Successive classes of freshmen would come in and prepare to take office; their incredible pride at joining the House or Senate, being part of history as an exclusive and small group of people ever to have served, was palpable. During much of that era, Rep. Bill Frenzel (R-MN), a first-rate lawmaker and member of the House Ways and Means Committee, would join with his wife, Ruthie, to address the new members and their spouses. He would urge them to move their families to Washington; he believed their time in the House would be the greatest experience of their lives and was something they should share with their families.

By the early 1990s, that appeal fell increasingly on deaf ears. Many members shrank from the idea of moving families to Washington, and not only because the anti-Washington political climate of the period made it politically unattractive. Our conversations with the new members revealed a different mindset. Many viewed Washington as an insidious place and were fearful that the more time they spent there, the greater the likelihood that they would catch the virus that caused Potomac Fever. The pride that members of both houses had in their institutions gave way to a skepticism. New and returning members increasingly saw their service in Congress not as a great and joyful time of their lives but as an unpleasant duty, like taking castor oil or serving in the trenches in France in World War I—something to endure, not savor, for the greater good of achieving a policy revolution in the country or winning the tribal war against the enemy in the other party. A number had run on a pledge of limiting their own terms to avoid the fever and to convey their distaste for Washington and congressional careerism.

The reaction of new members has been matched by the growing indifference of committee and party leaders to the history and independent role of their own institutions and by a widespread acceptance by congressional leaders that the ends justify the means.

One small but meaningful example of this is the House Historian. The historian's office was created in 1983 and was ably filled by historian Ray Smock until January 1995, when he was fired by incoming Speaker Newt Gingrich. Gingrich then moved to appoint Christina Jeffrey, a political scientist from Kennesaw State College in Georgia. Jeffrey lasted a few days—when controversial comments she had made several years earlier caused enough of an outcry that Gingrich fired her. He did not replace her, and the post of House Historian stood vacant for a full decade, with neither Gingrich nor his successor, Speaker Dennis Hastert, interested enough to fill the job or energize the office. Finally, in 2005, Hastert appointed the veteran historian and author Robert Remini from his home state of Illinois to fill the position. But the decade-long indifference to the importance of the history of the House underscored the decline in institutional identity in the House.

Indifference to Reform

There were other signs as well. Our experiences in and around Congress have been wrapped up in a variety of reform movements—attempts by members and leaders to improve committee systems, ethics processes, campaigns and elections, congressional support agencies, congressional-executive relations, and so on. From our first efforts, in the late 1960s, through our involvement with the joint committee on congressional reform in the early 1990s, it was clear that many rank-and-file members, senior lawmakers, and party leaders understood the need for periodic reform and tried to convince their colleagues that the upheaval that would result from institutional reform was worth the cost. They often failed, but they regularly tried.

In the past ten years, after a real sense in the first year of the Gingrich-led Republican Congress that they would clear the decks and implement sweeping change in the way Congress did business, there has been a complete expunging of any sense of need or desire for congressional reform— and worse. The modest movement in 1995, led by David Dreier, to implement the committee-system reforms recommended by the joint committee, was largely quashed by entrenched committee interests. That was the end of any effort to examine the committee system, reorganize jurisdictions, or streamline bloated assignments—such as a House Appropriations Committee with sixty-six members, an Armed Services Committee with sixty-two, or, most egregious, a Transportation and Infrastructure Committee with, count 'em, *seventy-five* members.

In neither house of Congress has there been anything like the efforts of the Bolling and Stevenson committees in the 1970s, the Quayle committee in the 1980s, and the joint committee exercise in the 1990s. The current leaders have expressed zero interest in reform—which means no interest in institutional well-being, maintenance, or renewal. Where there has been action, it has either been defensive or negative. In the defensive category, consider the reaction of the Speaker and the Senate Majority Leader to the new Department of Homeland Security (DHS). At first, neither leader suggested any reorganization within the House or Senate. After months of criticism, the Speaker moved to create a select committee on homeland security—one with a credible chair, Chris Cox of California, but with no substantive jurisdiction and stacked with the powerful chairs of committees, such as Judiciary and Transportation, whose only role on the committee was to protect their own turf from encroachment by the new panel. The Senate did nothing. Grudgingly, the House and then the Senate finally created subcommittees on homeland security to coordinate appropriations for the behemoth.

Belatedly, after the heralded 9/11 Commission recommended much more serious changes in the committee system, the two leaders acted—limply and inadequately. The House committee was made permanent, but with severe limits on its jurisdiction and the continuing presence of turf-conscious chairs from competing panels. The Senate renamed its Government Affairs Committee the Homeland Security and Governmental Affairs Committee and gave overall authorization jurisdiction over DHS to the panel—but left jurisdiction over key areas, such as the Coast Guard, in other committees, consigning the HSGA committee at best to secondary status. Also responding to the 9/11 Commission, Congress in late 2004 changed the intelligence structure within the executive branch and created a new overall director of intelligence. At the same time, both houses addressed their own inadequacies in oversight of intelligence—but barely, falling far short of the constructive recommendations of the 9/11 Commission.

Disappearance of Oversight

In October 2005, John Dingell of Michigan reached the fifty-year mark for service in the House. We have known Dingell since we came to Washington—and suffered his wrath in the early 1990s when we proposed taking sizable chunks of jurisdiction away from his Energy and Commerce Committee. But we also watched Dingell operate through seven presidents, Democrats and Republicans, mostly as chairman of the committee, often as chair of its vaunted Oversight and Investigations subcommittee. There were times when we winced as he grilled bureaucrats mercilessly and excessively. But what we saw consistently was a man of the House who viewed his role, regardless of the occupant of the White House, as overseeing the executive branch and making sure that the laws were faithfully executed without bias or malfeasance. He made Democratic and Republican presidents alike uncomfortable, but the result was better execution of policy in a host of areas.

John Dingell is a unique figure on Capitol Hill. But during the 1980s and into the 1990s, he was not alone. Serious oversight was done by the Appropriations Committees in both houses and by a number of authorizing committees. When the Republicans took control of Congress, there was substantial aggressive oversight—for the period when Bill Clinton was president, that is—although the oversight of policy was accompanied by a near-obsession with investigation of scandal and allegations of scandal. But when George Bush became president, oversight largely disappeared. From homeland security to the conduct of the war in Iraq, from the torture issue uncovered by the Abu Ghraib revelations to the performance of the IRS, Congress has mostly ignored its responsibilities. The exceptions—for example, the bipartisan efforts in several areas by House Government Reform Committee Chair Tom Davis with his ranking member Henry Waxman—glaringly prove the rule.

Consider homeland security. To any student of organizational behavior, governmental or otherwise, and especially to students of mergers and reorganizations, it comes as no shock that, since its inception, the Department of Homeland Security has been beset by a series of management problems, a lack of consistent focus, and a failure to sort out its numerous responsibilities. This was evident long before the scathing White House report on the institutional failures surrounding Hurricane Katrina.

The department has had a near-revolving door in its top management team, major problems integrating agencies, and less-than-stellar success creating an integrated and functional information management system for the department, much less coordinating its computers with others in such places as the FBI.

The failures in oversight here are particularly crushing. No one other than Congress can ride herd over a massive new department like DHS, prodding the nascent conglomeration to make sure that when mad cow disease looms or self-initiated "Minutemen" patrol the border that the Animal and Plant Inspection Service and the Immigration and Naturalization Service, both now part of the new department and charged with their new priority of homeland security, can concurrently handle the responsibilities in the old areas for which they still have the burden. The same, of course, is true of the Federal Emergency Management Agency (FEMA), which lost its robust independent status when it was subsumed into DHS and had mass confusion about its role in dealing with domestic emergencies as well as preparing for a catastrophe precipitated by a terrorist attack.

However, for three years after the creation of the department, there was no significant oversight—nothing to make sure that all the preexisting functions of the twenty-two components of the new department were maintained while the new functions were added. The House committee, under Chris Cox, tried at times to assume that job. Knowing the relative powerlessness of the House select committee, which had no legislative jurisdiction and no control over the budget or actions of the department, top officials at DHS treated it with indifference or contempt or a combination thereof. The lack of a committee in the Senate—or any entity committed to general oversight of the area or specific authorization of DHS—meant there was no serious oversight of the department. The problem was perversely compounded by the incessant demands of a gaggle of committees and subcommittees (as many as eighty-eight of them) to grab a piece of homeland security jurisdiction and political cachet and cover by demanding that the DHS Secretary or other top official testify before them. The top management of the agency had to spend huge chunks of time at Congress but almost no time participating in a serious examination of the department's functions and performance.

One result, tragically, was the abject failure of DHS and its emergency management unit, FEMA, after the catastrophe of Hurricane Katrina. Ornstein wrote soon afterward:

> The performance of the federal government in the Hurricane Katrina disaster—the policy wing of the federal government, not the dedicated employees—has been abysmal. Sen. David Vitter (R-La.) was right: The grade should be an F. But the failures . . . are a symptom of the bigger fiasco, one that should leave all of us furious—and nervous. And in that fiasco, Congress stands front and center in the line of miscreants.
>
> On 9/11, the inability of firefighters and police in New York to work their radios contributed to the loss of many lives. At the Pentagon, the inability of emergency workers from Montgomery and Prince George's counties in Maryland and Fairfax and Arlington counties in Virginia to communicate with each other made the response there much more difficult.
>
> Now, four years have passed. A few metropolitan areas, on their own and without adequate federal assistance, have acted

to make their own radio systems interoperable. The broader problems? They're the same, in essence, as they were before and during 9/11.

On 9/11, it became obvious that the resources and training available to the nation's first responders—fire, police, emergency medical technicians, public health clinics and so on—were woefully inadequate to deal with the new threats, not to mention larger natural disasters. No capability for dealing with chemical or biological threats, not enough gas masks (or appropriate ones), no training to deal with the collapse of large buildings. Four years later, regrettably, we can say the same thing. Instead of allocating the resources necessary to deal with these problems, we have in fact cut them in many areas.

On 9/11, a new set of broad threats emerged: the international network of terrorists out to kill as many of us as it could. The threat had existed beforehand, but suddenly it took on a new magnitude. The Hart-Rudman Commission, understanding this threat, had recommended prior to 9/11 the creation of a new Department of Homeland Security to bring together agencies and bureaus with other missions to incorporate the new missions of combating the terrorist threats and responding to a disaster that terrorists could bring—disasters of a different form and magnitude than a natural catastrophe, but with many similar characteristics.

Four years after 9/11, we have a DHS, and it's much larger than the Hart-Rudman Commission had envisioned. Its bureaucracy is still reeling from the task of integrating more than twenty separate entities into one—the largest reorganization in federal government history. When Katrina struck, DHS was not the centerpiece of federal response that its outside framers had foreseen, but rather a bloated bureaucracy that was unable for days to figure out what to do, and which produced a leaderless response that only compounded the tragedy.

The idea of creating such a department was a solid one; the magnitude and form of such a department was more debatable. But it was never debated. After vehemently resisting the idea of a department for almost nine months, the president turned around virtually overnight and embraced it, unveiling a plan much more sweeping than the original, and which had been hatched in secrecy by several key administration aides working in the situation room to ensure confidentiality. The normal debate and deliberative process that would have questioned the sweep of the reorganization plan and its breakneck pace was absent. Absent, too, was the notion of starting with a new Department of Border Security and moving in increments to something grander.

When the Department of Homeland Security bill came to Congress, it ended up facing one and only one serious area of controversy and deliberation: the question of sweeping civil service changes to eliminate many of the regular protections for the 70,000 DHS employees. That issue became a political tool—a major campaign point in the 2002 elections—even as the larger and important questions of what kind of department, and how to fulfill all the real and serious government functions, were ignored. . . .

Much of the failure to implement the changes needed over the past four years can be laid at the feet of Congress and its leaders.[6]

Why? The most logical explanation, reinforced by the comments made to us by many members of Congress, is that lack of institutional identity. Members of the majority party, including the leaders of Congress, see themselves as field lieutenants in the president's army far more than they do as members of a separate and independent branch of government. Serious oversight almost inevitably means criticism of performance—and this Congress has shied away from anything that would criticize its own administration.

One result has been that executive agencies that once viewed Congress with at least some trepidation because of its oversight activities now tend to view Congress with contempt. Consider the Senate Armed Services Committee hearing in May 2004 on torture in the Abu Ghraib prison. During Senator John McCain's tough questioning, Secretary of Defense Donald Rumsfeld said that the military brass with him had prepared a thorough chart. When one of the generals said they had forgotten to bring it, Rumsfeld said, "Oh my." As Ornstein wrote in *Roll Call* at the time:

Could anything more clearly demonstrate the contempt this department has for Congress? This was not a routine authorization hearing—this was a hearing testing the very core reputation of the Defense Department and the military. And they forgot the key chart!

How could this happen? I think the answer is rooted in a larger problem, and it is fundamentally a problem of and for Congress. The White House, the Defense Department, and a whole lot of other departments and agencies have no fear of Congress, because Congress has shown no appetite to do any serious or tough oversight, to use the power of the purse or the power of pointed public hearings to put the fear of God into them. . . .

The House and Senate Armed Services committees have held a lot of hearings since we prepared to go into Iraq and since we went in. How many have dealt with the military takeover and occupation of Iraq? Less than a handful. . . . How many were tough and tough-minded, pushing Rumsfeld, Deputy Secretary Paul Wolfowitz, Joint Chiefs Chairman Richard Myers or other military and Defense Department figures to justify their actions or inactions? Even fewer.

It is hard not to like and admire Senate Armed Forces Chairman John Warner (R-Va.). He is smart, decent, and a true patriot. But he has seen his role far more in terms of defending and explaining the administration than in providing penetrating public criticism. The larger problem of this Congress, which to be sure is far more true in the House than in the Senate, is that the Republican majority has gone out of its way to avoid serious criticism or tough challenges to its own administration. The idea of public hearings to really dig into policy and administrative failures is abhorrent to Congressional leaders and most committee chairmen. They are doing it now only reluctantly, only out of necessity, and bending over backwards to minimize the damage.

The administration, for its part, knows its Congressional party well. It has demanded fealty, ignored Congress when it can get away with it, and when challenged by Congress, usually offers the back of its hand. Sen. Dick Lugar (R-IN) and the Foreign Relations Committee have tried to explore the key foreign policy issues in depth and have found neither cooperation nor openness from the White House, but rather attempts to marginalize the panel. It is so interesting that the two most prominent administration figures with Congressional backgrounds—Vice President Cheney, who was his party's Whip, and Secretary Rumsfeld, a key Congressional reformer in his greener days—have little if any sympathy for an independent and critical role for Congress.

The two Appropriations Committees have shown a little more appetite for searching questions and tough oversight, fitting their long traditions and pedigrees, but they are better than other panels only by comparison. Appropriators have only become exorcised when it became clear to them that Defense officials were putting together tons of military construction projects that had not been appropriated by them and were a direct challenge to their core responsibilities.

To be sure, the failure to ask tough questions of the military, or to challenge decisions made during wartime, is not new to Congress and not limited to Republicans. Richard Russell, a legend in the Senate (and a Democrat), never used the gavel of the Armed Services Committee to raise any of the tough issues about Vietnam that he did in private. Had he done so, we might have conducted that war in a much better fashion.

The Democrats who ran the Senate in 2001–2002 did not exactly distinguish themselves with penetrating oversight on Iraq and defense. But the lack of any strong sense of independent legislative authority, and the pervasive sense of Congress as a subsidiary body to the presidency, is much stronger in this Republican Congress than I have seen it in three and a half decades, and unusual in American history. [7]

These examples are illustrative of the pattern that has developed in recent years. Initially, a centralization of political control in the Congress, and the marginalization of committees, contributed to a sharp reduction in congressional oversight of the executive. UCLA political scientist Joel Aberbach reports that the number of oversight hearings—excluding the appropriations committees—dropped from 782 during the first six months of 1983 to 287 during a comparable period in 1997. The falloff in the Senate between 1983 and 1997 was just as striking: from 429 to 175. [8] That decline was then reinforced and exacerbated with the return of unified party government. The Republican Congress had even less incentive to oversee an executive controlled by its own party.

The problem in the Senate goes beyond obsequiousness to the executive to maddening passive deference to the House. Anyone who hung around the Senate through the past several decades would have seen its members' intense pride in the heritage and trappings of the body almost as part of its institutional DNA. Thus, to watch the Senate disregard that heritage and its honor over the past few years has been particularly jarring. The attitude in the body during debate on bankruptcy—bowing to the take-it-or-leave-it demands of the House to pass the bill the House wanted without change—has been more typical than not; the Senate has frequently bent to threats from the House, and on such key issues as the Medicare prescription drug bill and the energy bill even cast aside its own rules to allow the House to bar elected Senate members of the conference committees from full participation.

Tolerance of Executive Secrecy

The passivity and indifference of Congress and its leaders to their independent and assertive role fit perfectly with the Bush administration's assertive and protective attitude toward executive power and its aversion to sharing information with Congress and the public.[9] Two months after Bush took office, White House Counsel Alberto Gonzales blocked the release of 68,000 pages of records from the Reagan presidency, which were scheduled to be made public under terms set by the Presidential Records Act of 1978 (PRA). Later that year the president issued an executive order that granted former presidents, vice presidents, or their representatives designated by family members, the right to block the release of documents "reflecting military, diplomatic, or national security secrets, Presidential communications, legal advice, legal work, or the deliberative processes of the President and the President's advisors."

The order also directed the Justice Department to litigate on behalf of any such claims.

Early on the administration also revealed its hand with respect to the Federal Advisory Committee Act, which established openness requirements for advisory bodies to the executive, and the Freedom of Information Act, which provides for public access to government documents. The administration rebuffed attempts by several members of Congress to use the Federal Advisory Committee Act to force Vice President Cheney to divulge information about his energy task force, a working group of industry lobbyists and government officials to formulate national energy policy. Bush officials argued that the Federal Advisory Committee Act was unconstitutional in that it authorized "extreme interference" and "unwarranted intrusion" into executive responsibility.

The Government Accountability Office (GAO) sued the Vice President on behalf of Congress—on its own, and not with any imprimatur from the Speaker or Senate Majority Leader—for access to the information, but the administration prevailed in the courts. It also successfully defended its position in related suits brought by the Sierra Club and Judicial Watch. Exemptions from the Federal Advisory Committee Act were written into the Homeland Security Act, the Medicare prescription drug law, the FY2004 Defense authorization bill, the President's Commission to Strengthen Social Security, and the President's Commission on Intelligence on Weapons of Mass Destruction. In 2003 the Office of Management and Budget issued a ruling that agencies could avoid the requirements of the Federal Advisory Committee Act if they hired contractors to manage advisory committees.

The Bush administration also found inappropriately burdensome requests for information under the Freedom of Information Act. In an October 2001 directive planned well before September 11, Attorney General John Ashcroft announced a new policy for handling these requests. The Clinton administration had established a "foreseeable harm" standard for the release of Freedom of Information

Act documents—agencies would have to make records public whenever possible as long as no foreseeable harm existed for their release. Ashcroft changed this standard to one of a "sound legal basis" so that agencies could withhold information so long as there was any legal basis to do so. The attorney general directed agencies to release information only after "full and deliberate consideration of the institutional, commercial, and personal privacy interests that could be implicated." The memo also stated that "you can be assured that the Department of Justice will defend your decisions [in court]."

In addition to resisting congressional and public access to information under the Presidential Records Act, the Federal Advisory Committee Act, and the Freedom of Information Act, the administration substantially increased, relative to previous presidencies, the number of documents it classified (while decreasing the number it declassified); blocked the release of documents and briefs requested as part of congressional investigations of the terrorist attacks; refused a House committee request for numbers adjusted for undercounting in the 2000 census; invoked executive privilege in denying Congress access to information concerning the FBI misuse of organized crime informants in Boston; was unwilling to share information on missile defense systems with the Senate subcommittee that oversees the project; delayed sending to Congress full cost estimates of the Medicare drug bill before it was signed into law; denied the Senate Governmental Affairs Committee information about undisclosed meetings between Enron executives and top administration officials; and restricted access by Congress to environmental records. And the administration engaged in many battles—with Congress and in the courts— over what information it had to release concerning the handling of terrorist detainees and enemy combatants.

While this behavior by the Bush administration justly earned it a reputation for secrecy, it was entirely consistent with its view of executive prerogatives. At times it was difficult to discern its motivations for denying information to

Congress, the 9/11 Commission, and the public. Surely avoiding political embarrassment factored in to some of its decisions. And the net effect of its actions to avoid transparency in executive decision making, as former Senator Daniel Patrick Moynihan argued in attacking secrecy in government, may well have done more harm than good to the country. But at least President Bush defended his branch of government and acted in a way he thought would leave a stronger institution for his successors.

Sadly, the same cannot be said of Congress during Bush's tenure in the White House. What we were struck by during this period was how supine the first branch of government was in responding to the president's aggressive denial of information that Congress thought was essential to its work. Members of both parties were quite open with us about the utterly dismissive attitude, indeed the contempt, with which Bush and Cheney greeted such requests from Congress. National security briefings were often considered a complete waste of time by members; reading the morning newspaper was much more informative. Yet again party trumped institution.

The minority Democrats had political, as well as institutional, incentives to demand such information, and they often did so with gusto. But without support from the majority, they had little chance of prevailing in battles with the executive. Individual Republican senators and representatives fought for the release of critical information, but they seldom had the support of their leadership or their colleagues. Such Republican Senate committee chairs as Charles Grassley and Susan Collins were often deeply frustrated by the resistance of the administration to their requests for information. Senators John McCain and Lindsay Graham fought many battles, unpopular with their party colleagues, to garner the information they felt was essential to conduct responsible congressional oversight of the wars in Afghanistan and Iraq.

In the House, former Government Reform Committee Chair Dan Burton had to subpoena documents related to his investigation of the FBI and threaten to sue the Justice Department before the administration relented. Representative Chris Shays, while chairing the Subcommittee on National Security, Emerging Threats and International Relations, encountered stonewalling in response to his request to the Defense Department, with ranking Democrat Henry Waxman, for audits of the Development Fund for Iraq, which finances the rebuilding of the war-torn country. Unfortunately, these efforts are exceptions to the general rule, "Don't do anything to embarrass the president." Hardly the vigorous defense of institutional interests planned by the Framers.

The Nuclear Option

Nothing underscores more the indifference to institution—and the decline in Senate pride—than the flap over Rule XXII and the filibuster when it came to President Bush's judicial nominations in 2003–2005. Unlimited debate defines the uniqueness of the Senate. As discussed in chapter 2, from its early days, the Senate had no way to stop debate. The "filibuster" as we know it—and the supermajority requirement for cloture—was actually a reform to expedite action, not to block it. Prior to 1917, there was, in effect, no limit on debate in the Senate. Any one senator, or any small group of senators, could keep debate going indefinitely.

That ability was a part of the unique role of the Senate, which was designed by the framers to slow the process and add to its deliberative nature. Just as the Senate itself is not representative of the majority of the country—senators from small states, which collectively represent a fraction of the overall population of the country, command a majority of votes in the body—the Senate's unique legislative procedures, including its reliance on unanimous consent and its tradition of sensitivity to minority viewpoints via unlimited debate, are extensions of the framers' conservative views on governance. The rules change that provided some limits on debate—creating a hurdle in that it required two-thirds of senators present and voting to end debate and proceed to a vote—was urged upon the Senate by then–President Woodrow Wilson and instituted after a handful of senators blocked action to arm merchant ships prior to American entry into World War I. The two-thirds rule remained in effect until 1975, when frustration over the use of filibusters led to a lowering of the bar to sixty senators. That is where it stands today—with one deliberate exception. Debate on any change in the Senate rules can only be halted by votes of two-thirds of senators present and voting—a clear sign of the determination of the Senate to preserve its longtime rules and practices. Real filibusters, by which the Senate comes to a screeching halt and debates around the clock to try to overcome the objections of intense minorities, are a thing of the past. Most middle-aged Americans remember them from the 1950s and early 1960s, when the filibuster was employed by Southerners trying to block civil rights legislation for blacks. Since then, filibusters have worked more as a threat than a reality—senators declare their opposition to a bill or a nomination, and the body works to pass a cloture motion, requiring sixty votes, to halt debate after one hundred hours.

But the tradition of the filibuster, the nod to the importance of each individual senator and to the centrality of minority rights and viewpoints in our constitutional system, has been central to the Senate for more than two centuries.

That tradition was shaken to the core in 2005 over judicial nominations. In the modern age of partisan parity and ideological polarization, few issues have had the impact and high stakes of federal judicial nominations. As the Congress has more frequently found itself stymied on controversial issues, one way out has been to pass the buck on to the courts, allowing policy decisions to be resolved through litigation. This has been true, for example, on many environmental matters in such areas as clean air. As left and right have found themselves losing on issues in the legislature, they have been more inclined to refuse to accept defeat and try to reverse the outcomes in the courts. As judges have been given more opportunities, they have not shrunk from a larger policy role, whether or not they label themselves strict constructionists.

As a consequence, the battles in the Senate over judges, including even district court and appeals court judges, have become more acrimonious and routine. During George W. Bush's first term, Senate Democrats employed many of the tactics used by Republicans under Clinton to challenge his judicial nominees. Most of the conflict occurred with circuit court appointments. Bush won confirmation of 87 percent of his district court nominees but only 53 percent of his circuit court appointees between 2001 and 2004 (slightly better than Clinton's record on the former, slightly worse on the latter).[10] Prior to the May 2001 change in the Senate majority, when Jim Jeffords of Vermont moved from Republican to independent status and gave the Democrats a one-vote opportunity to take the helm, Judiciary Committee Chairman Orrin Hatch had scheduled no hearings on the president's judicial nominees. When Patrick Leahy took over as committee chair, he reinstituted the ABA review of nominees, which further delayed their consideration. The summer recess, September 11 attacks, and anthrax-laced letters sent to the Senate, including Leahy's office, kept them waiting in the queue.

More serious obstacles were looming, however. Leahy complained that Bush, unlike Clinton, refused to negotiate with the chairman of the Judiciary Committee; nor would the president work with home-state senators of judicial nominees. Democrats considered several of his nominees especially provocative. In March 2002, the Judiciary Committee rejected a nomination for the first time in Bush's term—that of Charles Pickering—on strict party lines. The battle was joined once again, with the parties simply switching positions and arguments. Now it was the Republicans who denounced Senate obstructionism and lamented the vacancy crisis on the federal bench while Democrats pointed to the large number and percentage of district court nominees confirmed and criticized some of the Bush appointees as being out of the mainstream. The most controversial nominees were bottled up in the Senate Judiciary Committee during the months leading up to the election and never brought to a vote, although several were confirmed in the post-election session when it was apparent that the Republicans would return to the majority in January. A week before the election, President Bush presented a proposal to "Ensure Timely Consideration of Judicial Nominees," which included mandating a ninety-day-or-less window between a presidential nomination and a Judiciary Committee hearing as well as an up-or-down vote in the Senate.

The return of unified Republican government with the 2002 elections did little to diminish the acrimony. Both sides spoiled for a fight. The president resubmitted thirty nominations that were not confirmed by the Senate during the 107th Congress, including Priscilla Owen, Charles Pickering, and Miguel Estrada. Encouraged by an alliance of liberal interest groups, the now minority Senate Democrats—no longer able to block the most controversial nominees in committee—resorted to the filibuster. While not without precedent, the systematic use of filibusters to defeat nominees with majority support in committee and on the floor was clearly an escalation of the war over the courts. In February, Democrats successfully filibustered the confirmation of Miguel Estrada to the District of Columbia Court of Appeals. Later in the year they blocked William Pryor and Priscilla Owen from being seated on the appeals court. Although many noncontroversial nominees were confirmed during 2003, leading to a very low vacancy rate (39 out of 859 seats),[11] the political struggle over the courts intensified. In early 2004 the president made a recess appointment of William Pryor to the 11th Circuit Court of Appeals. Later in the year, Michigan's two Democratic senators blocked three Bush nominees, admitting that their move was also retaliation for Republicans blocking Clinton's appointees to those same seats for years, keeping the slots vacant for the time when their president could fill them.

That struggle further intensified after Bush was reelected in 2004 and Republicans picked up four seats in the Senate—increasing their majority to fifty-five, but leaving them still five short of a so-called filibuster-proof margin. Bush quickly resubmitted his most controversial court nominations, those that had been successfully filibustered by the Democrats.

No effort was made by the White House to negotiate a settlement with Senate Democrats on the disputed nominees. Instead, Majority Leader Bill Frist seized on an issue that had been raised in 2003 and began building an aggressive public case for a radical change in Senate procedures—dubbed the "nuclear option" by Senator Lott—to prohibit the filibuster on judicial appointments.

Senate rules and precedents were clear: the Senate is a continuing body because every election involves only one-third of its members, and the rules are a constant, able to be changed only if two-thirds agree. Frist proposed a radical alternative: achieve the same result by making a parliamentary point of order that extended debate on a pending judicial confirmation is out of order. He would then have that point of order upheld by the president of the Senate (Vice President Dick Cheney) and follow with a vote of a simple majority upholding the ruling of the chair. Doing so would require ignoring or overruling the Senate Parliamentarian, since a constitutional point of order is itself debatable (and could be filibustered).

The ploy here was laid out by Senate rules guru Martin Gold, an adviser to Frist. While he and other former Republican Senate staff members built the case that such a move was consistent with Senate precedents, the argument was lame. There was no mistaking the purpose and potential consequences of the nuclear option. The Senate would by fiat overrule an established procedural principle to serve the immediate interests of the president and respond to the demands of a vocal constituency. And in so doing, it would establish a precedent that would threaten to change the essential character of the institution, making the Senate much more like the House.

This was at many levels a struggle over arcane procedural chess moves. But it became a major political issue. A vigorous public debate ensued, featuring television ads run by groups on both sides of the debate, all of whom saw this battle as critical to the upcoming struggle to fill expected vacancies on the Supreme Court. Proponents of the nuclear option argued that never before had filibusters been used to block judicial nominations. Columnist Charles Krauthammer wrote, "One of the great traditions, customs and unwritten rules of the Senate is that you do not filibuster judicial nominees." He called the threats by Democrats to filibuster several of the Bush nominees "historically unprecedented" and "radical," saying they have "unilaterally shattered one of the longest-running traditions in parliamentary history."[12] Frist, in a *USA Today* op/ed, said there had been a 214-year-old tradition of having up-or-down votes in the Senate on judicial nominations. He added that, since President Bill Clinton's judicial nominees only required fifty-one votes, "why should George W. Bush's be treated differently?"[13]

Here was the reality: For more than two hundred years, hundreds of judicial nominees at all levels had their nominations buried, killed, or asphyxiated by the Senate, either by one individual, a committee, or a small group of senators, before the nominations ever got anywhere near the floor. To be sure, most were not filibustered in the "Mr. Smith" sense, or in the modern and direct version.

Consider the history of Supreme Court nominations—the most visible and prized of all. Of the 154 nominations to the Supreme Court between 1789 and 2002, thirty-four were not confirmed. Of these, eleven were rejected by a vote of the full Senate. The remaining twenty-three were postponed, referred to a committee from which they never emerged, reported from committee but not acted on, or, in a few cases, withdrawn by the president when the going got tough. At least seven nominations were killed because of objections by home-state senators. Five others were reported to the Judiciary Committee (which was created in 1816) and never made it out. And, of course, there was the case of Abe Fortas, whose nomination by Lyndon Johnson to be chief justice was filibustered in 1968 until other problems forced Fortas to withdraw.[14]

As for other levels of judicial nominations, there is a long-standing tradition, exercised countless times, giving one or two senators from the home state a veto power over district court nominees. (This is the unwritten rule, incidentally, that was shattered by Orrin Hatch, then the Judiciary chairman, when Clinton was president.) This "blue slip" power was applied less frequently to appeals court nominees, but many in the past were killed far short of a vote on the Senate floor. Why weren't more of them filibustered? Because it was easy enough to kill most of the controversial ones without resorting to a filibuster.

Some retired conservative Republican senators, including Malcolm Wallop of Wyoming, understood this history and the implications of an abrupt change in the rules and deplored the move. But as Frist moved closer and closer to detonating the nuclear option, the silence of Republican pillars of the institution—Thad Cochran, Pete Domenici, and Dick Lugar—was deafening. Lugar warned that the consequences of pulling the nuclear trigger could be severe and backfire against Republicans and conservatives, but he then said that if the Republican leader asked him for support to do so, he would give it.

As many of us thought and wrote at the time, if they won't defend their institution, who will? In the end, a bipartisan group of old bulls, mavericks, and moderates—referred to as the Gang of 14—pulled the Senate back from the brink. Their informal agreement, entirely self-enforcing, to oppose both the nuclear option and filibusters on judicial confirmations except under extraordinary circumstances forced a temporary de-escalation of the judicial arms race. How long it would last was far from certain.

There *is* a long-standing tradition in the Senate regarding judicial nominations. That tradition calls for a vigorous and independent Senate playing its role of advice and consent. Because they represent lifetime appointments that cannot and should not be easily rescinded, judicial nominations require higher hurdles than simple legislation, which can always be amended or repealed. Charles Krauthammer called the nuclear option "restoration." It's not even close. And the willingness of dozens of senators to apply it spoke volumes about their indifference to the body's essence when they confronted short-term political expedience.

The Decline of Deliberation

When we first came to Congress, members from New York, Pennsylvania and other parts of the Northeast were notorious for their commuting schedule. Many would try to limit their time in Washington to three days, spending long "weekends" back home. They were known as the Tuesday to Thursday Club. That meant coming down to the Capitol early on Tuesday morning, during routine morning business and before the substantive legislative schedule began, and returning home late Thursday night after the last votes, or early Friday morning.

The Shrinking Schedule

Although these days the Tuesday to Thursday Club encompasses the vast majority of members, the schedule is even more attenuated. Members from all over the country straggle in late on Tuesday, insisting that there be no votes until the end of the day, and scramble to get out of town as early on Thursday as possible. Of course, it doesn't work every week—sometimes, votes actually take place on Mondays and Fridays, and sometimes emergencies or pressing business require full weeks and even occasional weekend sessions. But the change from the past—and the lack of time spent in meaningful floor debate—has been striking. For 2006, the second session of the 109th Congress, the House set a grand total of seventy-one days in which votes are scheduled to take place and an additional twenty-six days with no votes occuring before 6:30 p.m. The total number of calendar days, even if counted generously, is ninety-seven, the smallest number in sixty years. This Congress is on track to set a record-low workload for an entire Congress since the 80th—famous as, in Harry Truman's words, the "Do-Nothing Congress"—in 1947–48.

During the 1960s and 1970s, the average Congress was in session 323 days. In the 1980s and 1990s, the average declined to 278. But the days in session have since plummeted, with the likelihood that the first six years of the Bush presidency will show an average below 250 per two-year Congress.[15]

Beyond the attenuation of meaningful action and debate on the floor, we have seen as well the decline of committees, and not only through the disappearance of oversight. Major bills that in the past would have required weeks of hearings and days of markups are now often reviewed in days of hearings and with little or no visible time spent by the committee on systematic analysis of the legislation line by line and word by word. Much of the action now takes place behind closed doors, with bills, as in the bankruptcy case, put together by a small group of leadership staff, committee staff, industry representatives, and a few majority party members and then rammed through subcommittee and committee with minimal debate. In the 1960s and 1970s, the average Congress had an average of 5,372 House committee and subcommittee meetings; in the 1980s and 1990s the average was 4,793. In the last Congress, the 108th, the number was 2,135.[16]

The Demise of Regular Order

But the lack of interest in the admittedly arduous process of going through multiple levels and channels of discussion, debate, negotiation, and compromise that make up a robust deliberative process has been a symptom of the broader malady in the contemporary Congress—the belief, especially in the House, that deliberation, fairness, bipartisanship, and debate are impediments to the larger goal of achieving political and policy success. In other words, the credo that the ends justify the means.

The House, unlike the Senate, is a majoritarian institution. With its complete control of the Rules Committee, the majority leadership may write special rules to control debate and amendments on the House floor. As long as its party members support the Rules Committee, the leadership may waive any standing rule not specified in the Constitution, such as the requirement that conference committee reports lay over for three days before they are considered by the House. By controlling the position of presiding officer, in committee or on the floor, the majority may also adopt less formal means to advance its legislative agenda and weaken the position of the minority.

During the last decade of their forty-year control of the House, Democrats made increasing use of this power to deny the minority Republicans opportunity to participate in any meaningful fashion in the legislative process. Republicans chafed under the increasingly heavy hand of the majority. In 1993 ranking Rules Committee member David Dreier and his Republican committee colleagues issued a stinging report criticizing the tactics used by the majority to shut down "deliberative democracy."[17] What was essential to the House but missing under the arbitrary rule of the Democrats, they argued, was a "full and free airing of conflicting opinions through hearings, debates, and amendments for the purpose of developing and improving legislation deserving of the respect and support of the people." Dreier acknowledged the majority's right to control the agenda and schedule and to structure legislation to advance its policy goals. But this can be accomplished, he asserted, without denying the minority an opportunity to be heard and have their ideas considered.

The 1994 election changed the majority party in the House but it did nothing to stem the decline of deliberative democracy. During more than a decade of Republican rule, the majority has tightened its grip on the House and the minority has been increasingly marginalized. Statistics on

House rules compiled by former Republican Rules Committee staffer Donald Wolfensberger document this trend.[18] The percentage of open or modified open rules dropped from 44 percent in the 103rd Congress (the last controlled by the Democrats) to 26 percent in the 108th Congress. During the same time span, the percentage of closed or modified closed rules jumped from 18 percent to 49 percent. Wolfensberger also documents an increasing use by the Republican majority of self-executing rules, which allow a bill to be altered without having a separate debate and direct vote on amendments, and of bills considered under suspension of the rules.

But this is only the tip of the iceberg. Committee deliberation on controversial legislation has become increasingly partisan and formalistic, with the serious work being done by the committee chair, party leadership, administration officials, and lobbyists. This pattern is repeated in conference committees, often without any pretence of a full committee mark-up with members of both political parties present. The Rules Committee routinely suspends its requirement of a 48-hour notice of meetings, invoking its authority to call an emergency meeting "at any time on any measure or matter which the Chair determines to be of an emergency nature."[19] Those meetings, at which 60 percent of all rules during the 108th Congress were reported (a lot of emergencies), often were scheduled with little advance notice between 8 p.m. and 7 a.m. And their primary purpose was to dispense with regular order.

For example, during the 108th Congress the Rules Committee, in structuring consideration of twenty-eight conference reports, almost always in emergency session, in every case waived all points of order against the conference report and against its consideration. This action made it virtually impossible to discover what was in each conference report before voting on it. Months after the adoption of the 850-page conference report on the Medicare prescription drug bill, which was filed in the House at 1:17 a.m. on November 21, 2003, and passed at 6 a.m. on November 22, members and the public were still unraveling what was in the bill that became law.

This Rules Committee practice has been employed to facilitate the now-routine process of folding many significant issues into huge omnibus bills and bringing them to the House floor for up-or-down votes without any notice or time for members to read or absorb them. House leaders have become particularly enamored of packaging several stand-alone appropriations bills into one omnibus bill that is brought up at the end of the session, as all the members are preparing to go home and do not want to vote to shut down the government. By forgoing nearly all floor debate, they can pack these bills with numerous provisions that could never pass in separate votes.

But this form of legislating—which often means that bills are passed and laws are enacted via all-night sessions whereby staff and a few members and party leaders try to slap all the pieces together under tight deadlines—results in stealth legislation that has not really passed majority muster and frequently has embarrassing consequences. One pungent example occurred in December 2004, when it was discovered that giant appropriations bill had a provision that would allow Appropriations staff access to individual tax returns and would exempt them from criminal penalties for revealing the contents of those returns.

When a press report disclosed the provision, after the bill had passed, it was denounced by subcommittee chair Ernest Istook, who said he had no idea that language was in the bill. It turned out that the provision had surfaced between 3 and 5 a.m. during an all-night staff negotiation just before the final 3,000-page document was slapped together and sent to the floor. It does not appear that the provision was a deliberately pernicious one—it was simply that no one understood what the language actually did. No wonder; they were operating, after all, sleep-deprived in the middle of the night after a series of crash sessions to put the omnibus together. Former Appropriations staffer Scott Lilly reflected eloquently on this process in a *Roll Call* op-ed:

While the flawed language should have been spotted, the circumstances in which it was added make such mistakes almost inevitable. Why do we conduct the people's business this way? Some say it's that Members of Congress have become too lazy to do their own work, and there may be some instances in which this is true. But my experience indicates that the vast majority of Members of both parties would love to revert to the old system in which the people elected to make these decisions actually do. I also know that nearly all of the staff who have been called on to participate in these exercises are deeply troubled by the process that has evolved.

The reason the old system of legislating no longer works is that the current leadership has not only assumed the role of passing the legislation required of Congress, but has also taken on the responsibility of insuring that the content of that legislation is consistent with a specific ideological criteria that is often not the will of a majority in the House.

They have committed to conservatives within the Republican Conference that legislation sent to the president will be consistent with the views of a majority of the Conference. On dozens of issues ranging from trade with Cuba to Canadian drug imports and the raising of the minimum wage, the majority position in the Republican Conference is not the majority position of the full House. Preventing the House from producing legislation that reflects the views of its Members requires circumventing a body of rules and procedures developed in the past 215 years.

The House was intended to be the centerpiece of our democracy. It can again function as a democratic institution if we return to the "regular order." When even subcommittee chairmen don't know the content of the legislation bearing their own name, the role of elected representatives has been diminished to the point that ordinary citizens can have little confidence that their views have any weight in decisions made by Congress.[20]

This is all part of a pattern, of which perhaps the most egregious practice has been the willingness of the majority leadership to hold open votes well beyond the fifteen minutes specified in the rules. As we discussed earlier, the vote on the Medicare prescription drug bill was the most extreme example—Republican leaders held the vote open for nearly three hours in order to muscle the decisive votes for its passage. But other bills have been accorded the same treatment, most recently the Central American Free Trade Agreement and the oil refinery bill brought up in the House in the aftermath of Hurricane Katrina. The latter bill, crafted behind closed doors and filled with provisions to waive or obliterate environmental regulations, took nearly an hour to pass (for what was supposed to be a five-minute vote).

Rules Committee Chairman Dreier acknowledges that he and his colleagues in the Republican leadership now use the tactics he condemned when he was in the minority. "We have had to do some of the things we criticized once. . . . But now that I'm in the majority, I have this responsibility to govern. It's something I didn't completely understand when I was in the minority."[21] He has a point—up to a point. The Republican majority is narrow. The parties are even more ideologically polarized. President Bush is pursuing a conservative agenda that requires an aggressive partisan start in the House. Democrats are remarkably unified in their opposition.

But what is significant is what Dreier doesn't say. His party has manipulated the process to serve partisan interests far beyond what the Democrats did during their forty-year reign in the House. Most maneuvers aimed to garner a hard-fought legislative victory, but some—as witnessed by well-publicized, heavy-handed actions by Judiciary Committee Chairman Jim Sensenbrenner and Ways and Means Committee Chairman Bill Thomas—were simply to spite the vanquished minority.[22] And their impressive successes have come at a steep price: in the suspect content of the legislative product, the diminished institutional standing of the Congress, and the rancorous tone of public life in Washington and the country.

The Explosion of Earmarks

Another sign of the decline of the deliberative process is the startling rise of earmarking—legislating specific projects for specific districts or states instead of leaving the allocation of resources to professionals. Earmark fever has completely taken over the appropriations process as it earlier had consumed public works. The conservative watchdog group Citizens Against Government Waste commented in an open letter released in 2004, "Over the past ten years, pork-barrel spending has increased exponentially, from 1,430 projects totaling $10 billion in 1995 to 10,656 projects, totaling $22.9 billion, in 2004."[23]

Scott Lilly, the longtime Democratic staff director of the House Appropriations Committee and a stellar career professional in the House, noted, "Earmarking has not simply grown in volume; the distribution of earmarks has also changed dramatically. In the 1980s, earmarks were largely rewards for Members who had persevered for years on the back benches and risen to positions of significant power on key committees. Today, earmarks are much more broadly distributed among the rank and file, and this most important advantage of incumbency affects election outcomes not just in a few districts of well-connected Members but in virtually all Congressional districts."[24]

The most startling development on the earmark front has been in appropriations. In the definitive treatment of the appropriations committees, Richard F. Fenno's magisterial *The Power of the Purse* published in 1966, there is no reference to *earmark* in the index. That is because historically, appropriations bills have not explicitly targeted funds for particular programs in particular districts. They have shaped the direction of spending and often encouraged specific programs in report language. But appropriators avoided earmarks because they inevitably would lead to a kind of circus or bazaar, with rising pressure to add funds for each district or to use the earmark as a weapon to reward friends and punish enemies.

The House especially saw the danger in this process. The Senate was much happier to open the spigots and use the appropriations process to logroll and make each member happy. Earmarks took off in the Senate in the 1990s and have risen logarithmically, with senators of both parties eager to take advantage. Only Senator John McCain (R-AZ) has stood up strongly against the practice. In the House, though, there were many voices opposing earmarks, including, particularly strongly, Republicans.

That is, until they took over the majority in the House. Now the House is at least as eager to use the earmarking process as the Senate, and the results are clear.[25] In 1992, there were 892 specifically earmarked programs or projects, adding up to $2.6 billion in spending. The number more than doubled in six years (1998) to 1,000 earmarks, with spending jumping to $13.2 billion. By fiscal year 2002, the number of earmarks rose to 8,341, with spending up to $20 billion. By 2005, the number had escalated to 13,997 at a cost of $27.3 billion. The trends are obvious for almost every area of discretionary spending—$7 billion or more in defense, $1.2 billion in military construction, one hundred more pages of earmarks in the Veterans, Housing, NASA and Environmental Protection Agency appropriations than in 1995, more than $1 billion in the Labor/HHS bill, which, under Obey, had no earmarks to speak of before 1995. Among the most avid proponents and users of these earmarks has been one (ex-) House Majority Leader Tom DeLay (R-TX).

As pragmatists and students of the legislative process, we have never been ardent foes of pork barrel spending. We understand that it takes grease to make the wheels of the legislative process move and that pork itself is not evil or even necessarily bad. Some of it is the price of getting things done in Congress, and much of it is beneficial to society. But you can reach a point where all the standards fall by the wayside and scarce funds are seriously misallocated—with important programs getting diminished funding so that picayune projects can prevail.

The problem is at its worst in the transportation arena. When the 1991 highway bill moved to the House floor, it was attacked scathingly by minority Republican members for its excessive earmarks, which totaled 538 by the time the bill reached the president's desk. To be sure, that number was the highest in history—up to then. As Scott Lilly noted, "Since the passage of the Federal Aid Highway Act of 1956, there have been twenty separate highway bills enacted, including the one signed by President Bush in August 2005. Prior to 1970, these bills let state highway commissions determine transportation priorities. In 1970, Congress passed a highway bill that included three specific projects to be built based on the directives of Congress. For the next sixteen years, highway legislation was passed every two or three years and the bills contained as few as two and as many as fourteen."[26]

The number went up significantly, to 155, in the 1987 highway bill as many rank-and-file members specifically demanded a piece of the action, leading to the 538 in 1991. Now look at what has happened in the two blockbuster transportation bills enacted since the Republicans took control of the House, in 1998 and 2005. The 1998 bill contained 1,850 earmarks, at a total cost of $9.5 billion. The 2005 bill contained a jaw-dropping 6,371 earmarks, worth $23 billion. Scott Lilly again: "Over the past fifty years there have been 9,242 earmarks in highway bills. Of those, 8,504, or 92 percent, have been inserted in the three highway bills enacted since Republicans took the House ten years ago."

The 2005 transportation bill, after years of struggle to get it passed—the president had long threatened a veto if it exceeded a specified limit in cost—was held over for an extra day so that earmarks could be used as bait or threats to secure votes to pass the Central America Free Trade Agreement. Republican leaders had not merely tolerated the explosion in earmarking but encouraged and even masterminded it. Earmarks became major tools for them to protect incumbents in marginal districts and to buy votes in extraneous areas.

Of course, the use of projects or pork to protect incumbents or to logroll for votes is nothing new. But the sheer scope of their use in the past few years is a sharp break with tradition; that it occurred on the watch of self-proclaimed fiscal conservatives has left many real fiscal conservatives boiling.

The Dominance of Machine Politics

Running the House of Representatives with an iron fist requires a high degree of unity and loyalty among members of the majority party. Indeed, strong leadership in the House is conditional on widespread agreement among rank-and-file members on major public policy issues. The growing ideological polarization between the parties set the stage for more aggressive and partisan leadership, initially while Democrats were in the majority, in the late 1970s through the early 1990s, and then more ambitiously under Republican rule. While party leaders were dependent upon policy consensus in their caucus to run the House, they sought other means of increasing loyalty among their members. Two proved to be of particular importance. The first was to play a more central role in congressional elections, especially in their financing; the second was to enlist sympathetic interest groups and their lobbyists to the partisan cause.

Money and Elections

During the rise of strong party leadership, campaign fundraising became an essential activity of party leaders and aspiring leaders. In addition to raising funds for their own campaigns, they appeared at fund-raisers for their party colleagues in Washington and in their districts; formed leadership PACs to contribute funds to their collegues' campaigns; exhorted interest groups to contribute to the party and its members; used nonprofits to cater to the personal and electoral interests of their colleagues; and raised substantial funds for the revitalized congressional campaign committees, allowing them to play a more strategic and consequential role. With the demise of seniority, aspiring committee and subcommittee chairs were obliged to raise large sums of campaign funds just to be considered for the posts they sought. Over time parties put in place systems for redistributing campaign funds from safe to marginal districts, through both transfers to the campaign committees and member-to-member contributions.

During the 1990s, the parties and their leaders discovered new ways of spending so-called soft money—large, unregulated contributions from corporations, unions, and individuals—in congressional campaigns. President Clinton and his political adviser, Dick Morris, broke new ground in the 1996 presidential campaign by using soft money to finance sham issue ads—those designed to influence elections but that avoided words that expressly advocate the election or defeat of a candidate, which would have triggered contribution limits. Both parties quickly followed suit. Before long, congressional leaders were deeply involved in soliciting—or extorting—large contributions from CEOs, labor leaders, and wealthy individuals for their party committees and leadership PACs. These developments made a mockery of campaign finance law, and it became all too easy for congressional leaders to abuse their authority as public officials.

Immediately after the 1996 elections, the two of us joined with several colleagues to develop a reform agenda—"Five Ideas for Practical Campaign Reform"—that dealt directly with the twin problems of soft money and sham issue advocacy. Several pieces of our agenda made their way into the legislation that was ultimately enacted. Over the course of the next seven years, working with the chief sponsors as part of a sustained effort to develop, enact, and constitutionally defend the Bipartisan Campaign Reform Act of 2002 (BCRA), we had a unique vantage point from which to observe the world of money and politics on Capitol Hill. We were deeply impressed by the courage and tenacity of the prime cosponsors of the legislation, Senators John McCain

(R-AZ) and Russ Feingold (D-WI), Representatives Chris Shays (R-CT) and Marty Meehan (D-MA); the resourcefulness of Senators Olympia Snowe (R-ME) and Jim Jeffords (R, I-VT) in sponsoring an amendment to more sharply define the electioneering communication that would be subject to regulation; the guts of twenty Republican House members who bucked their leadership to sign a discharge petition that allowed the Shays-Meehan legislation to be considered on the floor; and the commitment and skill of Democratic leaders Tom Daschle (D-SD) and Dick Gephardt (D-MO) in holding their party together in support of the bill. The latter was particularly notable in light of the strong opposition of Democratic election-law lawyers and political consultants, union leaders, and a number of prominent liberal interest groups.

BCRA did not reduce the amount of money in federal elections (it was never intended to) nor did it marginalize the role of congressional leaders in campaign finance. They continue to be deeply involved, a reality that fuels party polarization in both the House and the Senate. But in limiting their efforts to raising only hard money—those funds subject to restrictions on source and caps on amount—the law removed one powerful means of abusing public power.

The electoral activities of congressional leaders went beyond campaign fund-raising. The old norm that constrained leaders, and the Speaker in particular, from campaigning against members of the other party fell by the wayside. Speaker Dennis Hastert campaigned hard against conservative Democrat Charles Stenholm, who often sided with the Republicans on economic policy votes. Not the best way of building bridges to the other party or of strengthening the political center. In the Senate, Majority Leader Frist publicly relished the opportunity to defeat his Democratic counterpart, Tom Daschle. His campaign trip to South Dakota was a first in Senate history.

Congressional party leaders also became more actively involved in trying to extract partisan gains from the decennial redistricting process. In an effort to control the bodies empowered with redistricting authority, they helped finance state legislative election campaigns and then had their staffs draw partisan maps for use in key states. The post-2000 round of redistricting strengthened the Republican advantage nationally, shored up the position of marginal incumbents in both parties, and reduced the overall number of competitive seats. House Majority Leader Tom DeLay was not content to rest on this success, however. Violating a century-long norm, he orchestrated a brazen effort to take a second bite of the redistricting apple. After gaining full control of the Texas legislature in the 2002 elections, in a campaign masterminded by DeLay, the Republicans pushed through a second post-2000 set of maps designed solely to elect more Republican representatives.

The Texas mid-decade gerrymander succeeded brilliantly, putting seven Democrats in the state delegation at severe risk. (Six of these districts subsequently moved into the Republican column: one Democrat switched parties, another retired in the face of certain defeat, and four lost in the general election; the seventh barely survived in a strong Republican district.) As one Republican U.S. House staffer working on the Texas redistricting plan put it in an e-mail not designed for public consumption: "The maps are now official. I have studied them and this is the most aggressive map I have ever seen. This has a real national impact that should assure that Republicans keep the House no matter the national mood."[27] So much for democratic accountability and responsiveness.

So much for propriety as well. To make his move work, DeLay and his associates crafted a scheme to evade the century-old Texas law forbidding corporate contributions to state races. They raised large sums from corporations, much of it in Washington, that was laundered through the Republican National Committee and then channeled back to specific candidates for the Texas legislature. Subsequently, DeLay and several associates were indicted for their part in this money-laundering ploy.

Lobbying

The second way of shoring up party support is to extend the whip operation beyond the halls of Congress. No one mastered this feat as well as Tom DeLay.[28] Together with Republican strategist Grover Norquist, he started in 1995 what became a formidable political machine, especially after the 2000 elections. The K Street Project is innocuously described on the website of Norquist's Americans for Tax Reform as "a non-partisan research of the political affiliation, employment background, and political donations of members in Washington's premier lobbying firms, trade associations and industries." The collection of data is perfectly innocent, but the objective clearly is to place party loyalists in all of the key lobbying positions in Washington and then to steer the formidable resources of the organizations they represent toward support of the Republican party's legislative agenda and the election of Republican candidates to Congress. As DeLay said in 1995, "There are just a lot of people down on K Street who gained their prominence by being Democrat . . . we're just following the old adage of punish your enemies and reward your friends. We don't like to deal with people who are trying to kill the revolution. We know who they are. The word is out."[29]

DeLay and the Republicans are hardly the first congressional majority to play hard ball with the business community in Washington. Early in the Reagan administration, Representative Tony Coelho, chairman of the Democratic Congressional Campaign Committee, reminded business lobbyists that the Democrats still controlled the House and were in a position to boost or retard their legislative priorities. He aggressively sought and achieved rough parity for his party on K Street with the Republicans, a balance that persisted until Republicans took control of Congress after their stunning 1994 election victory.

But nothing in Washington has come close to the ambition and daring of DeLay's operation. As Nicholas Confessore aptly described it, "Like the urban Democratic machines of yore, this one is built upon patronage, contracts, and one-party rule. But unlike legendary Chicago Mayor Richard J. Daley, who rewarded party functionaries with jobs in the municipal bureaucracy, the GOP is building its machine outside government, among Washington's thousands of trade associations and corporate offices, their tens of thousands of employees, and the hundreds of millions of dollars in political money at their disposal."[30]

Joined later by Rick Santorum in the Senate and Roy Blunt in the House, DeLay had great success with his K Street strategy. He became the point man for headhunters and industry executives making hiring decisions—they knew to seek his approval. As retaliation for the Electronic Industries Association's hiring of former Democratic Representative Dave McCurdy as its president, DeLay held up two intellectual property treaties in the House that the Electronic Industries Association supported. While later admonished by the House Ethics Committee for this behavior, DeLay eventually got his way with the Electronic Industries Association (which hired two Republicans to do its lobbying), and the message was received loud and clear by other trade associations and lobbying firms. Since the late 1990s, some twenty-nine former DeLay staffers have moved to lobbying positions in Washington. No other congressional leadership office comes close. They represent about 350 energy, finance, technology, airline, auto manufacturing, tobacco, health care and pharmaceutical companies and institutions. They also represent thirteen of the biggest trade associations. DeLay alumni also work for conservative Republican organizations, including several high-powered communications firms.

The Collapse of Ethical Standards

In early 2003, the *Washington Post* reported that the staff of House Financial Services Committee chair Mike Oxley, personal and committee, had pressured the Investment Company Institute to fire its chief lobbyist, Julie Domenick, and replace her with a Republican (Domenick was a Democrat with ties to John Dingell). According to the *Post,* committee staffer Sam Geduldig "told a group of lobbyists...that Oxley's probe of the mutual fund industry was linked to Domenick's employment at the mutual fund group."[31]

Following on DeLay's unethical effort to strong-arm the Electronics Industries Association, the effort to bludgeon the Investment Company Institute by threatening legislative retribution if its lobbyist were not canned made it clear that the K Street Project was more than merely another effort to extract money and jobs from interest groups.

The difference was dramatized—perhaps typified—by lobbyist Jack Abramoff, a close friend of Grover Norquist since their mutual efforts in college Republican and conservative movements and a close ally and associate of Tom DeLay (and Bob Ney, among others). Abramoff rose dramatically to visibility, power, wealth, and notoriety as a lobbyist in Tom DeLay's Washington who used his connections to DeLay and other majority insiders to represent a range of clients, most notably Indian tribes who were trying to get or keep gambling casinos—or stop other tribes from getting them—and the Northern Marianas Islands (Saipan), which was trying to keep preferential treatment for its sweatshop garment industry.

In just three years, Abramoff and his associates, including former DeLay key staffer Michael Scanlan, pulled in $82 million from the Indian tribes. This bonanza included taking fees from one tribe to prevent another from getting a casino and then taking fees from the second tribe to try to reverse the decision. Some of the money went to his law firm; but $66 million went to Scanlan's public affairs firm and to a series of nonprofits, including charities organized by Abramoff and the American International Center, a "think tank" Abramoff set up that was headquartered in the beach community of Rehoboth, Delaware, and run by a former lifeguard with no public policy experience. Some of the money was turned into fees for Grover Norquist and Ralph Reed, the former executive director of the Christian Coalition and former head of the Bush presidential campaign's Southern region, to help the Indian gambling effort by lobbying to block the licensing of rival casinos; other money was channeled to conservative organizations, including some affiliated with Norquist.

Abramoff spread his largesse around widely, hosting lavish trips abroad for members of Congress and other officials, in some cases to golf resorts in St Andrews, Scotland, where he paid greens fees that approached $5,000 a day. DeLay and Ney were among the golfing junketeers. At the same time, Abramoff was pursuing other business ventures, including the leasing and acquisition of federal properties and the purchase of gambling boats in Florida. In each case, he enlisted lawmakers and administration officials to help.

In 2004, the Senate Indian Affairs Committee began to investigate Abramoff's alleged rip-offs of Indian tribes and other chicanery associated with them. In early 2005, Abramoff was indicted for wire fraud in his purchase of the gambling boats, amid numerous federal investigations into his other activities. During the first week of October 2005—the same week that Tom DeLay was indicted by a grand jury in Texas for the money transfers that sent corporate money through the Republican National Committee and on to Texas legislative candidates—there were three separate stories about Abramoff's activities, all linked to key legislators and officials in the administration:

- David Safavian, the chief federal procurement officer inside the White House and a former lobbyist with both Abramoff and Norquist, was arrested and subsequently indicted for obstructing justice and lying to federal investigators about his ties to Abramoff during his time with the General Services Administration and his golfing trip to St Andrews with Abramoff and Rep. Bob Ney.
- Three men were arrested for the gangland-style murder of Gus Boulis, the man from whom Abramoff and his partner, Adam Kitan, had purchased the gambling boats. The three men had at one time worked for or otherwise been associated with Kitan.

- The Justice Department's inspector general confirmed that it was investigating the circumstances behind the demotion in 2002 of Frederick Black, the longtime acting U.S. Attorney in Guam, only days after he had notified the Public Integrity Section of the Justice Department that he had opened a criminal investigation into Abramoff's lobbying activities in Guam. Frederick Black was not only returned to his position as Assistant U.S. Attorney, but he was barred from continuing corruption investigations, which effectively killed the Abramoff probe.

During the second week of October, two more stories came to light. The first was an AP account of how, in 2000, Tom DeLay and his deputy whip Roy Blunt of Missouri had set up a series of complicated exchanges of funds in which they deliberately raised far more soft money for parties at the Republican Convention in Philadelphia than they needed or would use and then shuffled the excess funds, totaling hundreds of thousands of dollars, back and forth between each other via their unregulated funds, ARMPAC (Americans for a Republican Majority PAC) and the ROYB (Rely on Your Beliefs) Fund. Some of the money ended up at the Alexander Group, a lobbying firm that was directed by former DeLay chief of staff Ed Buckham and employed DeLay's wife. Some ended up with the Missouri Republican Party, which in turn made generous contributions to Matt Blunt, Roy's son, then running for Missouri Secretary of State (he won). Some of the funds came from Northern Marianas Islands–based Concorde Garment Manufacturing, part of a coalition that had hired Abramoff as a lobbyist.

The second was the withdrawal of Tim Flanigan from his nomination for Deputy Attorney General. As general counsel to Tyco International, Flanigan had presided over a lobbying contract given to Abramoff, who had boasted of his ties to Tom DeLay and Karl Rove, to help Tyco, based in Bermuda, avoid paying additional U.S. taxes. Abramoff had persuaded Flanigan to give $2 million to another lobbying firm, Grass Roots International—and $1.5 million of it was diverted to unrelated Abramoff-controlled entities.

Following Abramoff's plea agreement with the Department of Justice, the various investigations threatened to metastasize into a broader set of charges against many other Washington players, including prominent conservative strategists, Republican operatives, former Hill staffers, and lawmakers in both houses—with many of the players in the same constellation as Tom DeLay. All reflected a culture of greed and arrogance that had permeated Washington. It was eerily reminiscent of the Gilded Age, the era named in an 1873 novel by Mark Twain and Charles Dudley Warner that was characterized by rampant corruption involving business trusts, members of Congress, and other government officials, all in a self-reinforcing loop of sloshing money around politics to gain riches through government policy, with the money contributing to keeping in power those politicians who were getting bribed or influenced in the first place.

Some members of the 109th Congress were willing and eager to get to the bottom of this ethics embarrassment, including John McCain and others on the Indian Affairs Committee. The Senate Finance Committee began a preliminary investigation into Abramoff's use of nonprofit organizations. The approach of Congress, however, especially in Tom DeLay's House, was neither outrage nor embarrassment, but rather a concerted effort to put the lid on any investigations and to employ large-scale damage control by punishing or silencing those who wanted to sanction the miscreants.

That was especially true with the broad set of charges that swirled around DeLay. In late 2004, the House Committee on Standards of Official Conduct—the ethics committee—unanimously issued three separate rebukes to DeLay, warning him that there was a pattern of conduct that he needed to reexamine if he were to be seen as a representative reflecting honor on the House. The admonishments involved his efforts to strong-arm Nick Smith on the House floor during the three-hour vote on Medicare prescription drugs; his enlistment of the Federal Aviation Administration to track Texas Democratic state legislators when they vacated Austin during the dispute over the re-redistricting of Texas; and his use of a golf tournament for charity.

The ethics committee had not particularly wanted to investigate DeLay. The process was almost forced upon the panel when Chris Bell, a Texas Democrat who lost a primary election after the re-redistricting, brought a bill of particulars offering specific accusations of wrongdoing and ethical violations to the committee challenging DeLay's conduct. Republican leaders were enraged, seeing it as a breach of the unwritten truce that had kept any lawmaker from bringing ethics cases to the committee against any other lawmaker. Indeed, a part of the price paid within the committee to obtain a unanimous vote on each of the three rebukes against DeLay was a letter of rebuke to Bell for exaggerating the charges against DeLay. But when faced with the issues involving DeLay, the ethics committee did its job thoroughly and well. It left one issue pending—the ongoing investigation by a Texas prosecutor of whether DeLay had violated the state's campaign finance laws.

Soon after the 2004 elections, with the fear of an impending indictment of DeLay in Texas, the House Republicans initiated changes in their own procedures, spearheaded by Texas Republicans Henry Bonilla and Kevin Brady, that would allow their leaders to stay in their leadership posts if indicted in state courts. It was an obvious effort to protect DeLay if such an indictment came down. The rules change passed by voice vote in the GOP conference—after Ways and Means Committee Chair Bill Thomas cautioned against allowing a secret ballot vote—but a small and courageous group of House Republicans, including Reps. Christopher Shays (CT), J.D. Hayworth (AZ), Mike Castle (DE), Phil Gingrey (GA), and Tom Davis (VA) condemned the change.

Weeks later, the press and public outcry against this move to alter their ethical standards in order to protect one member under challenge forced the House Republicans to reverse course and reinstate the old caucus rule. But an undaunted Speaker Dennis Hastert found another means of protecting DeLay and other members who might come under scrutiny for unethical conduct. The Speaker ousted ethics panel chairman Joel Hefley, along with two committee members whose terms had not expired, Kenny Hulshof and Steve LaTourette. Hulshof had been the head of the subcommittee on the DeLay issues.

The actions taken by the Speaker—in effect firing those Republican members who had done their job and upheld the ethical standards of the House—were unprecedented. The pretext used to remove Chairman Hefley was that his term of service on the committee had expired and the Speaker had no choice. But the same day he fired Hefley, Speaker Hastert gave a waiver to David Dreier to serve an additional term as chair of the Rules Committee despite the fact that he had filled his three-term limit as chair. Hefley, in fact, had not served three terms as chairman (although he had served that long as a member of the committee).

Hulshof and LaTourette were another matter; they had not even met the limit on terms of service on the committee. Compounding the offense, Hastert replaced the two with Reps. Lamar Smith of Texas and Tom Cole of Oklahoma, both of whom had given substantial sums to DeLay's legal defense fund. Smith had previously served on the ethics panel during the Gingrich investigation, the only member of the committee to vote against the recommended penalties. Hefley was replaced by Doc Hastings of Washington, who as a senior member of the Rules Committee was a clear contender to move up to chair (the Speaker's decision) when Dreier left—with his performance as ethics chair clearly a factor in that prospective career advancement.

The signals by the Speaker could not have been more clear: take your responsibilities as guardians of House ethics seriously and you will be the ones stigmatized; play the game and make sure that no ethics issues are raised about your party colleagues or are downplayed and diluted, and career enhancement awaits.

When the ethics committee met to organize for the 109th Congress, Chairman Hastings announced that he was going to employ his own personal staffer to help lead the committee staff—violating the long-standing procedure that all staff on the committee were bipartisan. Ranking Democrat Allan Mollohan objected, and the Democrats on the committee boycotted, preventing the panel from having a quorum and from organizing to do business. After months of stalemate, with further criticism of the House Republicans' stance on ethics, Hastings relented, allowing the panel to get set to do business. But months later, understaffed and still divided, the ethics committee was in no position to deal with the post-indictment issues facing DeLay, much less the larger set of issues flowing from the Abramoff case, or other ethics questions hitting members of both parties, including a long-standing one involving senior Democrat Jim McDermott of Washington.

In effect, there was no ethics process in place to deal with a set of problems hitting the House with full force—and no acknowledgment of the problem, or the fundamental challenge to the integrity of the body, by the Speaker or any other major leader in the majority. Whatever the problems in the 1990s—and there were significant ethical issues then—at least the leaders in the majority under Speakers Wright, Foley, and Gingrich had made sure that the ethics process moved forward with significant insulation from a partisan tilt and from the self-interest of the members being investigated. Not so the House of Speaker Hastert and Majority Leader (now former Majority Leader) DeLay.

SIX

The Case of Continuity

ON THE BRILLIANTLY CLEAR and beautiful morning of September 11, 2001, when hijacked planes hit the World Trade Center buildings and the Pentagon, the Capitol was a busy place. The House of Representatives was in session, doing morning business. Lots of committees were meeting formally and informally. Many members, staffers, lobbyists, and tour groups were on the grounds, outside or on the steps on the East Front.

News that a plane had hit the World Trade Center was met with intense interest but no notable reaction. The second hit—and the visible sights and sounds of the plane hitting the Pentagon only a few miles away—brought a reaction akin to chaos. The top congressional leaders—Speaker, House Minority Leader, Senate Majority and Minority Leaders—were quickly hustled away to an undisclosed location. The rest of the lawmakers, staff, and others were not given any directions or news. Without an evacuation plan, many lingered for several hours on or near the Capitol grounds. Others, including a number of leaders, went to the Capitol Police headquarters a block from the Senate office buildings to wait for further information.

By late afternoon, as word emerged that a fourth plane had crashed in rural Pennsylvania, it became clear that United 93 had indeed been hijacked as well and had been headed to a fourth target—almost certainly the Capitol. The 9/11 Commission report, released three years later, noted that Mohammed Atta had focused on the first part of September as his target time "so that the United States Congress would be in session."[1]

With the House in session, one can easily imagine what the consequences would have been had a large jetliner with lots of fuel in its tanks hit the Capitol dome at full speed. Molten cast iron, burning jet fuel, and chunks of marble and metal would have rained down upon lawmakers, staff, and everyone else within hundreds of yards of the dome itself, causing widespread death and destruction. Perhaps hundreds of members of the House would be dead or missing—and many others would have been in intensive care and burn units in hospitals for months or longer.

And the House itself? Given the constitutional requirement that a quorum of half the membership of the body was necessary in order to conduct official business, the House would have been shuttered, out of business, until it could get enough members back in place to meet the quorum requirement. Since the House, unlike the Senate, can fill vacancies only by election, and since special elections in recent decades have taken four months on average to conduct—in single districts, without widespread disruption—that would mean the House and the legislative branch would have been inoperative for many months at a critical moment in the nation's history. It might have been even worse; if a majority of members were alive but incapacitated, there would have been no vacancies to fill, no elections, and no quorum for much longer than four months—possibly, if such a catastrophe had occurred on 9/11/2001, until January of 2003.

Soon after the stunning events of 9/11, another horror story hit Capitol Hill. High-grade fine particles of anthrax were placed in a series of letters sent to prominent Senate leaders, including Tom Daschle and Pat Leahy. This was neither a frivolous nor amateurish effort; some people who came into contact with the envelopes died and others became infected with serious forms of inhalation anthrax. After weeks of near-panic and intensive investigations, the envelopes stopped coming, but with no explanation of where they originated or where the anthrax had been obtained. Years later, the case remains unsolved.

What was clear was that if terrorists had secured larger quantities of such weapons-grade anthrax and had introduced it into the ventilation systems in Senate office buildings, sixty or more senators might have been hospitalized for months. Vacancies in the Senate, in accord with the 17th Amendment, may be filled by executive appointment if states desire—and virtually all states do so. But sixty incapacitated senators would leave the Senate without a quorum indefinitely—probably for more than two years given the six-year terms of its members—since appointments only apply to vacancies. Over the history of the Senate, a number of individual members have served for years while comatose or clearly unable to perform their duties.

During the Cold War, Congress and the executive branch had engaged in some continuity planning—including setting up a secret, large hardened "bunker" at the Greenbrier Resort in West Virginia that would accommodate all the members of both houses, with food, water, a mini-chamber, and protection against radioactivity in the event of a nuclear strike on Washington by the Soviet Union. Only top congressional leaders knew about its existence. It was based on the assumption that the government would have advance notice to evacuate if missiles were launched from Siberia, enough time to hustle the lawmakers by car, helicopter, train, or other means to the Greenbrier, some two hundred miles from Washington. With the end of the Cold War, the secret was breached and the bunker is now a tourist attraction. It is not relevant during an era where terrorist attacks come suddenly, without notice or an opportunity to evacuate—an era the framers could scarcely have contemplated when they wrote the Constitution.

These worst-case and previously far-fetched scenarios suddenly moved into sharp relief. Three weeks after 9/11, Ornstein wrote a column in *Roll Call*, "What If Congress Were Obliterated? Good Question," the first discussion in print of these horrific possibilities. He wrote:

> It is simply not practical to have the possibility exist of Congress being unable to operate because of massive deaths and incapacitations, or operating for many months with a skeleton crew that is highly skewed in regional or partisan composition. Congress must consider this horrible possibility and reform the process to deal with it. There is no simple answer, but there are ways to create a better balance.
>
> The best start is to create a small, short-term task force of constitutional scholars and former lawmakers to report to the top four Congressional leaders with suggestions for reform. It should consider laws that would expedite special elections under emergency circumstances.
>
> Unfortunately, it may also be necessary to consider a constitutional amendment, crafted narrowly and carefully, to lay out ways to fill Congress temporarily if disaster or an act of war reduces its ranks below the regular quorum. These might include interim appointments to both houses by state governors until special elections can be held, redefinition of a quorum if large numbers of Members are physically incapacitated, delegation of emergency powers to Congressional leaders, and/or provisions for emergency meeting places. . . .
>
> No doubt, Congress doesn't want to think about that nightmarish situation. But it should, and then act responsibly and quickly to minimize the potential disruption to our way of governing.[2]

Soon after the column appeared, Ornstein was contacted by Rep. Brian Baird (D-WA), who had come to the same conclusion on 9/11 as he and his colleagues milled around aimlessly after the attacks. Baird drafted his own constitutional amendment[3] to provide for temporary appointments to the House in the event of a catastrophic attack affecting Congress; the draft was not meant to be definitive since it did not address all the most difficult and delicate questions—under what circumstances does one make temporary appointments, who makes the decision, who makes the appointments, for how long, and so on. But Baird found, as did Ornstein, that few members of Congress were eager to jump on the issue. Human nature—the same reasons many people do not write wills—left many uneasy about contemplating their own demise. Other issues, including the response to the attacks, distracted many.

A tepid response from rank-and-file lawmakers was not surprising. The lack of any interest or urgency from congressional leaders, who have the fiduciary responsibility to protect the integrity of Congress, was less understandable. Over the months that followed 9/11, Ornstein wrote frequently on the continuity issue, honing the ideas for reform, but he found the attitude of the Speaker of the House was, in essence, "I will act on this only when my members demand that I do so."

Faced with a passive and indifferent leadership, Mann and Ornstein created an informal working group to discuss the issues, doing in effect what we had hoped Congress would do in the weeks after 9/11. Our interlocutors included former speakers Newt Gingrich and Tom Foley. In the meantime, Baird went about collecting signatures from his colleagues to urge action in Congress.

Prodded by columns, articles, and Baird's inside efforts, the House Judiciary Committee's subcommittee on the Constitution held one hearing in February 2002 on the constitutional issues surrounding the continuity of government. Chaired by Steve Chabot of Ohio, the subcommittee called four witnesses, including Ornstein, for a morning of interesting testimony and give-and-take. But subsequent conversations with Chabot made it clear that Judiciary Committee Chair James Sensenbrenner (R-WI) saw the hearing as a way to deep-six any initiative in the area—not as the beginning of a legislative process to find a constructive policy that could be implemented. There would not be another hearing. A press conference convened by Baird in

March 2002 brought together several other members, including Jim Langevin of Rhode Island, and focused on alternative proposed amendments, including one by Rep. Zoe Lofgren of California, but it did not result in any additional action by congressional leaders.

Following Ornstein's op-ed piece on continuity issues in the *Wall Street Journal* in March 2002,[4] former White House Counsel Lloyd Cutler contacted him to discuss how he might help move the issue along; the result, several months later, was the creation of the blue-ribbon Continuity of Government Commission, jointly run by AEI and Brookings and with Lloyd Cutler and former Senator Alan Simpson as co-chairs. The commission comprised a broad array of former members, such as former speakers Foley and Gingrich and former minority leader Bob Michel, former Cabinet officials and White House chiefs of staff, academics, and others. In March 2002, Baird had two hundred signatures on a letter to congressional leaders asking for the creation of a bipartisan panel of House and Senate members to study and report on the problem.

Faced with some pressure and public scrutiny, Speaker Hastert and Minority Leader Pelosi held a series of joint meetings beginning in May 2002; these resulted in the creation of a task force on continuity, co-led by Republican Chris Cox and Democrat Martin Frost. Thus began a conscientious effort to examine the problems and possible avenues for solution. Cox made clear to us early on that the mandate from Speaker Hastert was to explore and exhaust all the alternatives short of a constitutional amendment or any form of appointment for the House. As a strategy, that was perfectly defensible—up to a point. Of course, if there were reasonable approaches that did not require a constitutional amendment but that would ensure the rapid reconstitution of Congress after a devastating attack, they would be vastly preferable. But what if such reasonable approaches were not possible? Cox also made clear that the Speaker would not then make the leap to consider, much less condone, any kind of amendment or emergency interim appointments.

Suzanne Nelson, a reporter who followed the continuity issue closely from its inception, wrote a postmortem in *Roll Call:* the Cox-Frost group "dissolved at the end of the 107th Congress without delving into the more difficult constitutional changes that almost all outside experts believe are necessary."[5]

Why? One reason became clear to Ornstein when he met with Rep. James Sensenbrenner, chair of the House Judiciary Committee. Before Ornstein could finish sitting down on the couch in Sensenbrenner's office, the chairman was loudly berating him for his push to allow appointments to the House—and for mentioning Sensenbrenner's name in press stories about who the key players were on continuity. Sensenbrenner made clear that he would do everything in his power to block any action that would encourage or allow for emergency interim appointments; he hinted that he had his own alternative in the works but would not let others know in advance. Subsequently, Ornstein met with David Dreier, the chairman of the Rules Committee, for a conversation that was more civilized but no more encouraging. Dreier's concerns were not his alone, and they did reflect a larger attitude among a number of House members. They saw the main distinction the House had compared to the Senate was the fact that it is an all-elected body. Vacancies have never been filled by appointment, but only by election. But Dreier's views in this area were not just a reasoned defense of the primacy of elections. He shared with Sensenbrenner a strongly visceral reaction against appointments and was unmoved by, and unwilling to consider seriously, the argument that the choice was not between an elected House and an appointive House, but having a House at all, having a house so depleted it would be wildly unrepresentative of the nation, or simply allowing martial law to prevail for months.

Then, of course, there was the Speaker. Zoe Lofgren (D-CA), who pushed hard on the issue, noted to Nelson in her postmortem, "The Speaker is obviously the leader of his party in the House, but he has an obligation not just to his party but also to his country. It would have been in keeping with that role to have stepped in and made something happen. I didn't see him playing that role."[6] A central reason was articulated by a key Democratic aide: "The Speaker hasn't been willing to take on Sensenbrenner . . . Sensenbrenner has just planted his feet in cement. Sensenbrenner has all but won this discussion by virtue of the fact that he had refused to hold a discussion."[7]

On June 4, 2003, the Continuity of Government Commission issued its first report, making a strong and unanimous case that the only effective way Congress could ensure its viability in a timely fashion after a devastating terrorist attack on Washington was via a constitutional amendment allowing for emergency interim appointments to the House in the case of widespread deaths and to either house in the case of significant incapacitation. The Commission members met over lunch with Vice President Cheney and went to Capitol Hill to present the report to the four top congressional leaders. The meetings with Senators Frist and Daschle and Representatives Hastert and Pelosi were cordial, but all four were noncommittal; Hastert, despite the active pleas to him by fellow Illinois Republican Lynn Martin and former Senate Republican Whip Alan Simpson, was strikingly detached.

The Senate, however, began its own exploration of continuity issues, initiated in a fashion that underscored the small town nature of the Washington community. In January 2003, at the annual Washington Press Foundation Salute to Congress, Ornstein sat next to newly elected Texas Senator John Cornyn. Cornyn asked him what he was working on, and when the conversation turned to continuity and the failure of Congress to act, Cornyn expressed interest in the issue—with the added comment that he happened to chair one subcommittee as a freshman, the Judiciary Subcommittee on the Constitution. Soon thereafter, Ornstein and Mann met with subcommittee staff director James Ho, who immediately grasped the significance of the issues and the need for action; he and Cornyn began a vigorous process to bring the continuity problem to the attention of the Senate and to work toward an appropriate constitutional amendment. They started with a well-publicized hearing in September of the full Judiciary Committee, chaired by Cornyn, followed a week later by a joint hearing of the Judiciary and Rules committees to explore presidential succession.

The House Responds—Badly

The efforts of the Continuity of Government Commission, Baird and his allies, and Cornyn had brought enough public attention to the issues and enough press inquiries that House Republican leaders felt some considerable pressure to act—to do something. So in July 2003, Reps. Sensenbrenner, Dreier, and Candice Miller (R-MI) introduced a bill to expedite special elections in the event of a catastrophe. The bill mandated that when the Speaker has declared that there are at least one hundred vacancies in the House, the states must hold special elections within twenty-one days. More accurately, since the parties were given fourteen days to choose candidates, the bill would require these elections to be held within seven days.

The week after their bill was introduced, Ornstein called it "loopy" in his column in *Roll Call*,[8] highlighting the stories then in newspapers about the pending California special election on the recall of the governor. The *Los Angeles Times* had noted the extraordinary difficulty California local election officials were having getting ready for an election that was seventy-five days off—not seven days. The story noted:

> "Time is really our enemy," [Los Angeles County Deputy Registrar Kristin] Heffron said.
> She usually reserves polling places six months in advance of an election, but many of the regular precinct locations—in

schools, churches and community centers—have already been booked for other uses. . .

Once the list of candidates is released, the presses at Sequoia [Voting Systems'] Porterville [Calif.] facility will start running twenty-four hours a day, churning out millions of absentee and regular ballots for Los Angeles and several other counties.

"We'll print three shifts a day until they're done," [Sequoia spokesman Alfie] Charles said.[9]

The California election made clear that a twenty-one-day period for one hundred or more special elections—all held after a national catastrophe of untold and unprecedented proportions—was simply unworkable. In his response to the column, David Dreier called the twenty-one-day/seven-day formula a "starting point"—the only response to the issue, in other words, coming nearly two years after 9/11, was not a well-crafted plan shaped by hearings in a deliberative process, but a starting point quickly slapped together. In fact, the sponsors had not consulted with scholars, election officials, local government officials, or anyone else before drafting and dropping their bill in the hopper. This was the "secret plan" alluded to by Sensenbrenner.

At the Senate Judiciary Committee's prime hearing in September that year, and at a House Administration Committee hearing merely a week later, the Sensenbrenner/Dreier/Miller bill came in for scathing criticism from scholars and election officials. Mann told the House Committee that the bill sponsors' emphasis on the unique constitutional principle that no person can serve in the House without first being elected by their constituents was more affectation than reality. The popular election of presidents and the provision for the direct election of senators in the 17th amendment gave them an electoral connection similar to that of the House. He went on to testify that:

Members of this body should not delude themselves into thinking that any form of election is preferable to emergency temporary appointments in the wake of a national catastrophe. After all, North Korea has elections. So too did Saddam

Hussein's Iraq and the Soviet Union. Only democratically legitimate elections merit our approval.

The House already has a problem with very limited competition and choice in the overwhelming majority of its districts. It would be a shame to exacerbate this pattern by creating a remedy to the continuity challenge that compounds it.

Congress should not accept a solution to the continuity problem that sacrifices democratic substance and administrative feasibility for democratic form.[10]

The bill was subsequently adjusted to extend the time for the emergency special elections to no more than forty-five days—with ten days allowed for parties to select candidates. This after Doug Lewis, speaking for many election officials, pleaded for at least sixty days for such a process.

In mid-November, at Sensenbrenner's behest, the House Administration Committee marked up the bill. Virtually no changes were allowed by Chairman Bob Ney, with amendments rejected on party-line votes. Committee members acknowledged the serious problems that were raised by ranking member John Larson (D-CT) but said there would be a response from the House Judiciary Committee. The brief, nonresponsive response arrived only after the bill had been reported from House Administration and sent on to House Judiciary. In January 2004, the bill was rammed through the Judiciary Committee with no amendments on a peremptory, party-line vote.

Suzanne Nelson described the hearing in the January 22, 2004, *Roll Call* as follows:

In front of a packed hearing room (full because the next item on the agenda was the divisive Unborn Victims of Violence Act), Judiciary Democrats repeatedly asked Chairman Jim Sensenbrenner (R-Wis.) to allow the panel to take more time to debate the measure and discuss alternatives.

Calling Congressional continuity a "matter of national constitutional import," Rep. Mel Watt (D-N.C.) chastised Sensenbrenner and the Republican leadership for stifling input on the issue, particularly from Members who believe expedited special elections alone are not sufficient to ensure the legislative branch's relevance in a crisis if large numbers of Members were killed or incapacitated. Watt was joined by ranking member John Conyers (D-Mich.) and California Democratic Reps. Adam Schiff, Linda Sanchez and Zoe Lofgren. Sanchez said the panel was giving the issue "short shrift."

Sensenbrenner shot back that "those issues were very, very adequately ventilated," citing a House Administration Committee hearing and subsequent markup last year. He also noted that the Judiciary subcommittee on the Constitution "has had hearings on this issue."

The subcommittee held one hearing on potential amendments in early March 2002.

As many lawmakers have done when discussing the subject, Watt prefaced his remarks by saying, "This is not a partisan issue."

But for at least the past year debate over continuity has played out primarily along party lines, especially in the House.[11]

In late April 2004, the House brought up the bill, with a modified closed rule under which virtually all amendments failed on largely party-line votes; the only change made was on relaxing absentee voting requirements for military personnel overseas. On the floor, after the mediation of Republican Whip Roy Blunt, Sensenbrenner agreed to bring up, at least for debate and a vote, the Baird-drafted constitutional amendment, but under very tight time limits.

On the floor, Baird engaged in a testy exchange with Dreier over the handling of the continuity issue. "You now give us two hours," Baird said. "Ask my colleagues, as I did yesterday, have they had sufficient time to study [a] matter of this magnitude before we vote on it. They will tell you, 'No, sir. I have not.' They will vote party line as we far too often do here. But they will not vote their conscience, because their conscience has not grappled with it."[12]

The bill that passed the House was filled with inconsistencies and loopholes. It preempted election laws in all fifty states, but in ways vague enough to leave most states in limbo as to which of the provisions in their own state laws can or cannot apply to these special elections. Left unaddressed and unanswered for many states with laws involving absentee voters, military voters, and party nominating processes that run afoul of this bill: What if they can't reconcile the two? What if their own communities have been hit by terrorist attacks? What if they fail to meet the forty-five-day deadline? Are their elections to the House then invalid?

With only ten days to choose nominees to go on the ballot, primaries were ruled out—meaning party insiders would handpick candidates. Sensenbrenner himself said if they could not get it done in ten days they would be out of luck and without a candidate for Congress. (Not much sympathy for presenting voters with a competitive choice of candidates, but then Sensenbrenner seldom had to deal with any real opposition in his safe Wisconsin district.) Minor parties and Independent candidates would be out of luck, period.

Thirty-five days to an election largely precluded absentee voting, including overseas military absentees. This violates federal law as well as many state laws. The change made on the floor to avoid embarrassment at disenfranchising the military left unresolved the tension between the thirty-five-day requirement to get elections done and the indefinite period allowed to count only those overseas absentee ballots.

Of course, even if the bill worked, America would, for sixty days or so at best—including the time to certify election results and get Members to Washington—be governed under a form of martial law. During this period there would be no Congress to declare war, give authorization for use of military force, appropriate emergency money, or oversee the waiver of civil liberties and the exercise of prosecutorial power.

The following month, May, the House Judiciary Committee held a markup on the Baird constitutional amendment— no hearings, and no alternatives were proposed to be taken to the floor. Once again, the exchanges were testy and partisan. The various sponsors of constitutional amendments on continuity wrote a letter to colleagues saying, "[T]he process in the House . . . has short-circuited any serious legislative process by denying hearings to develop the issue properly, educate the Members and the American public, and perfect the most appropriate language from among the very different ideas. . . proposed."

In early June, 2004, the House voted against the Baird amendment, but the "debate" on the floor was instructive. Again, Suzanne Nelson in *Roll Call:*

> The debate was subject to a closed rule, preventing Rep. Dana Rohrabacher (R-Calif.) and two Democrats from offering their amendment proposals as substitutes. Baird and a handful of his Democratic colleagues said the closed rule contradicted Rules Chairman David Dreier's (R-Calif.) assertions that the GOP leadership has worked "in a strong bipartisan way" to ensure an open deliberative process. So instead of spending the allotted 90 minutes discussing the measure's merits, much of that time was instead dedicated to discussion of whether the duration and nature of the deliberation was appropriate to an issue so fundamental to the institution.
>
> Rep. Doc Hastings (R-Wash.) said the measure "deserves to have a debate. This rule provides for that debate, 90 minutes."
>
> "How indicative," Baird replied. "Ninety minutes to debate the future of this country in the event of a terrorist attack. Ninety minutes."
>
> . . . Rohrabacher, too, was incensed Wednesday. "I asked the Rules Committee yesterday to make my proposal in order, and I was denied," he said. "That's why I voted present." Asked before the vote if he was given a rationale, he said no, but indicated that Dreier told him "the leadership made the decision."[13]

After this vote, Ornstein put continuity in the broader context of deliberation in the House.

> It would have been easy for [congressional leaders] to mak[e] last Wednesday's debate and vote open, nonpartisan and deliberative. . . . Several interesting and creative alternative amendments are circulating out there, offering a variety of approaches to the continuity problem, sponsored by such House

Democrats as Baird, John Larson (Conn.), and Zoe Lofgren (Calif.) and from Republicans such as Dana Rohrabacher (Calif.).

None of their measures was expected to gather the two-thirds vote necessary to pass the House, but a real debate, for a full day or so, about the alternatives would have been educational for the nation and for the majority of Members of the House.

Instead—almost inexplicably—there was a closed rule. It was one vote, one amendment, and an amendment which the author himself admitted has flaws. Dreier, as a minority member of the Rules Committee, argued regularly and eloquently against the use of closed rules by Democrats, and he swore things would be different under a Republican majority.

Well, they have been different: There are more closed rules than ever. Dreier has said that, as a minority member, he didn't understand the difficulty of governing from the majority, and that doing so is far harder with the narrow majorities Republicans have had in the past two Congresses. He has a point: There are issues, from fiscal to foreign policy, in which the majority needs to constrain choices if it is to prevail. And there are amendments designed more to structure 30-second campaign commercials than to offer constructive changes or genuine alternatives.

But the amendments on continuity were different altogether: They were all legitimate and honest. To force this issue to come up under a closed rule was an insult to Democrats, and to Rohrabacher. It was utterly unnecessary. Why do it? It is more than sheer partisanship; it is sheer power. The Republican leadership did it because they could, and they knew they could hold their own troops on a procedural vote.

Most news stories on the floor vote mentioned only the vote on final passage, which was lopsided. The real story, as reported in *Roll Call,* was the near party-line voting on the rule and on the motion to recommit—a motion in which Baird himself led the way, arguing for more time to debate this important issue.

Sensenbrenner even refused to let Brian Baird speak on his amendment's behalf—the kind of common courtesy that used to be, well, common in the House. Though a number of Democrats share Sensenbrenner's misgivings about a constitutional amendment, that issue melted away, as Democrats united in outrage against the chairman's bullying tactics. . . .

Every day we get reminders about the real threat to the Capitol from vicious terrorists. The issue of ensuring a continuing Congress should have been the subject of vigorous debate from the early stages after 9/11. It is a complicated problem, and it takes time and effort for Members to get their minds around it. Far more of them should be engaged now.

Of all the issues out there, this one should be the least partisan. There was no earthly reason for the Judiciary Committee to vote on strictly partisan lines on the Sensenbrenner alternative, or on the constitutional amendment. There was no reason for the House to split on partisan lines on the rule and on the motion to recommit, no reason to limit the debate to a pathetic 90 minutes, no reason to slap Dana Rohrabacher, Zoe Lofgren and John Larson in the face. It is the middle-finger approach to governing, driven by a mind-set that has brought us the most rancorous and partisan atmosphere I have seen in the House in nearly 35 years.[14]

Redefining the Quorum

With passage of the expedited elections bill and rejection of the Baird constitutional amendment, the House Republican leaders were prepared to declare victory on continuity. But they remained stung by another potent argument used against them: expedited elections did not address the problems of incapacitation, which had become particularly clear and powerful with the anthrax attack on the Senate and the panic in the House when a rumor hit the body that anthrax might be migrating over to the other side of the Capitol. Expedited elections were a fix, albeit a bad and inadequate one, for widespread deaths. But if large numbers of lawmakers were incapacitated, say in intensive care units with burns or anthrax, there would be no ability to meet the constitutional quorum requirement of half the members to do official business.

So in late July 2004, the House moved to change its rules to redefine the quorum in the event of a catastrophe. This move was, to say the least, highly controversial. The

Constitution's language on the quorum requirement is clear and unambiguous—a majority of the members of the body. The framers left no wiggle room, and the debate at the time made it clear that they were worried about allowing a much smaller number of members to conduct themselves as if they represented the entire country. To be sure, the Congress has itself applied rules defining the quorum as a majority of those elected, sworn, and living. But that exception, never tested in the courts, is a far cry from defining the quorum down sharply from that standard.

Earlier, in the spring, the House Rules Committee held a hearing on this subject. The committee struggled beforehand to find a single reputable scholar who would not object to the idea. Most major constitutional scholars in this area had signed a letter to Senator John Cornyn (R-TX) asserting that a smaller quorum would be clearly unconstitutional. The one scholar who was brought in to testify, Walter Dellinger, said that even if it were unconstitutional, the House could likely get away with it under catastrophic circumstances. But even Dellinger cautioned that such a change would require a trigger that was accepted by a broadly bipartisan consensus.

Despite his caveat—and despite the open calls from Democrats such as Martin Frost and from the scholarly community to make the decision dependent on the joint action of both Speaker and Minority Leader—the Rules Committee passed through a rules change that let the Speaker alone, along with the Sergeant-at-Arms, decide when members would be considered incapacitated.

Senator Cornyn addressed the House move in an article in *Roll Call:* "The proposal to eviscerate the quorum requirement is unconstitutional because it turns Members into non-Members."[15] Just as significant, a move by the House to contravene a constitutional requirement by allowing a simple majority to change the rules set a dangerous precedent—opening up the possibility in the future of changing the rules to require supermajorities to pass tax increases, for example. The objections were ignored by the majority, which steamrolled the rules change through the House.

The lack of concern with comity and the regular order on continuity issues did not end with that rules change. The expedited election bill that passed the House died in the Senate, which had no interest in taking up a flawed bill despite the active importuning of Jim Sensenbrenner and Dennis Hastert. In 2005, in the 109th Congress, the House once again brought the bill up and once again passed it, without an additional hearing or move to restructure the bill or amend it to take up even noncontroversial perfecting amendments that had been suggested by Rep. John Larson of Connecticut. Once again, it sat in the Senate. This time, Speaker Hastert used a different parliamentary ploy—repassing the bill as an amendment to the legislative appropriations bill and pressuring the Senate to incorporate it into the conference bill.

Legislating on an appropriations bill has long been considered a no-no by the House—substantive provisions are supposed to be handled by authorizers, even if they have appropriations consequences. In this case, the expedited election bill had no link to federal appropriations. But that did not stop the Speaker and Chairman Sensenbrenner. The Speaker ordered Appropriations Committee Chair Jerry Lewis to include the measure; an embarrassed Lewis admitted during the committee markup that he did not know anything about the issue but was adding it to the bill at the direction of the leadership. When the legislative appropriations bill went to the Senate, the Speaker made it clear that the entire bill would go nowhere unless the Senate went along with the expedited election provision. The Senate reluctantly went along, making the bill law.

The Senate's reluctant move was at least a move on its part. Despite the heroic efforts of Senator Cornyn and his ability to get a constitutional amendment that would deal with the incapacitation issue through the Judiciary Subcommittee on the Constitution (supported by Democrat Russ

Feingold of Wisconsin, among others), the Senate Republican leaders, including Bill Frist and Orrin Hatch, showed no interest in taking the amendment or any other legislation further. If House leaders at least had a reason for killing debate and consideration on the appointment solution, Senate leaders were driven more by indifference to the problem. Some people in the Senate involved with the process added another reason: a dollop of unease over promises of retaliation by Chairman Sensenbrenner if the Senate leaders moved the amendment along.

More than four years after 9/11 shook the Capitol to its foundations, the Congress had stubbornly—and negligently—failed to protect itself and the constitutional system in the event of another terrorist attack focused on the Capitol, opting instead for poorly designed, even unconstitutional actions in the House and no action in the Senate. At every stage along the way, when forced to confront the issues, the House had made sure to abandon any part of a deliberative or bipartisan process on an issue with no partisan or ideological coloration. The expedited special-election bill was purely symbolic and ineffectual; the House quorum rule unconstitutional and potentially dangerous. So much for Congress dealing responsibly with the continuity of its own institution.

SEVEN

Conclusion

IT IS EASY AND TEMPTING to romanticize the past and demonize the present. The "Good Old Days" were rarely as beneficent as old-timers remember them, and the problems of the day seldom seem as awful or intractable with the passage of time or comparison to other eras. But we are both convinced that the Congress we have observed and experienced in recent years is qualitatively different than its predecessors in important and dismaying ways.

To be sure, the change was not abrupt. It did not begin with the election of a Republican Congress in 1994 or the elevation of George W. Bush to the White House in 2000. Cracks in the institution began to show in the 1980s and early 1990s, during the last decade of the forty-year hegemony of Democrats in the House. They were exacerbated during that time by the appearance of a Democratic president, Bill Clinton, after a full twelve years of Republican control of the White House. The sudden arrival of one-party control of both ends of Pennsylvania Avenue crystallized the minority and sharpened the partisan conflict, already high during the late 1980s as the parties became more unified and ideologically polarized and the permanent campaign became an ever-present fact of life.

Then a Republican Congress under a new-style leader, Newt Gingrich, created an alternative power center and, ultimately, a war between the parties that culminated in the impeachment attempt against the president. The more serious problems that beset the institution, however, now are largely post-Gingrich. These problems have been heightened by new generations of leaders in both houses and by the arrival of an ambitious Republican president under extraordinary circumstances, facing a Congress with the narrowest majorities in seven decades.

Signs of a Broken Branch

A casual visitor to the Capitol or occasional viewer of C-SPAN might not see much difference from a decade or more ago. The language on the floor or in committee is pretty much the same, the lawmakers look no different, the physical structures differ only because of security barriers and the massive construction that represents the coming Capitol Visitors Center. But to grizzled veterans like us, with more than thirty-five years of Congress-watching, the differences are palpable and painful. Taken together, they have made for a broken branch, one that needs major change if it is to recapture its proper role in the constitutional system.

We saw signs of this coming for years, including the gradual collapse of the center in Congress as the parties became more homogeneous by shedding sizable shares of their moderates and moving toward the respective ends of the ideological spectrum. The rise of a sharper and more corrosive partisanship, bordering on tribalism, was driven by the permanent campaign, the higher stakes in elections with majorities regularly at stake, and the growing role of more fundamentalist forces in politics, with issues framed in starkly black-and-white terms and adversaries transformed into enemies. This deeply partisan era was also shaped by the changing nature of individuals coming into the elective arena, characterized by fewer politicians—a term we view with respect, not disdain—who care about compromise, product, and institutional health and more individual activists, ideologues, and entrepreneurs interested in purity and personal advancement. During this period public discourse, reinforced by transformations in the media, degenerated into a clash of ideological extremes— the "Crossfirization" of dialogue—that has coarsened and trivialized debate in every arena.

These combustible elements—a long time in developing— combined with more contemporary events to lay waste to the first branch of government. In the House, much of the malady stems from the ardent desire of Republican leaders, gifted in 2001 with the first fully Republican Washington in forty-six years, to enable their new president to succeed— and a president and vice president who saw success less as a partnership with Congress and more as one with a dominant executive branch and a subordinate legislature.

They all viewed their chances of policy success and its concomitant political success as flowing from the creation of a neoparliamentary system on the House side of the Capitol—something difficult to achieve under the best of circumstances in our constitutional system, but even more challenging with tiny majorities in Congress. Speaker Hastert proudly announced that his primary responsibility was to pass the President's legislative program, which often required ensuring that majority sentiment within the majority party, even if it reflected a distinct minority position in the full House, prevailed. In spite of the obstacles— relatively weak electoral and public support and paper-thin majorities in the House and Senate—President Bush and his congressional leaders found ways to make it work. But to do so meant bending the rules, precedents, and norms of legislative behavior in ways that left the institution in tatters. Winning at all costs consumed Republican leaders in Congress, which meant not merely shutting the minority Democrats out of the lawmaking process but also regularly marginalizing the views and roles of rank-and-file Republicans, moderates, and staunch conservatives alike in order to advance the president's program.

It led them to radically expand the use of earmarks so they might have chits to use to reward the compliant and punish the stubborn among them, while losing control over the federal purse-strings for a large share of discretionary spending. It led to a regular process of inserting significant policy changes stealthily into omnibus bills and conference reports that would not likely pass if conducted by the usual, open process—offending Republicans, as well as Democrats, when their handiwork was belatedly discovered. But for several years, the techniques worked well enough that Republicans were able to pass most of their party's legislative agenda, gain seats in successive elections, and help their president win reelection against the odds.

Holding the reins of power is a heady experience. Having them work, as Republicans believed they had in the late 1990s and through the first Bush term, led as well to an "anything goes" atmosphere in Washington. The desire to hold power and advance their ideological vision required a formidable political machine, one greased by money, staffed by loyalists in lobbying shops, and unabashedly adept at smash-mouth politics. Highlights—or lowlights—included the unprecedented re-redistricting effort in Texas in 2002, which after strenuous efforts that shattered any remaining bipartisanship in the state resulted in an election triumph for the GOP and then subsequently to the indictment of Tom DeLay and two of his cronies. The anything-goes atmosphere also led to the rise and fall of Jack Abramoff, whose multiple scandals, most playing off his access to Tom DeLay and other influential Republicans in Congress, along with players in the White House, the Interior Department, and such outside groups as Americans for Tax Reform, threatened to mushroom into the biggest corruption scandal in Washington in 125 years. By spring 2006, with Abramoff and several of his cronies copping pleas and turning on others, the situation was on the verge of doing just that.

As we have documented in earlier chapters, the problems that make this Congress sharply different from past ones and clearly, in our view, a broken branch, are manifold. They include a loss of institutional identity, an abdication of institutional responsibility vis-à-vis the executive, the demise of regular order (in committee, on the floor, and in conference), and the consequent deterioration of the deliberative process—the signature comparative advantage of Congress as a legislative body.

Current members of Congress simply do not identify strongly as members of the first branch of government. Whether they place their ideology or partisan identity first, too many members of Congress now think little if at all about their primary role and responsibilities as members of the legislative branch. This is reflected in the Tuesday to Thursday schedule that prevents adequate time for sustained lawmaking and oversight; a tolerance of extraordinary measures, such as the nuclear option on judicial confirmations, that undermine institutional health for short-term political gains; and an unwillingness to meet their constitutional responsibility to police the conduct of members of Congress with a strong and independent ethics process.

The arrival of unified Republican government in 2001 transformed the aggressive and active GOP-led Congress of the Clinton years into a deferential and supine body, one extremely reluctant to demand information, scrub presidential proposals, or oversee the executive. The uncompromising assertion of executive authority by President Bush and Vice President Cheney was met with a whimper, not a principled fight, by the Republican Congress.

It is ironic that the methods used by the passive legislative branch to achieve the presidential goals were themselves super-aggressive, abrasive, and over-the-line. Regular order in a legislature—produced by an elaborate set of rules, precedents, and norms governing the conduct of business in committee, on the floor, and in conference—is designed to facilitate orderly and deliberate policy making, ensure fairness, and maintain the legitimacy of Congress and the constitutional system. Majorities are always tempted to dispense with regular order to advance their immediate policy and political objectives. Democrats were not reluctant to do so during their long rein in power, especially in the latter years. But Republicans have far exceeded Democratic abuses of power. Committees have been marginalized in myriad ways, from central party direction to ad hoc groups to omnibus bills. Floor debate and decision making is tightly controlled with restrictive rules and extended time for roll-call votes. Conferences to reconcile differences between the House and Senate are now the setting for breathtaking abuses: minority party members excluded from negotiations, entirely new provisions added in the stealth of night, and routine waivers of time for members to learn what is contained in the reports they must vote on.

These practices have produced a measurable decline in the quantity and quality of deliberation. The essence of lawmaking in Congress is deliberation. The dictionary defines deliberate as: 1. To think carefully and often slowly, as about a choice to be made. 2. To consult with another or others in a process of reaching a decision. 3. To consider (a matter) carefully and often slowly, as by weighing alternatives. Congress was designed to be deliberative, through its checks and balances, its decentralized decision making in committees and subcommittees, its large membership, its emphasis on debate and give-and-take, and its openness to individuals and organized groups in the society, all of which allow it to take time, consider alternatives, consult widely, discuss, negotiate, and compromise. Yet it is hard to look at the contemporary Congress and see deliberation as a core value in these terms.

Consequences

We believe these developments have serious consequences for policy and governance. The absence of institutional regard among its leaders diminishes Congress in the constitutional scheme and encourages more unilateral and less responsible behavior in the executive. The failure of Congress to insist on more information from the executive translates into less effective congressional oversight of such crucially important matters as the war in Iraq and homeland security. The suspension of regular order in Congress creates greater opportunities for parochial, special interest provisions to be added to legislation out of public view and for poorly constructed laws to get enacted without being properly vetted and corrected. The failure to discern and make explicit the true costs of important policy initiatives—from tax cuts to Medicare prescription drugs to the war in Iraq—make it impossible for a realistic cost-benefit analysis to enter the calculus before they are approved. And the sharply partisan strategies and tactics embraced by this unified Republican government further poison the tone of public discourse.

Manifestations of these maladies are littered throughout the record of the last several Congresses. We have described the absence of genuine deliberation, the shamefully deceptive cost accounting, and the special interest payoffs associated with the successful effort to add a prescription drug benefit to Medicare. The projected long-term costs of the law are staggering, dwarfing the projected shortfall in Social Security. The cost is not the only issue: as the law was implemented, liberal and conservative critics alike criticized its structure, complexity, and policy gaps.

The unprecedented intervention by Congress in the Terri Schiavo end-of-life care controversy—in which the Republican leadership moved rapidly, without the benefit of hearings, much less deliberation in committee or on the floor, to try to compel the federal courts to overrule Florida courts and initiate a *de novo* consideration of the case—was rejected by the judiciary and, with the exception of conservative activists, widely panned by the public. The energy bill that finally cleared Congress in the summer of 2005 manages to distribute generous public subsidies to producers—some large and transparent, others small and privately targeted to beneficiaries—without addressing in any serious way the need to reduce consumption of fossil fuels or expand alternative sources of energy. The highway bill enacted that same season uses chicanery and legerdemain to stay within striking distance of the president's bottom-line number. Its authors simply added $10 billion to the authorization while at the same time pretending to take that amount away.[1]

The highway bill became especially notorious because of its outrageous laundry list of earmarks, including especially the "bridge to nowhere," a $223 million allocation for a bridge from a town of 14,000 in Alaska to an island with a population of fifty. After a major and sustained public outcry, Congress with great fanfare announced it was rescinding its funding for the bridge to nowhere, but in the fine print of the announcement, it was clear that not a dime was being rescinded; Alaska was set to receive the same exact sum in federal dollars, with the state able to set its own priorities. And state officials made it clear that the bridge would be on that list of priorities.[2]

The costs of doing business in the contemporary Congress for policy and governance are vividly illustrated in the two most ambitious and fateful initiatives of the Bush administration—the 2001 tax cuts and the war in Iraq.

2001 Tax Cuts

Set aside for the moment differences of opinion over the economic consequences of tax increases and tax cuts (illustrated by the contrasting policies of Clinton and Bush), the changing rationale for tax cuts (long-term investment and growth, budget surpluses—"the people's money"—that ought to be returned to the people, short-term stimulus in the face of an economic slowdown), and the legitimacy of sharp distributional effects of tax cuts. Whatever one's ideological disposition on these matters, there is no avoiding the conclusion that this bill was enacted in a recklessly dishonest fashion and was itself a dishonest product.

Gimmicks of one sort or another have long been used by legislators to get around complying with their own targets.

For example, shifting back or forward by one day (out of the budget window) a month's worth of spending or tax cuts can provide instant relief to the budget bottom line but does nothing to cut spending or increase revenues. But in 2001, Congress with the encouragement of President Bush set a new standard for accounting chicanery. As longtime budget analyst Robert Greenstein commented then: "None of us can remember any major budget or tax bill in recent history that comes close to this bill in the magnitude of budget gimmicks included."[3] Even many of those sympathetic with the president's tax proposals, such as Clive Crook of the *National Journal,* were appalled by the final product: "The tax bill is scandalously bad. It's filled with a whole series of outright frauds and outrageous lies."[4]

If the congressional budget resolution adopted by both House and Senate was to be believed, the president's proposal to cut taxes by $1.6 trillion over the following ten years was reduced to $1.35 trillion, a $100 billion economic stimulus in the immediate year (FY2001) and $1.25 trillion in the following decade. Yet by the time the architects of the conference report on the tax bills writing these targets into law were through, a more realistic accounting of costs to the Treasury put the figure at $1.8 trillion in the first decade and $4.1 trillion in the second.[5]

What tricks were up their sleeves? Sunset all of the tax-cut provisions a year before the end of the ten-year budget window. Phase in some of the cuts over the course of the decade; phase out other popular cuts after several years; and avoid a long-term or permanent fix for the Alternative Minimum Tax, which was initially created to prevent wealthy taxpayers from avoiding their obligations through loopholes and deductions but expected, with the other tax cut provisions, to affect 35.5 million households by 2010. Then plow these "savings" back into additional tax cuts.

The sunset provisions, combined with the late phase-ins of some of the other cuts, make for very peculiar hypotheticals. One of the most bizarre is the situation confronting wealthy estate-bearers at the end of 2010: The legislation calls for the gradual decrease and repeal of the estate tax by 2010, yet it reverts to its 2000 levels in 2011. As Paul Krugman writes: "So in the law as now written, heirs to great wealth face the following situation: If your ailing mother passes away on Dec. 31, 2010, you inherit her estate tax-free. But if she makes it to Jan. 1, 2011, half the estate will be taxed away. That creates some interesting incentives. Maybe they should have called it the Throw Momma From the Train Act of 2001."[6]

The tax cuts, combined with the economic downturn and willful congressional decisions to sharply increase spending, turned a projected $3.5 trillion surplus over the next decade into a deficit of equivalent size. Revenues dropped to 16 percent of GDP, the lowest in a half century—since before the establishment of Medicare and Medicaid. More ominously, the pressure to extend or make permanent the tax cuts that are included in the bill, even as the same Congress presides over the most rapid acceleration in federal spending in history, promises to accelerate our fiscal imbalance at the very time the retirement of the Baby-Boom generation will put great strain on our retirement and health insurance programs. The Republicans in Congress were delighted to let lapse the pay-as-you-go rules enacted during the 1990 budget compromise, which forced every budget increase or tax cut to be offset, despite the fact that they had brought about impressive fiscal discipline that had contributed mightily to the surpluses of the late 1990s. Dishonest and irresponsible is precisely the way in which this political victory should be characterized. Just as bad was the impact the structure of this tax cut had on future policies. It led to a series of additional diversionary debates over extending the tax-cut provisions with artificial deadlines that took attention away from the needed debates over fiscal policy, including what kinds of tax revenues and what broad tax policy ought to be pursued into the twenty-first century.

War in Iraq

If the damage done to fiscal policy by Congress was an act of commission, its role in approving and overseeing the war and reconstruction in Iraq is best viewed as a failure of omission. No decision made by democratic societies is as weighty as that dealing with war; this is especially true when the war in question is not a response to an attack or an imminent threat of attack on the United States or its citizens and interests abroad. Although the Constitution gives Congress the power to declare war, presidents have launched dozens of military operations without such a declaration and largely on their own initiative. In recent decades, presidents typically declare they have full authority to act on their own but then seek congressional authorization short of a declaration of war without committing in advance to be bound by Congress. The War Powers Resolution, passed over President Nixon's veto in 1973, while successfully imposing some formal communications and notifications between the branches, has failed to elevate Congress to a position of a genuine partner to the president in decisions to use military force.

By several accounts, George W. Bush decided shortly after the attacks of September 11 to depose Saddam Hussein's regime. After Taliban forces were routed in Afghanistan, planning for Iraq began in earnest. The case for military action varied over time, but alleged Iraqi links to al Qaeda and September 11 and the threat from Iraqi weapons of mass destruction were cited most frequently by the president and vice president in the long run-up to the war. They both firmly believed in the conditions and the case. But the hard evidence on both was sketchy; in retrospect, neither proved accurate.[7]

Members of Congress complained frequently during 2002 about the inadequacy of information on the threat from Iraq that was provided by the administration to Congress. Senator John McCain, a strong supporter of military action against Iraq, called the "top secret" briefings provided to Congress "a joke."[8] Concerns were expressed by individual senators and representatives from both parties about the imminence of the threat, the size and composition of the forces necessary to depose Saddam and to secure the peace, the likely costs of the war and its aftermath, planning for postwar security and reconstruction, and the impact of a war on attitudes toward the U.S. and on the recruitment pools for radical Islamic terrorists. But these were lonely voices in a sea of silence. Republican leaders in Congress emphasized the importance of supporting the president and discouraged systematic hearings by committees that might raise embarrassing questions. Democratic leaders Tom Daschle and Dick Gephardt cautiously supported the president, the former more reluctantly than the latter, and did relatively little to elevate to public attention the concerns being raised by their Democratic colleagues. The single oasis in the desert of congressional obeisance was the Senate Foreign Relations Committee, under the leadership of Joe Biden and Dick Lugar. They conducted a series of important and prescient hearings—raising precisely the kinds of difficult questions about the war and its aftermath that should be raised—that were largely ignored by the administration and their colleagues in Congress.

The fragility of the case for war against Iraq being made by the president came home to the two of us in a private Pentagon briefing in the summer of 2002 conducted by Secretary Donald Rumsfeld and Assistant Secretary for International Security Affairs J. D. Crouch II. The briefing was designed as a dry run for the unveiling on Capitol Hill, and for our allies and the American public, of a PowerPoint presentation that documented the threat from Iraq and other countries possessing weapons of mass destruction. About twenty Washington hands—some Republican and Democratic operatives, others, like ourselves, from think tanks— were invited to react to a declassified version of the presentation. The case was built around the nexus of terrorists, rogue states, and weapons of mass destruction. The aesthetics of the charts projected on the far wall of the Secretary's conference room left much to be desired. Uneven rows across several columns made it difficult to read. One Republican wag quipped: "It looks like it was designed by the Palm Beach County Elections Board."

The virtually unanimous reaction of our group, which leaned strongly in support of military action, was that the presentation diminished rather than elevated the threat from Iraq relative to other countries. North Korea and Iran, at least, qualified by the stated criteria as higher-priority targets. The Secretary did not take these reactions well. A vigorous discussion ensued, touching on the prevalence or absence of terrorists and WMD in Iraq and on the efficacy of continued strategies of containment and deterrence of Iraq. But this was seen as ideological crossfire by Pentagon officials, not as an opportunity to profit from the perspectives of others, many of whom were naturally sympathetic to them.

Congress received no more compelling information from the administration but did little to remedy that situation. Once President Bush decided on a course of action—to appear before the United Nations and to seek an authorization from Congress before the 2002 election—he largely dictated terms of the engagement. A National Intelligence Estimate on the threat of WMD was belatedly made available to Congress only after Senate Intelligence Committee chair Bob Graham of Florida demanded it from the CIA, but there is no sign that more than a handful of its members read it and pursued the conflicting evidence contained in it.[9]

The outcome of the congressional vote was never in doubt. Congress made minor revisions in the resolution submitted by the president that proved of little consequence. The concerns expressed by Biden and Lugar were further marginalized when Gephardt cut his own deal with the president in support of the war. The debate was desultory— a far cry from what had ensued in the House and Senate a decade earlier on the eve of the first Gulf War. The president won authorization to take unilateral action, if necessary, against Iraq, without being forced to confront in advance the critical questions surrounding how to win the peace. Neither armed services committee pursued questions of force size, post-invasion plans, or the role of reserves and National Guard. Months and years after the passage of the resolution, Congress continued to play an episodic and inadequate role in overseeing the planning for and conduct of the Iraq campaign. Not until the fall of 2005, after the public had clearly soured on the war, did Congress begin to seriously engage the issue and challenge the president. We can't help wondering whether some of the disastrous consequences in Iraq after Saddam's regime fell might have been avoided if Congress had done its job.

Roots of the Problem

It is not unreasonable to ask whether these patterns of dysfunctional behavior in Congress are natural and understandable if not inevitable responses to powerful forces in its political and social environment. American democracy has been deeply affected by the rise of the most partisan era since the late nineteenth and early twentieth centuries. This is an era characterized by strong and ideologically polarized parties competing from positions of rough parity. These features of the party system are evident among elected officials in government and in the electorate. They are reinforced and strengthened by teams of aligned activists, interest groups, community organizations, and media outlets. Competition for control of the White House and Congress is intense, but it is waged on an increasingly restrictive playing field. Fewer states are up for grabs in presidential elections and the number of competitive contests for the Senate and especially for the House has dropped markedly. This environment encourages an intense struggle for control of government and an unabashed manipulation of electoral and governing institutions to achieve one's political and policy goals.

The roots of this distinctly partisan era are deep and complex. Fissures in the New Deal coalition of the Democratic Party were evident in the 1960s, with the rise of the counterculture and opposition to the war in Vietnam. The 1964 Goldwater campaign initiated a long-term struggle among party activists to develop a more distinctly conservative Republican agenda. The passage of the Voting Rights Act in 1965 and the economic development of the South broke up the uneasy coalition between blacks and conservative whites that had allowed Democrats to dominate the region for many decades and eventually led to a safe Republican South. The Supreme Court's 1973 abortion decision in *Roe v. Wade* prompted a pro-life movement that years later would form the core of the Republican Party's largest and most reliable constituency—the religious conservatives. California's tax-limiting Proposition 13 and the emergence of its governor, Ronald Reagan, on the national political scene lent the Republican Party a more distinctive economic platform. President Reagan's robust challenge to the Soviet Union added national security to the set of new issues dividing the parties.

As these developments played out over time, party platforms grew more distinctive, those recruited to Congress became more ideologically in tune with their fellow partisans, and voters increasingly sorted themselves into the two parties based on their ideological views. At the same time, voters were making residential decisions that reinforced the ideological sorting already under way. Citizens were drawn to neighborhoods, counties, and states where others shared their values and interests. This ideological sorting and geographical mobility produced many areas dominated by one party or the other, which diminished electoral competition and increased partisan polarization among elected officials. Both bipartisan and partisan gerrymanders contributed further to these effects. And they were reinforced by interest groups that increasingly aligned themselves with one party or the other and radio and cable news and talks shows that pitched to distinctive partisan and ideological audiences.

These developments in the social and political environment facilitated the actions within Congress that are chronicled in this book and that led to a broken branch. But politicians are not merely waifs amid forces. They make choices about how to organize and run their institution and how to conduct themselves personally, albeit choices constrained by the external environment and the incentives it creates. In recent decades, leaders and members of Congress acted in ways that exacerbated the partisan polarization and intensified the forces leading to institutional decline. They are not powerless to take steps that might begin to reverse these disturbing trends.

What Is To Be Done?

We wish we could now turn and provide a solid blueprint for recovery, a set of steps that would directly and clearly mend the broken branch and restore Congress to what it should be and at times has been. Unfortunately, there is no quick fix for a dysfunctional institution. Our analysis of the features and roots of the current partisan era confirms just how much Congress is a captive of its political and social environment. It also counsels against an overreliance on remedies that appear to treat symptoms rather than causes, such as reforms aimed at blocking the corruption of Randy "Duke" Cunningham or Jack Abramoff without treating the broader systemic problems that have created the climate in which a Cunningham and Abramoff could operate.

In chapter 2, we discussed the powerful role electoral forces played in shaping the internal organization of Congress between 1890 and 1912. As the parties came to represent distinctive constituencies—industrial interests by the Republicans, Southern, agricultural, rural interests by the Democrats—they became more internally unified and ideologically polarized.[10] That set the stage for a centralization of power within the House and, to a somewhat lesser extent, the Senate. Party leaders came to dominate committees in a fashion not dissimilar to the current situation. The rise of the Progressives within the majority Republican Party, encouraged by the presidency of Theodore Roosevelt, attenuated those constituency differences, creating divisions within the party that left a significant number of Republicans in both chambers unwilling to cede authority to their party leaders. The successful revolt against Speaker Cannon, engineered by a coalition of Democrats and progressive Republicans, eventually led to a decentralization of power, the establishment of the seniority system, and the elevation of committees relative to parties in the power structure of both the House and Senate.

The lesson for our purposes is that major change within Congress is most likely to originate outside. Citizens at the polls are the most powerful agents of change. But their actions can be shaped by leaders intent on shaking up the existing party system. Progressive reformers Teddy Roosevelt and Robert LaFollette of Wisconsin played critical roles in the early twentieth century in diversifying interests within the Republican Party and destroying the unity that made dominant and over-weaning congressional party leadership possible.

Might such forces be gathering in our politics today? The turbulent political waters encountered by President Bush in 2005 and 2006, the first years of his second term, suggest just that possibility. An increasingly unpopular war in Iraq, high energy prices, and an initially diffident and clearly inept response to Hurricane Katrina contributed to a precipitous decline in public support for the president. Nervous Republicans on Capitol Hill are less willing to lend automatic support to their president or party leaders in Congress. Long-submerged policy differences began to surface, making strictly partisan governing strategies increasingly untenable. While still in the minority, Democrats in late 2005 remained remarkably unified, unwilling to enter into negotiations they believe would be entirely self-defeating. Were they to return to the majority as a result of the 2006 midterm election, the political logic of divided government might well produce some reduction in partisan rancor and at least occasional cross-party policy agreement—although it would be difficult because any sizable Democratic Party gains would come at least in part at the expense of the remaining few Republican moderates. Moreover, our recent experiences with divided government, including a brief period in 2001–2002 during the Bush first term, after Senator James

Jeffords of Vermont switched from Republican to Independent status and changed the Senate's majority, and during the last six Clinton years, show at best a mixed bag in terms of constructive engagement between the branches. Much of the oversight done by a Republican Congress over a Democratic president was focused on alleged scandals and not on policy administration; much of the dynamic of the Bush presidency–Democratic Senate period was partisan and posturing rather than serious governance.

Still, major electoral setbacks for the Republicans, if seen as a reaction to the consequences of its agenda, might trim the party's ideological sails and diminish the degree of polarization, while giving Democrats the self-confidence and incentive to work for policy change. One might also imagine steps taken by candidates in one or both parties in the wide-open 2008 presidential sweepstakes that would ease rather than exacerbate the partisan divide. While the current presidential nominating system tends to elevate the importance of each party's core constituencies and true believers, the desire to hold or capture the White House introduces a certain level of pragmatism into the system. On the Democratic side, there are already signs of the party trying to deescalate the religious/culture wars by appealing directly to mainstream sentiment on abortion and other potentially explosive social issues. Democrats might also find that the setbacks in Iraq and the return of huge budget deficits under Republican government offer them opportunities to challenge the national security and tax-cutting policies of the GOP in ways that reduce the ideological distance between the parties.

As for the Republicans, a presidential candidate might emerge in TR-fashion to try to build a political center where none now exists. The appeal of Senator John McCain among independents and Democrats, in spite of his conservative views on many social and economic issues and his hawkish posture on national security, suggests how a candidate might fill a vacuum in the political market and scramble the coalitional bases of the parties while also building a coalition in Congress that would cut across party lines. McCain's unique appeal aside, the reality is that presidential leadership, far more than any other kind, has the potential to alter the dynamic of institutional behavior and decision making in American politics and governance. A different style of leadership, one more inclusive, less partisan, and less divisive than we have seen in recent years, could make a significant difference.

These examples hint at ways in which the current system might generate changes in the political system that eventually reverberate in the halls of Congress. But we cannot simply wait and hope for these changes to occur. We must also push for broad changes in the electoral system that encourage movement toward less ideological polarization and partisan tension. Competitive districts and states tend to produce more moderate elected officials, ones less driven by ideological agendas and more inclined to listen to voters and groups on both sides of the partisan divide. Increasing the level of electoral competition is a worthy objective for those who want to mend the broken branch.

We understand full well that achieving that objective is no simple task. Convincing the national party committees to spread their resources to a larger number of contests, instead of concentrating as they do now on a few states and congressional districts, would help. So too would any changes in campaign finance law that steer resources to challengers. Free air time, incentives for small donors, subsidized voter brochures, other forms of public financing and more permissive contribution limits for start-up funds are a few ideas worthy of consideration. But near the top of the list has to be dealing with the problem of gerrymandering.

Redistricting is not the only or even the major cause of the ideological polarization and partisan tension that have beset Congress. One need only look back at the last partisan era, when redistricting was not a significant factor, or to the contemporary Senate, whose ideological and partisan patterns mirror those of the House, to realize that other, more powerful forces are at work. In recent years, scholars have demonstrated that bipartisan gerrymanders in individual states with divided party control have protected incumbents and diminished competition. They have also documented how some states under unified party control have shaped partisan gerrymanders that severely distort the relationship between votes and seats.[11] But the net national effects of these gerrymanders are relatively modest.[12] For example, most of the decline in the number of competitive House districts has occurred outside the window of redistricting after each decennial census. Ideological sorting and geographical mobility have created enclaves of like-minded voters that dampen political competition and encourage politicians to operate at their ideological poles.

Nonetheless, redistricting makes a difficult situation considerably worse. Lawmakers have become more insular and more attentive to their ideological bases as their districts have become more partisan and homogeneous. Districts have become more like echo chambers, reinforcing members' ideological predispositions with fewer dissenting voices back home or fewer disparate groups of constituents to consider in representation. The impact shows in their behavior; and reform of the way in which legislative boundaries are redrawn would make a difference.

Over the past forty years, the Supreme Court has focused almost exclusively on equal population and racial gerrymandering in its constitutional and statutory review of legislative redistricting. Indeed, the Court's almost monomaniacal insistence on exact mathematical equality in the population of congressional districts within states has inspired more mischief in line-drawing than good. While the Court has said that partisan gerrymandering in theory can be unconstitutional, it has in the past set the standard for such a violation so high as to render it meaningless.

The Court's willingness in early 2006 to reconsider the Texas mid-decade redistricting case created a slight hope that it would provide a vehicle to set one or more standards for identifying unconstitutional political gerrymandering. Whatever the Court does, hope for serious change in the way districts are redrawn has to focus on the states. The most promising idea, drawing on the experience of a small set of states such as Arizona and Washington, is to transfer redistricting authority to an independent commission operating under a number of explicit standards and guidelines.[13] Building competition and partisan fairness into the mix should increase the number of competitive districts and prevent majority parties from manipulating the rules of the game to perpetuate their hold on power. And even a modest increase in competition could help the system reach a tipping point that sets in motion a very different dynamic.

To be sure, the road to reform is plagued by potholes and dangerous twists and turns—as the defeats in 2005 of the Ohio and California initiatives to establish independent redistricting commissions demonstrate. Careful craftsmanship and public education and mobilization are essential. But this is an idea well worth pursuing in a number of states and in as many forums as possible.

We also need serious institutional reforms inside Congress to respond to the systemic corruption and to improve both process and climate. From our vantage point after decades in the reform trenches, we are more aware than most of the limits of reform. No package of reforms will force lawmakers to develop a strong sense of institutional identity and loyalty, to strengthen an empty ethics process, to open up the policy process for serious deliberation, or to develop a new fealty to the regular order. Reforms will not eliminate arrogance, greed, insensitivity, or impropriety.

If a few leaders believe that they can swing the vote for just about anything, they will be sorely tempted to use the tools available to them to do so, and not only in areas which are sharply divided by party or ideology, or areas of top priority to the party in power. Restrictive rules cannot and should not be banned; they are a vital tool that enables a majority to work its will in the House. Strong parties have an important and constructive role to play in the legislative process. But Rules Committee chairmen and their bosses in the leadership, if they are not rebuffed, will exhibit no restraint and instead will use them routinely just because they can and not only when it is absolutely necessary. Members will try to make lobbying firms hire their own and fire the other side's people as long as they can get away with it—and especially so long as the watchdogs out there in the press pay little sustained attention to their shenanigans. Most importantly, as long as there is an "anything goes" atmosphere that envelops the legislative process, it will almost inevitably bleed over into an "anything goes" atmosphere when it comes to wheeling and dealing and individual corruption.

A sense of fair play, of balanced rules that cover everybody, and of concern for the very integrity of the institution would go a long way toward restoring confidence in the First Branch. And there are changes that could minimize mischief and bad behavior and the opportunities for it, and help restore some sense of a viable, even vibrant legislative branch. Some are fairly simple, internal alterations. For example, Congress should adopt a new schedule, going two weeks on and two weeks off, with the two weeks on beginning early Monday morning and going to late Friday afternoon—in other words, a typical work week and not the Tuesday late afternoon to Thursday early afternoon schedule that has become the norm. (An alternative would be to make at least twenty-six weeks a year five-day weeks in Washington.) That kind of schedule change may sound trivial—it is not. If members were at the Capitol for extended periods, including, most likely, the weekends in between the "on" weeks—they would interact with each other more frequently and more directly, including across party lines, developing interpersonal relationships that are now often nonexistent. Weekends spent in Washington would include more socialization with colleagues and their families and build the kinds of links that used to be commonplace and now are not. It might even encourage more members to bring their families to Washington, adding to the stability of legislating.

Full weeks spent in Washington would provide Congress with more opportunities to do extended legislating—more time to have real debate or discussion on the floor, more time to consider omnibus bills, more opportunities to do real hearings and real markups. Schedule changes should be combined with rules changes that would enforce deliberation and restore regular order. Every bill should have a period of at least twenty-four hours, but preferably three days, from the time it is reported to the time it is debated on the floor, so that lawmakers know what they are voting on. No vote in the House should last more than twenty minutes unless both party leaders or both party floor managers consent. Conference committees should not exclude any conference members; nor should they be able to include provisions never considered in either house, eliminate provisions included in identical form by both houses, or add provisions after conferees have signed off on the final product. Pernicious and pervasive earmarks should be curtailed, with every lawmaker required to disclose when he or she had a direct interest, financial and otherwise, in the contracts or projects steered to his or her district or state, and parliamentary options made available for striking individual earmarks from bills on the House and Senate floors.

These commonsense recommendations are a part of a package suggested in December 2005 by four House Democrats— David Obey, Barney Frank, David Price, and Tom Allen—that we helped construct, with the objective of making them part of a bipartisan coalition for constructive reform.

These four, along with Rahm Emanuel and Marty Meehan, Russ Feingold, Barack Obama, Chris Shays, Joel Hefley, and other lawmakers in the House and Senate, also turned their focus to lobbying and ethics reform. Shays and Senator John McCain expanded the coalition for reform in these areas by introducing a major bill at the end of 2005 to address the abuses uncovered by the Abramoff scandal. The McCain-Shays bill focused appropriately on disclosure; it greatly expanded public disclosure by lobbyists of all varieties and broadened the definition of lobbyists and lobbying to include, for example, grassroots activities. Their bill also put a special focus on trips for members and staff who were financed either directly or indirectly by lobbyists and/or were accompanied by lobbyists.

Not surprisingly, when it became clear that the Abramoff scandal was going to extend to many members of Congress, the number of reform plans dramatically increased, as did their authors, some of whom included Senate Democrats and, for the first time, such leaders as Pennsylvania Senator Rick Santorum and House Rules Chair David Dreier, who had been designated as point men respectively by Majority Leader Bill Frist and Speaker Dennis Hastert. The House Republicans quickly embraced and enacted a proposal to deny former members access to the House or Senate floors and to the House gym. But an early pronouncement by Speaker Hastert that called for a total ban on privately financed travel by lawmakers met stiff resistance from many of his rank-and-file members, among them John Boehner, then-candidate for majority leader who was subsequently elected to the post—a sign that the rhetorical call for reform would result in legislative action only if public pressure intensified.

By the time we both testified in front of the House Rules Committee about reform in March 2006, the signs of resistance to serious change were palpable. The Senate Rules Committee reported out a bill that included several watered-down proposals: one for a point of order on the Senate floor to challenge individual earmarks added in conference, with sixty senators then required to keep the earmarks in the bill; and another for a ban on all gifts from lobbyists except meals. But proposals that would require lawmakers to pay full value when using private jets for travel and to put a two-year moratorium on lobbying for ex-senators were both rejected, largely along party lines.

A plan proposed in the Senate Governmental Affairs Committee to create an independent Office of Public Integrity was rejected in that committee in an 11 to 5 vote and then in the Senate by a comparable margin, although the two-year moratorium was recommended as well as the expansion of lobbyist disclosure to include quarterly reports and grassroots lobbying activities. But that proposal, too, failed to deal effectively with such problems as lobbyist campaign contributions, private jet travel, or the gigantic loophole in the law, set in the separate laws regulating campaign finance, that would enable a lobbyist to continue to provide lavish meals or trips to lawmakers as long as they were accompanied by a campaign contribution or a campaign fund raiser.

Our testimony called for much more significant change. Mann laid out the problems made clear by the contemporary scandal:

> The Abramoff case is appalling in many dimensions, not least the brazenness and financial ambitions of the man and his close associates. From the perspective of those looking for appropriate reforms, I would point to his cultivation and recruitment for well-paid lobbying positions of staff in key congressional offices; the market among some members and staff for privately financed, first-class travel with tenuous connections to official responsibilities or public policy education; the reality that the abuses of Abramoff—and Cunningham—were initially detected by journalists in spite of, not thanks to the official reporting and disclosure systems; and the fact some private groups and individuals apparently believe that hiring well-connected lobbyists and showering campaign and other funds on members of Congress as directed by those lobbyists is essential to protecting or advancing their interests. These lessons suggest dealing more effectively with the revolving door (for members and staff); ensuring that privately financed travel is legitimate and consistent with chamber rules and guidelines; setting up more effective reporting and disclosure systems; and reducing the opportunities available to members to deliver—or appear to deliver—special benefits for narrow interests.

Ornstein noted:

> The problem goes beyond corrupt lobbyists or the relationship between lobbyists and lawmakers. It gets to a legislative process that has lost the transparency, accountability, and deliberation that are at the core of the American system; the failure to abide by basic rules and norms has contributed, I believe, to a loss of sensitivity among many members and leaders about

what is and is not appropriate. Three-hour votes, thousand-page-plus bills sprung on the floor with no notice, conference reports changed in the dead of night, self-executing rules that suppress debate along with an explosion of closed rules, are just a few of the practices that have become common and that are a distortion of the regular order. They should become a thing of the past.

Both of us emphasized a fundamental reality: no lobbying reforms would mean anything unless they were accompanied by real enforcement provisions, including a reiteration of our longtime call for an independent, outside role in ethics adjudication consistent with Congress's constitutional requirements.

We explored the two main ideas in front of Congress: One was the creation of an Office of Public Integrity, an idea that had been endorsed by several reform groups, embodied in a bill introduced by Reps. Chris Shays and Marty Meehan, and proposed by Senators Susan Collins and Joe Lieberman in the Senate Governmental Affairs Committee only to be rejected. The second, embodied in a bill introduced by Senator Barack Obama, called for the creation of an independent commission, which would include some former members and that would screen complaints, handle initial ethics investigations, and process and audit lobby disclosure forms.

The idea of a chief officer for public integrity was drawn from the experience of the British; the idea of an independent commission was drawn from the successful experience of several states, such as Florida and Kentucky. In our testimony, we noted that these are not mutually exclusive ideas. In fact, the British have a distinguished outside commission that oversees its head of public integrity.

The best idea, we said, was to blend the two approaches: to establish an office with a robust permanent professional staff that would keep and disclose lobbyists' reports as well as proactively educate members and staff on the rules and permissible behavior; and to designate a chief ethics officer whose role and independence would be akin to that of the comptroller general. But we also recommended that an outside commission—composed of members of impeccable integrity, such as former legislators Lee Hamilton, John Porter, and Nancy Kassebaum Baker—oversee the office and make the preliminary tough decisions about whether or not to pursue complaints against individual lawmakers. Then, should the commission recommend further action, the ethics committees would follow up with an investigation, after which the House and Senate would make the final judgments—as the Constitution requires.

The tendency in Congress and in the press is to think of lobbyists as victimizers and lawmakers as victims. We know, however, that the opposite is often true. The lawmakers themselves, in the zeal to raise ever-increasing bundles of campaign cash, regularly shake down lobbyists for money, using even more brazen threats to demand that the lobbyists contribute personal and PAC funds to their fund raisers. Some have suggested barring members from raising money outside their districts or banning fund raising between January and June every year, as some state legislatures do, to provide some breathing space for lawmaking without the crushing demands and corrupting atmosphere of fundraising. The latter idea has some real appeal, but it could likely only be done as an ethics matter, not as a law, and would thus leave challengers unfettered during those restricted times. We can live with that; can lawmakers?

Two other ideas on campaign money merit strong support. One is to ban so-called leadership PACS. When the House Appropriations Committee chairmanship was up for grabs at the beginning of the 109th Congress, there were three contenders for the throne, all longtime, solid legislators: Reps. Ralph Regula (R-OH), Hal Rogers (R-KY), and Jerry Lewis (R-CA). But it was clear that the choice was going to be made not solely, or even primarily, on the basis of legislative acumen or leadership skills, nor even by ideology. Rather, the ante to get into the race itself was to raise a ton of money for "the team."[14]

We watched them scramble to raise hundreds of thousands of dollars, turning to everyone they knew and everyone with any business before the committee. It was wrenching. Subsequently, news reports suggested that the winner, Jerry Lewis, altered his view on a defense program soon after attending a fund raiser for his leadership PAC run by an investment firm in New York that benefited handsomely from the policy change.[15]

It is a fact of life; watch any leadership race, for a party post or for a committee or subcommittee gavel, and it has become clear that setting up and exploiting a leadership PAC is now a necessity in both parties. It fuels the party polarization in Congress. And it intensifies the phenomenon that lobbyists have reported privately for years—that they are more and more often pressured by members and their aides for money.

A core part of the K Street Project was to create a loop in which former lawmakers and staffers would be placed in lucrative lobbying posts that paid two to ten times what they earned on Capitol Hill, with the understanding that they would reciprocate by maxing out on contributions to the party and its candidates as well as to the leadership PACs of major lawmakers. The shakedown did not begin with Republicans and has not been confined to them, but of course it is more often a majority-party phenomenon. It is wrong. We need to ban or sharply restrict leadership PACs.

It is time as well to find a more direct means to stop the shakedowns. It is probably not constitutional to ban a class of citizens, such as lobbyists, from contributing to congressional campaigns. But we believe that it is possible to enact a rule that makes it a violation of House and Senate ethics for a member to solicit or accept a contribution from a lobbyist with business before the body.

Still, we must face the reality that even if we could get the procedural, ethics, and electoral reforms through just as we would draft them, and even if we could include serious reform of the committee structure and of the budget process, it would not change Congress dramatically unless and until the leaders of Congress change their approach to governance.

The current leaders of Congress have no interest in change—unless change is forced upon them or they are replaced. The way in which issues, personalities, politics, and policy outcomes were coming together early in 2006 suggested that both may occur. Fitting with the typical pattern of second-term presidents, majority members of Congress, including party leaders, have shown less interest in being loyal to the president since he became a lame duck, and even less interest after his approval rating dropped below 40 percent.

In addition, there were signs in late 2005 that rank-and-file members of both parties were becoming increasingly frustrated with their limited voice. Consider the Republican rebellion against its leadership in November 2005, when a combination of moderates and conservatives first forced the leaders in the House to pull their major budget reconciliation bill from action on the floor after they were unable to get within striking distance of 218 votes for it, and then contributed to the stunning defeat on the House floor of the massive Labor-HHS Appropriations bill, the first such setback in a decade.[16] Both were signals that business as usual would not work any more. To be sure, this was not a sign of incipient revolution. Eventually, after making multiple compromises, such as taking out the provision for drilling in ANWR (the Arctic National Wildlife Reserve), a streamlined budget bill did pass, even if it took the tie-breaking vote of the vice president in the Senate to do so.

But the first budget votes, and a successful filibuster in the Senate over the eleventh-hour attempt there to add the ANWR drilling provision to the Defense Appropriations bill, showed that unhappiness with the abuse of the regular order was becoming more palpable. After their success in removing drilling in ANWR from the budget bill in the House, the group of Republican moderates known as the Main Street Coalition were ebullient and vowed to act as a moderating force in the House more aggressively and more often. Also striking was the demand by many rank-and-file House Republicans for leadership elections in January 2006—even before Tom DeLay's permanent resignation from the majority leader post in the middle of the term, an unprecedented action and another sign of simmering discontent.

Still, the simmering discontent did not spill over into revolutionary action. Faced with three options for majority leader, House Republicans eschewed both the straight status quo and more dramatic change, embodied respectively by acting leader and whip Roy Blunt and maverick John Shadegg, and instead took the route of moderate change, choosing John Boehner. A member of the leadership during the early Gingrich years, Boehner had been supplanted in 1998 as Gingrich departed but kept his hand in the process through his chairmanship of the Education and the Workforce panel. Blunt stayed on as whip, as the Republican conference showed its reluctance to break with the past by declining to allow votes on the entire leadership slate from top to bottom.

Boehner ran as a reformer—reminding his colleagues that he had been an original member of the "Gang of Seven," those House Republicans in the minority who had dramatized the corruption of the majority and helped turn the House Bank issue into a major scandal. But his reformist zeal did not last long in the leadership campaign, and there were few signs by mid-2006 that the basic behavior of the Republican leadership team had shifted in any significant way.

Other signs suggested modest hopefulness in such areas as oversight. Some Republican members, for example, Virginia's Tom Davis, were outspoken in their belief that Congress needed to be more aggressive in its oversight activities. His committee issued a stinging report on the administration's handling of Katrina, even though Democrats had boycotted the investigation. When the revelation emerged that the president had circumvented the Foreign Intelligence Surveillance Act to tap into conversations of Americans and others suspected of terrorist links, many members of Congress expressed public outrage, including

Senator Arlen Specter, chairman of the Senate Judiciary Committee. He, and Democrats, vowed serious hearings to right the balance between the branches, while at the same time there was conspicuous silence from Republican congressional party leaders or, from some, a vigorous defense of unlimited presidential authority in wartime.

There have been signs as well that many members will toy with drastic changes in House or Senate rules and norms but will draw back as they approach the abyss. The nuclear option outcome is the best example; the ability of the "Gang of 14" in the Senate to get the body to pull back from the ill-considered threats of its Republican leader to trigger the so-called nuclear option shows that such lawmakers exist in sufficient numbers on both sides of the aisle, at least in the Senate. But once the idea of a unilateral change-by-majority of Senate rules on the floor is out in the discourse, it is hard to put it back in the bottle. Another confrontation, whether over a judicial nominee or on a high-priority bill, might well blow up Senate precedents and devastate the comity that has largely characterized the institution.

The way in which many Democrats are handling their criticism of the contemporary Congress is also encouraging. From the Nancy Pelosi–led Minority Bill of Rights to the Obey-Frank-Price-Allen initiative, out in public before the Abramoff plea led to the flurry of other proposals, these leaders began early to build their campaign to recapture the majority on a firm pledge to do business in a different and more equitable fashion. These reform proposals are constructive and fair-minded. But there is no assurance in this continuing hothouse of partisan enmity, closely divided allegiances, tribal politics, a disappearing center, and overall acrimony—none of which will magically disappear in the near future—that in the end they would be willing or able to follow that pledge. Democratic leaders swear they mean what they say. We believe them when they say it. But the Republican experience post-1994—including sincere promises made by the likes of Gerald Solomon and David Dreier—does not represent an encouraging precedent.

A Final Note

A contentious, partisan, name-calling Congress is nothing new in American politics; some historians might argue that it is the norm. House Democrats went ballistic in November 2005 after freshman Republican Jean Schmidt of Ohio called veteran Democrat John Murtha (D-PA) a coward on the House floor[17]—but that, after all, is not much compared to duels on the House floor in the early nineteenth century or a senator caned nearly to death on the Senate floor by a bitter House colleague in the middle of that century.

Still, the problems now are different and worrisome. The frontier atmosphere that characterized Congress through much of our early history occurred during a time when Congress convened almost part time and when the role of the federal government was much more limited. There was no mass mobilization, no mass media, no twenty-four-hour cable news. Now, Congress is much larger, more potent, and part of a federal government with remarkable scope and sweep. Each of its actions or inactions has more consequences. The decline in deliberation has resulted in shoddy and questionable policy—domestic and international. The unnecessarily partisan behavior of the House majority has poisoned the well enough to make any action to restrain the growth of entitlement programs and to restructure health care policy impossible and has badly strained the long tradition of bipartisanship on foreign policy at a particularly delicate time. The failure of both houses of Congress to do meaningful oversight contributed to the massive and unconscionable failures of the Department of Homeland Security and, after Hurricane Katrina, of its FEMA arm. The broken branch distresses us as long-time students of American democracy who believe Congress is the linchpin of our constitutional system. But the consequences go far beyond our sensibilities, resonating in ways that damage the country as a whole. Perhaps we can do little, as larger forces in society, driven by technological change, overwhelm any efforts to alter course. But we believe that individuals can make a difference, that every step must be taken and no stone unturned to try to mend the broken branch and restore the needed balance in our political system.

Notes

CHAPTER ONE

1. Robert Pear and Robin Toner, "A Final Push in Congress: The Overview," *New York Times*, Sunday, November 23, 2003.
2. "Night of House Drama Yields a Narrow Medicare Victory," *National Journal's Congress Daily*, Monday, November 24, 2003.
3. Jill Zuckman, "Medicare Bill Has Close Call," *Chicago Tribune*, Sunday, November 23, 2003.
4. Amy Fagen and Stephen Dinan, "Arm-Twisting Wins 202–215 Medicare Vote," *Washington Times*, Sunday, November 23, 2003, A1.
5. Janet Hook and Vicki Kemper, "A Long Night's Journey into Yes in the House," *Los Angeles Times*, Sunday, November 23, 2003.
6. As reported by Damon Chappie, "Justice Dept. to Review Allegations of Bribery," *Roll Call*, December 8, 2003.
7. As reported by R. Jeffrey Smith, "GOP's Pressing Question on a Medicare Vote; Did Some Go Too Far To Change a No to a Yes?" *Washington Post*, Tuesday, December 23, 2003, A1.
8. Ibid.
9. Edward Epstein, "Democrats Decry Republican Tactics in Marathon Vote," *San Francisco Chronicle*, Tuesday, December 9, 2003, A17.
10. Report of the Committee on Standards of Official Conduct, September 30, 2004, iii.

11. Norman Ornstein, "...And Mischief," *Washington Post,* Wednesday, November 26, 2003, A25.
12. Associated Press, Jim Abrams, "Civility Drops to a Low Point in Congress," in *Washington Post,* June 25, 2004.
13. Donald R. Wolfensberger, "The House Rules Committee Under Republican Majorities: Continuity and Change," paper prepared for the annual meeting of the Northeastern Political Science Association, 2002.
14. Barbara Sinclair, "The New World of U.S. Senators," in Lawrence C. Dodd and Bruce I. Oppenheimer, eds., *Congress Reconsidered*, 8th ed. (Washington, D.C.: CQ Press, 2005), 1–22.
15. See Nelson W. Polsby, "The Institutionalization of the U.S. House of Representatives, *American Political Science Review,* March 1968, 144–68.

CHAPTER TWO

1. The following sections draw heavily from Michael J. Malbin, "Congress during the Convention and Ratification," in Leonard W. Levy and Dennis J. Mahoney, eds., *The Framing and Ratification of the Constitution* (New York: Macmillan, 1987), 185–208; Malbin, "Framing a Congress to Channel Ambition," in *This Constitution: Our Enduring Legacy*, American Political Science Association and American Historical Association (Washington, D.C.: Congressional Quarterly Press, 1986), 55–72; *Congressional Quarterly Guide to Congress,* 5th ed., vol. 1 (Washington, D.C.: CQ Press, 2000); and Paul J. Quirk and Sarah A. Binder, eds., *The Legislative Branch*, (New York: Oxford University Press, 2005), especially the essays of Charles Stewart III and Eric Schickler.
2. Nelson W. Polsby, "Legislatures," in Fred I. Greenstein and Nelson W. Polsby, eds., *Handbook of Political Science: Governmental Institutions and Processes*, vol. 5 (London: Addison-Wesley Publishing Company, 1975), 257–319.
3. Michael J. Malbin, "Congress during the Convention and Ratification," 186.
4. Richard F. Fenno, Jr., *The United States Senate: A Bicameral Perspective,* (Washington, D.C.: American Enterprise Institute for Public Policy Research, 1982), 5.
5. *The Federalist 70* (New York: New American Library, 1961), 424.
6. Edward S. Corwin, *The President: Office and Powers, 1787–1957,* 4th rev. ed. (New York: New York University Press, 1957), 171.
7. This discussion draws from Robert A. Katzmann, *Courts and Congress* (Washington, D.C.: Brookings Institution Press, 1997), 1–8.

8. Montesquieu, quoted in *The Federalist 78* (New York: Bantam Books, 1988), 394.
9. Michael J. Malbin, "Congress during the Convention and Ratification," 185–208.
10. Much of this discussion is drawn from ibid.
11. Gordon S. Wood, *The Radicalism of the American Revolution* (New York: Alfred A. Knopf, 1993), 367.
12. Charles Stewart III, "Congress and the Constitutional System," in Quirk and Binder, *The Legislative Branch*, 3–34.
13. This section draws heavily from Eric Schickler, "Institutional Development of Congress," in Quirk and Binder, *The Legislative Branch*, 35–62.
14. Ibid.
15. Eric M. Uslaner, "Comity in Context: Confrontation in Historical Perspective," *British Journal of Political Science* 21 (January 1991): 66–69.
16. The following account draws from Uslaner, "Comity in Context," 67–69, and David Donald, *Charles Sumner and the Rights of Man* (New York: Knopf, 1970), 7–8.
17. The following two paragraphs draw from Richard B. Cheney and Lynne V. Cheney, *Kings of the Hill: How Nine Powerful Men Changed the Course of American History* (New York: Simon & Schuster, 1996), 96–116; and Booth Mooney, *Mr. Speaker: Four Men Who Shaped the United States House of Representatives* (Chicago: Follett Publishing Company, 1964), 49–87.
18. Source quoted in Cheney and Cheney, *Kings of the Hill*, 98.
19. Schickler, in Quirk and Binder, *The Legislative Branch*, 43.
20. This paragraph and the next are based on Cheney and Cheney, *Kings of the Hill*, 117–37; and Mooney, *Mr. Speaker*, 89–127.
21. Mooney, *Mr. Speaker*, 93.
22. Cannon, quoted in Mooney, *Mr. Speaker*, 90.
23. Ibid., 94.
24. Roosevelt, quoted in Cheney and Cheney, *Kings of the Hill,* 125.
25. This section draws from James Sundquist, *The Decline and Resurgence of Congress* (Washington, D.C.: Brookings Institution, 1981), 15–36; and *Congressional Quarterly Guide to Congress*, 5th ed., vol. 1 (Washington, D.C.: CQ Press, 2000).
26. Quoted in Sundquist, *The Decline and Resurgence of Congress*, 24.
27. Ibid., 25–29.

28. This section draws from Charles G. Geyh, "Judicial Independence, Judicial Accountability, and the Role of Constitutional Norms in Congressional Regulation of the Courts," *Indiana Law Journal* 153 (Winter/Spring 2003): 154–220.

29. Ron Chernow, "Chopping Off the Weakest Branch," *New York Times,* 6 May 2005, A1.

30. William H. Rehnquist, "2004 Year-End Report on the Federal Judiciary," www.supremecourtus.gov/publicinfo/year-end/2004year-endreport.pdf. Last accessed December 1, 2005.

31. Jeffrey Rosen, "The GOP v. the Judiciary: Out of Order," *New Republic* (30 May 2005): 12–13.

CHAPTER THREE

This chapter draws from an essay written by Ornstein in 1977, "Congress: The Democrats Reform Power in the House of Representatives, 1969–1975," in Allan P. Sindler, ed., *America in the Seventies* (Boston: Little, Brown, 1977).

1. Charles O. Jones, *The Minority Party in Congress* (Boston: Little, Brown, 1970), 183.

2. David Rohde, *Parties and Leaders in the Postreform House* (Chicago: University of Chicago Press, 1991), 66–67.

3. "Minority Report; Ignored by Their President, Ill-used by Their Democratic Colleagues, House Republicans Are in a Mutinous Mood," *The Atlantic* (December 1985).

4. Janet Hook, "House GOP: Plight of a Permanent Minority," *Congressional Quarterly* (June 21, 1986).

5. David Rohde, *Parties and Leaders,* 111–12.

6. William F. Connelly, Jr., and John J. Pitney, *Congress' Permanent Minority?* (Lanham, Md.: Rowman & Littlefield, 2004), 82.

7. James A. Barnes, "Partisanship," *National Journal* (November 7, 1987): 2825, quoted in Connelly and Pitney, 83.

8. Julian E. Zelizer, *On Capitol Hill: The Struggle to Reform Congress and Its Consequences, 1948–2000* (Cambridge: Cambridge University Press, 2004), 201.

9. The name was subsequently changed to Government Accountability Office.

10. "Congress Confidential," *Washington Post,* November 3, 1991.

11. Alan Ehrenhalt, "In the Senate of the '80s, Team Spirit Has Given Way to the Rule of Individuals," *CQ Weekly Report* (September 4, 1982): 2176.

12. Ann Cooper, *CQ Weekly Report* (September 2, 1978): 2, 307, quoted in C. Lawrence Evans and Daniel Lipinski, "Obstruction and Leadership in the U.S. Senate," in *Congress Reconsidered,* 8th ed. (Washington, D.C.: CQ Press, 2005).

13. *Renewing Congress* (Washington, D.C.: American Enterprise Institute and Brookings Institution, 1992), 2.

14. Ibid., 3.

15. Ibid., 54–55.

16. Ibid., 14–15.

CHAPTER FOUR

1. Richard F. Fenno, Jr., *Learning to Govern: An Institutional View of the 104th Congress* (Brookings, 1997), 5–36; and Linda Killian, *The Freshmen: What Happened to the Republican Revolution?* (Boulder, Colo.: Westview Press, 1998), 3–31.

2. From a CBS–*New York Times* poll cited in Killian, *The Freshmen*, 6.

3. Killian, *The Freshmen,* 3.

4. *Roll Call,* September 11, 1995.

5. *Roll Call,* December 1, 1994.

6. Pat Towell, "GOP; Drive for a More Open House Reflects Pragmatism and Resentment," *Congressional Quarterly* 52, no. 45 (1994): 3320.

7. *CQ Weekly Report,* November 19, 1994.

8. Barbara Sinclair, "The New World of U.S. Senators," in Lawrence C. Dodd and Bruce I. Oppenheimer, eds., *Congress Reconsidered,* 8th ed. (Washington, D.C.: CQ Press, 2005), 6–13.

9. R. A. Zalvidar, "Veto Readied for GOP's Latest Plan. The Budget Wrangling Continues," *Philadelphia Inquirer,* November 7, 1995, A10.

10. George Hager, "Budget Battle Came Sooner Than Either Side Expected," *CQ Weekly Report,* November 20, 1995.

11. Sarah Binder, Forrest Maltzman, and Alan Murphy, "Op. Chart: History's Verdict," *New York Times*, May 19, 2005, A27.

12. Quoted by Carl Tobias, "Filling the Federal Courts in an Election Year," *SMU Law Review* 49 (1996): 309.

13. Richard Carelli, "Far from Spotlight, Judgeships Getting Filled," Associated Press, June 9, 1995.

14. Quoted in David Broder, "Partisan Sniping on Judicial Vacancies Gets Louder," *Washington Post,* January 3, 1998, A7.

15. This discussion draws from Thomas E. Mann, "Citizens to the Rescue," *Brookings Review* (Winter 1999): 2–3.

16. Nicol C. Rae and Colton C. Campbell, *Impeaching Clinton: Partisan Strife on Capitol Hill* (Lawrence: University Press of Kansas, 2000), 8–19; and Benjamin Ginsberg and Martin Sheffer, *Politics By Other Means: Politicians, Prosecutors, and the Press from Watergate to Whitewater*, 2nd ed. (New York: W.W. Norton, 1999), 23–25.

17. John F. Harris, *The Survivor: Bill Clinton in the White House* (New York: Random House, 2005), 431–37.

18. This section draws from John C. Fortier and Norman J. Ornstein, "President Bush: Legislative Strategist," in Fred I. Greenstein, ed., *The George W. Bush Presidency: An Early Assessment* (Baltimore: Johns Hopkins University Press, 2003).

19. Norman J. Ornstein, Thomas E. Mann, and Michael J. Malbin, *Vital Statistics on Congress 2001–2002* (Washington, D.C.: American Enterprise Institute Press, 2002), 68.

20. Lori Nitschke, "Estate Tax Phaseout Passes House But May Be Scaled Back in Senate When Finance Panel Begins Work," *Congressional Quarterly* 59, no. 14 (2001): 775.

21. Adriel Bettelheim, "Homeland Security's Big Hurdle: Ceding Power to White House," *Congressional Quarterly* 60, no. 30 (2002): 2030.

22. Adriel Bettelheim, "Workers' Rights Issues Looming Over Homeland Security Debate," *Congressional Quarterly* 60, no. 34 (2002): 2294.

23. Adriel Bettelheim and Mary Dalrymple, "Chafee Holds Key to Decision on Union Rights for Homeland Staff," *Congressional Quarterly* 60, no. 36 (2002): 2442.

24. Ibid.

25. Quoted in Dana Milbank, "In Cheney's Shadow, Counsel Pushes the Conservative Cause," *Washington Post*, October 11, 2004, A21.

Chapter Five

1. "Expected surge in Katrina-related bankruptcies may be too late," Associated Press, October 5, 2005.

2. "Bankruptcy Law Stands; Some rules are eased for Katrina's victims, but the full impact of the storm's wrath may not be felt for years," *Cards and Payments* (November 2005): 35.

3. "A Bankrupt 'Reform,'" *Washington Post*, Sunday, March 13, 2005, B7.

4. Henry J. Sommer, "Trying to Make Sense Out of Nonsense: Representing Consumers Under the Bankruptcy Abuse Prevention and Consumer Protection Act of 2005," *American Bankruptcy Law Journal* 79 (2005): 191.

5. Donald R. Matthews, *U.S. Senators and Their World* (Chapel Hill: University of North Carolina Press, 1960), 101–2.

6. "Congress Should Share a Big Part of the Blame for Katrina Response," *Roll Call,* September 7, 2005.

7. "Abu Ghraib Hearings Put Dismissal of Congress on Display," *Roll Call,* May 12, 2004.

8. Shailagh Murray, "Storms Show a System Out of Balance: GOP Congress Has Reduced Usual Diet of Agency Oversight," *Washington Post,* October 5, 2005, A21.

9. This discussion draws on Adam Clymer, "Government Openness at Issue as Bush Holds on to Records," *New York Times,* January 2, 2003, A1; David Nather, "A Rise in State Secrets," *CQ Weekly,* July 18, 2005; and Minority Staff, House Committee on Government Reform, "Secrecy in the Bush Administration," September 14, 2005.

10. Sarah Binder, Forrest Maltzman, and Alan Murphy, "Op. Chart: History's Verdict," *New York Times*, May 19, 2005, A27.

11. David Savage, "Vacancy Rate on Federal Bench Is at a 13-Year Low," *Los Angeles Times,* November 6, 2003, A14.

12. Charles Krauthammer, "Nuclear? No, Restoration," *Washington Post,* May 13, 2005, A23.

13. Bill Frist, "It's Time for an Up-or-Down Vote," *USA Today,* May 16, 2005, 12A.

14. Proponents of the nuclear option argued that Fortas had not been filibustered, even though virtually every news account at the time and the comments of Fortas opponents viewed the actions against him as a filibuster. Moreover, the official Senate Web site, in its section on history, has as its headline "October 1, 1968: Filibuster Derails Supreme Court Appointee."

15. Vital Statistics on Congress, 2001–2002, updated by author.

16. Ibid.

17. *Congressional Record,* April 21, 1993, H 1956.

18. Donald R. Wolfensberger, "A Reality Check on the Republican House Reform Revolution at the Decade Mark," Introductory Essay for Congress Project Roundtable on "The Republican Revolution at 10: The Lasting Legacy or Faded Vision?" Woodrow Wilson International Center for Scholars, January 24, 2005.

19. House Rules Committee Minority Office, Official Congressional Report, "Broken Promises: The Death of Deliberative Democracy: A Congressional Report on the Unprecedented Erosion of the Democratic Process in the 108th Congress," March 2005.

20. Scott Lilly, "When Congress Acts in the Dark of Night, Everyone Loses," *Roll Call,* December 6, 2004.

21. Andrea Stone and William M. Welch, "GOP Comes Around to a Majority View," *USA Today,* June 17, 2004.

22. A good example of Sensenbrenner's gratuitous partisanship presented itself in April 2005; the House Judiciary Committee, in its GOP-drafted report on a bill to make it illegal to evade parental-consent laws by taking minors across state lines for abortions, described amendments that had been offered by Democrats—to exempt from prosecution adult siblings, grandparents, and public transportation drivers of buses and taxis who take minors across state lines—as efforts to protect "sexual predators." Amendments offered by committee members are customarily described in the terms of their authors. When Democrats asked Chairman Sensenbrenner to change the report or to apologize, he refused. Rep. Jerry Nadler (D-NY) called the report "a rape of the rules of the House." After Democrats brought the House to a halt on grounds of personal privilege, the Republican leaders of the House persuaded Sensenbrenner to back down. See "Democrats Slam Sensenbrenner," by John Bresnahan, *Roll Call*, June 13, 2005. For his part, Ways and Means Chairman Bill Thomas summoned Capitol police to remove committee Democrats forcibly from a committee meeting room after they left the hearing room to protest his tactics on a tax bill; see "Intervention Time: GOP Should Rein In Chairman Thomas," by Norman J. Ornstein, *Roll Call*, July 23, 2003.

23. "CAGW Identifies Record $22.9 Billion in Pork," Citizens Against Government Waste release, April 7, 2004.

24. Scott Lilly, "Is the Politics of Pork Poisoning Our Democracy?" *Roll Call,* August 15, 2005.

25. Ibid.

26. Scott Lilly, "Despite Earmarks, Many Districts Are Worse Off," *Roll Call,* October 6, 2005.

27. Edward Walsh, "GOP Report Feeds Furor Over Texas Redistricting," *Washington Post,* October 11, 2003, A1.

28. The following discussion draws on Louis Jacobson, 2003, "The DeLay Factor on K Street," *National Journal* 35, no. 1; Nicho-

las Confessore, "Welcome to the Machine: How the GOP Disciplined K Street and Made Bush Supreme," *Washington Monthly,* July/August 2003; and John Judis, "Tammany Fall," *New Republic,* June 20, 2005.

29. David Maraniss and Michael Weisskopf, "Speaker and His Directors Make the Cash Flow Right," *Washington Post,* November 27, 1995, A1.

30. Nicholas Confessore, ibid.

31. Kathleen Day and Jim VandeHei, "Congressman Urges Republican Lobbyist; Oxley Staff Pressuring Mutual Funds," *Washington Post,* February 15, 2003, A3.

CHAPTER SIX

1. National Commission on Terrorist Attacks Upon the United States, *The 9/11 Commission Report*; Dan Eggen, "Al Qaeda Scaled Back 10-Plane Plot," *Washington Post,* June 17, 2004.

2. Norman J. Ornstein, "What If Congress Were Obliterated? Good Question," *Roll Call,* October 4, 2001.

3. *Proposing an amendment to the Constitution of the United States regarding the appointment of individuals to serve as Members of the House of Representatives in the event a significant number of Members are unable to serve at any time because of a national emergency,* HJ Res. 67, 107th Cong., 1st sess., *Congressional Record* 147 (October 10, 2001): H 6505.

4. Norman J. Ornstein, "Preparing for the Unthinkable," *Wall Street Journal,* March, 11, 2002.

5. Suzanne Nelson, "What Happened with Continuity, and Why," *Roll Call,* December 6, 2004.

6. Ibid.

7. Ibid.

8. Norman Ornstein,"It's Not the Time to Add Members to the FEC Hall of Shame," *Roll Call,* July 30, 2003.

9. Allison Hoffman, "The Recall Campaign; Clock Ticking, Election Officials Scrambling," *Los Angeles Times,* July 26, 2003.

10. House Committee on House Administration, *Hearing on the Continuity of Government,* 108th Cong., 1st sess., 2003, 112.

11. Suzanne Nelson, "Parties Divided Over Continuity," *Roll Call,* January 22, 2004.

12. *Continuity in Representation Act of 2004,* HR 602, 108th Cong., 2nd sess., *Congressional Record* 150 (April 22, 2004): H 2319.

13. Suzanne Nelson, "Baird Amendment Goes Down in Flames; Debate Focuses on Split Over Rule Not Continuity Measure's Merits," *Roll Call*, June 3, 2004.

14. Norman Ornstein, "GOP's Approach to Continuity: Not Just Unfortunate, Stupid," *Roll Call*, June 9, 2004.

15. John Cornyn, "Congress Must Pass a New Amendment to Ensure Continuity," *Roll Call*, May 12, 2004.

CHAPTER SEVEN

1. Richard Wolf, "Congress' spending draws fire," *USA Today*, August 5, 2005, A4.

2. Associated Press, "Alaskan Bridge Project That Drew Ridicule May Be on Ice, but State Will Still Get the Cash," *Los Angeles Times*, November 17, 2005, A26.

3. Quoted in Jonathan Weisman, "Analysts: Tax-cut bag full of tricks," *USA Today*, May 31, 2001, A1.

4. Clive Crook, "How to Take a Flawed Tax Bill and Turn It Into a Joke," *National Journal* 33, no. 23, June 9, 2001.

5. Joel Friedman, Richard Kogan, and Robert Greenstein, "New Tax-cut Law Ultimately Costs as Much as Bush Plan Gimmicks Used to Camouflage $4.1 Trillion Cost in Second Decade," *Center on Budget and Policy Priorities* newsletter, June 27, 2001; www.cbpp.org/5-26-01tax.htm. Last accessed November 28, 2005.

6. Paul Krugman, "Reckonings; Bad Heir Day," *New York Times*, May 30, 2001, 23.

7. See the accounts in George Packer, *The Assassins' Gate* (New York: Farrar, Straus, and Giroux, 2005), and Bob Woodward, *Plan of Attack* (New York: Simon & Schuster, 2004).

8. Quoted in Jim VandeHei, "Iraq Briefings: Don't Ask, Don't Tell; GOP and Democratic Lawmakers Frustrated as White House Reveals Little," *Washington Post*, September 15, 2002, A4.

9. Bob Graham, "What I Knew Before the Invasion," *Washington Post*, November 20, 2005, B7.

10. David Brady and David Epstein, "Intraparty Preferences, Heterogeneity, and the Origins of the Modern Congress: Progressive Reformers in the House and Senate, 1890–1920," *Journal of Law, Economics, and Organization* 13, no. 1 (April 1997): 26–49.

11. Michael P. McDonald, "A Comparative Analysis of Redistricting Institutions in the United States, 2001–02," *State Politics & Policy Quarterly* 4, no. 4 (Winter 2004): 371–95.

12. See Thomas E. Mann and Bruce E. Cain, eds., *Party Lines* (Brookings, 2005); and Alan I. Abramowitz, Brad Alexander, and Matthew Gunning, "Incumbency, Redistricting, and the Decline of Competition in U.S. House Elections," *Journal of Politics* 68, no. 1 (February, 2006): 75–88.

13. Trevor Potter and David Skaggs, "The Shape of Representative Democracy: Report of the Redistricting Reform Conference, Airlie, Virginia, June, 2005."

14. See Norman Ornstein, "Yes, Reform Lobbying, but Don't Forget Leadership PACs," *Roll Call,* January, 28, 3006.

15. Matt Kelley, "The congressman & the hedge fund," *USA Today,* January 19, 2006, A1. The article begins, "One day after a New York investment group raised $110,000 for Republican Rep. Jerry Lewis, the House passed a defense spending bill that preserved $160 million for a Navy project critical to the firm. The man who protected the Navy money? Lewis."

16. Jim Abrams, "House rejects education and health spending bill," Associated Press, November 17, 2005.

17. Dana Milbank, "Opening the Door to Debate, and Then Shutting It," *Washington Post,* November 22, 2005, A4.

Acknowledgments

In the most immediate sense, this book had its origins in a generous invitation from the Institutions of American Democracy Project, funded by the Annenberg Foundation Trust at Sunnylands, and its leaders, Kathleen Hall Jamieson and Jaroslav Pelikan, to write a volume about Congress that would be accessible to a broad public audience. Tim Bartlett, our initial editor at Oxford University Press, helped shape the prospectus, garner its approval, and encourage us along the way. From the outset, we profited from the project's parallel effort, led by Paul Quirk and Sarah Binder, to produce a collection of original scholarly articles, which were published last year as *The Legislative Branch*.

We were receptive to the invitation because, after much collaboration on scholarly and specialist volumes on Congress and American democracy, we had long contemplated writing a popular book on the first branch of government. At the end of our Renewing Congress Project in the early 1990s, we promised our program officer at the Carnegie Corporation of New York, Geri Mannion, that we would do just that. We are pleased to finally deliver on that promise.

Our interest in and knowledge of Congress was piqued in our undergraduate years—Mann at the University of Florida, Ornstein at the University of Minnesota. Ornstein in particular recalls the riveting stories about Congress told by Eugene Eidenberg, who put his time on Capitol Hill to very good use on the Minneapolis campus. We both learned much about Congress from John Kingdon, who gave an excellent seminar on the legislative process while we were graduate students at the University of Michigan and who continued to counsel us after we set off for Washington as congressional fellows.

In writing this book, we have drawn on the knowledge and wisdom of scores of colleagues in the scholarly, political, and reporting communities, too numerous to list here. We would like to offer special thanks to Richard F. Fenno, Jr., who read a draft of the entire manuscript and offered particularly constructive and consequential comments. Others who read all or parts of the manuscript and offered helpful reactions include David Price, Sarah Binder, Michael Robinson, Sheilah Mann, Pietro Nivola, Charles O. Jones, Nelson Polsby, and Jonathan Rauch.

At Brookings, Mann had the benefit of several very talented and productive research assistants (Alan Murphy and Mark Hiller) and interns (Jane Hendrick and Dedi Kuo). He also had the good fortune to schmooze about Congress and American politics on almost a daily basis with his Brookings colleagues, especially E. J. Dionne, Jr.

At the American Enterprise Institute, Ornstein also profited from great assistants, including Chris Trendler, Matt Weil, and Bryan O'Keefe, and colleagues such as John Fortier and Karlyn Bowman. The atmosphere of openness and collegiality made the difficult chore of writing a book much easier. Ornstein also benefited from his association with *Roll Call* and is sincerely appreciative of the editors who have given him great freedom in his weekly column on Congress to cause heartburn in many prominent members of Congress in both parties. He is grateful, also, to the editors and publisher of the *Atlantic* for permission to use excerpts from columns and an article respectively.

We have pulled few punches in this book. We have several role models in this area, especially John McCain, David Obey, and Chris Shays, who taught us that speaking honestly and bluntly is the best, if not the most comfortable, course to take.

Our editor at Oxford University Press, Dedi Felman, brought focus, clarity, and brevity to the manuscript while being a genuine champion of our efforts. Others at OUP who helped smooth the way to publication include Michele Bové and Joellyn Ausanka.

While we stand on the shoulders of many, we alone are responsible for whatever errors and misjudgments remain.

Index